P9-EDA-643

SAN FRANCISCO ALMANAC

Hansen, Gladys C., 1925-
San Francisco almanac :
everything you want to k
c1975.
33305004326470
cu   09/25/21

SAN FRANCISCO

ALMANAC

Everything you want
to know about The City

by GLADYS HANSEN

San Francisco Archivist

625636

Chronicle Books / San Francisco

SANTA CLARA COUNTY LIBRARY

■ 3 3305 00432 6470

SANTA CLARA COUNTY LIBRARY
SAN JOSE, CALIFORNIA

Copyright ©1975 by Gladys Hansen
All rights reserved. This book or any portion thereof, may
not be reproduced in any form without the written permission
of the publisher.

Library of Congress Catalog No. 75-299-40
ISBN 0-87701-073-0

Chronicle Books
870 Market Street
San Francisco, CA 94102

Contents

History & Vital Statistics

Vital Statistics

Highest Point - Mount Davidson, 938 ft.
Lowest Point - Sea level
Land Area - 45 square miles

"The waters of the Pacific Ocean rise 0.1 foot per year. Thus the land area of the city of San Francisco has been reduced 1.25 feet around its water periphery from 1864 as far as it applies to this phenomena.
(Schlowitz, A. L., *Shore and Sea Boundaries*, U.S.C. & G.S. Pub. 10-1, Vol. II, 1964)

Latitude & Longitude - Planetarium, Golden Gate Park 37° 46' 11" North 122° 27' 53" West

Geographical Center - Lies between Alvarado and Twenty-third Street on the east side of Grandview Ave. (City Engineer's Office)

Outside Lands - 1,706.61 outside acres consist of 492.09 being Camp Mather in Tuolumne County; 454.72 in Sharp Park Golf Course in San Mateo County; and the other 760 acres in Kern, Fresno and Monterey Counties as assets of a trust fund.

Population

Dec. 31, 1798 Presidio of San Francisco 206
Mission de San Francisco 625*
2**
—
627

(First census of California taken by order of the King of Spain)
*Indians
**Spanish or other caste

1800 Presidial-Pueblo of San Francisco 223
Mission de San Francisco (Indian) 644

1815 Presidial-Pueblo of San Francisco 373
Mission de San Francisco (Indian) 1,115

1830 Presidial-Pueblo of San Francisco 131
Mission de San Francisco (Indian) 219

(Dwinelle, John W., *Colonial History of the City of San Francisco*)

1846 "On the 7th of July, A.D., 1846, the then pueblo, now city of San Francisco, was a town of the population of about one thousand inhabitants, and on the 3rd of March, A.D., 1851, the population thereof amounted to about thirty thousand persons, and that on the said 7th of July, and on said third of March, the said pueblo or city, under and by virtue of the grant aforesaid, and under and by virtue of the laws, usages and customs of the government of Mexico and California, all and singular the premises aforesaid, except as aforesaid, were part and parcel of the land and premises of said pueblo or city."

(Documents, depositions, and brief of law points raised thereon on behalf of the United States, in case No. 280, before the U.S. Board of Land Commissioners. *The City of San Francisco* vs. *the United States.* San Francisco: Commercial Power Presses, 1854.)

1847 "San Francisco, last August, contained 459 souls, of whom 375 were whites, four-fifths of these being under 40 years of age. Some idea of the composition of the white population may be gathered from the following statement as to the nationality of the larger portion: English, 22; German, 27; Irish, 14; Scotch, 14; born in the United States, 228; Californians, 89."

(*St. Louis Reville*, Feb. 12, 1848)

"In 1847, we find her with a population of less than 400, with no commerce, no wealth, no power, and without a name, save as a small trading post and mission station."

(*Rincon de las Salinas, Part of the Bernal Rancho, Fronting on the Bay, and Immediately South of the City of San Francisco, California.* New York: Latimer, Bros. & Seymour, 1857)

1848 "A school census recently completed in the town indicates the population as follows: 575 Males; 177 Females; 60 Children, totaling 812 white population."

(*California Star*, March 18, 1848)

1850 "The first directory, of Sept. 1850, contained 2,500 names, and the votes cast in Oct. reached 3,440. Hittell assumes not over 8,000 in Nov. 1849, on the strength of the vote then cast of 2,056, while allowing about 25,000 in another place for Dec. *The Annals of San Francisco* insists upon at least 20,000 probably nearer 25,000."

(Bancroft, Hubert Howe. *History of California.* Vol. VI, page 168)

1852 . . . . 34,776*	1900 . . . . 342,782**	1930 . . . . .634,394**
1860 . . . . .56,802**	1906 . . . . 175,000 †	1940 . . . . .634,536**
1870 . . . . .149,473**	1907 . . . . .*est.* 300,000	1950 . . . . .775,357**
		1960 . . . . .740,855**
1880 . . . . .233,959**	1910 . . . . .416,912**	1970 . . . . .715,674**
1890 . . . . .298,997**	1920 . . . . .506,676**	1972 (July) . . . 685,600‡

*State Census   **U.S. Census   †After the earthquake & fire; estimate by General Greely
‡Calif. State Department of Finance

Categories of Non-whites

	1940	1950	1960	1970
Negro	4,846	43,502	74,383	95,900
Chinese	17,782	24,813	36,445	97,332*
Japanese	5,280	5,759	9,464	
Others**	3,820	7,517	15,621	2,863†

*Chinese and Japanese combined total
**Filipino, Southeast Asians, Indians, Samoans, etc.
†American Indian

Dept. of Public Health estimates that Spanish-surnamed population is 10% of white population: 71,567 (1970).

The Foreign-Born

Almost half the people enumerated in San Francisco during the 1970 Census were foreign-born or the children of foreign-born parents.

The total number of residents of foreign stock was 317,045 or 44.3 percent of The City's total population of 715,674; as shown in this table produced by a U.S. Census Bureau computer.

	Number	%
Foreign Stock, total	317,045	100.0
Austria	4,145	1.3
Canada	12,079	3.8
China	48,384	15.3
Cuba	1,357	0.4
Czechoslovakia	1,714	0.5
Denmark	2,515	0.8
Finland	1,294	0.4
France	5,639	1.8
Germany	19,610	6.2
Greece	4,285	1.4
Hungary	1,906	0.6
Ireland	16,690	5.3
Italy	29,040	9.2
Japan	9,161	2.9
Lithuania	825	0.3
Mexico	18,519	5.8
Netherlands	1,450	0.5
Norway	3,335	1.1
Philippine Islands	26,645	8.4
Poland	5,326	1.7
Portugal	1,347	0.4
Rumania	1,187	0.4
Sweden	4,724	1.5
Switzerland	2,795	0.9
U.S.S.R.	13,603	4.3
United Kingdom	14,165	4.5
Yugoslavia	3,269	1.0
All other	62,036	19.6

(Sunday *Examiner* & *Chronicle*, 10/29/72)

Mother Tongue

About 41.9 percent of San Francisco's population spoke a language other than English in their homes when they were children, according to a new U.S. Census Bureau report.

Here is the Census Bureau's breakdown of the population's mother tongue:

	Number	%
Total Population	715,674	100.0
English only	387,587	54.2
French	13,219	1.8
German	26,283	3.7

Hungarian	1,343	0.2	Swedish	3,797	0.5
Italian	30,232	4.2	Yiddish	5,917	0.8
Polish	2,986	0.4	All other	123,074	17.2
Russian	8,549	1.2	Not reported	48,291	6.7
Spanish	64,395	9.0	(Sunday *Examiner* & *Chronicle*, 10/29/72)		

Chinatown's Home on Dupont Street in San Francisco

San Francisco's historic Chinatown has remained in the same location for well over a hundred years despite several attempts to dislodge it and current mounting pressures from an expanding financial district for some of its valuable space.

Why and how the Chinese came to settle along Grant avenue (originally called 'Dupont') and Sacramento street, has always eluded the researcher, perhaps because there is no specific answer. We do know, however, that Chinatown began at a very early date and exactly where due to the fastidious record-keeping of Hubert Howe Bancroft. In the 1880s this historian and his assistants, carefully reconstructed Gold Rush San Francisco with this comment on Chinatown:

"Sacramento st[reet] was already becoming known as Little China, from the establishment of some Mongol merchants upon its north side, on either side of Dupont st . . ."

Sacramento was simply the most natural place in 1849 for Chinese immigrants to find lodgings and open small trading shops for the wharf at its feet was the most prominent landing for merchandise in the city. With the exception of a few laborers, all of the earliest Chinese were merchants from the port city of Canton, China and to remain near the wharves and water must have been a natural inclination.

Not unexpectedly too, the old traditional name still occasionally used by the Chinese for Sacramento is *Tong Yan Gai* or "Chinese street."

The very first recorded Chinese in San Francisco arrived in February, 1848 under labor contract to a Charles Gillespie. They shared his home on Dupont and Clay street—Clay being but one block north of Sacramento. An early hotel-keeper, Charles Brown once recalled that he believed himself to be the first importer of Chinese labor to California, utilizing them in the construction of his inn at Clay and Kearny. (He was wrong, Gillespie preceded him by eight months at least.)

And one block north again of Clay, at Jackson and Kearny, the city's first Chinese restaurant opened in late 1848. Here at the "Canton Restaurant" was held on December 10, 1849 the first gathering of California Chinese to discuss mutual problems and goals.

No one has yet been able to determine the first real estate purchase by Chinese and thus who might have lent such invaluable aid to the founding of their first permanent settlement. Such records were, no doubt, destroyed in the 1906 earthquake and fire. The French settlers were, it seems, the most sympathetic to early Chinese housing and employment needs and when they slowly abandoned the old Gold Rush French quarter along Dupont street, the Chinese remained.

Ironically, although the French restaurants served some of the best food in those early years, at least part of the cooking was under the direction of Chinese chefs! Alexander Dumas in his 1852 book *A Gil Blas in California* expressed the Frenchman's indignation at another race tampering with French culinary art by calling it "abominable" (naturally). Other argonauts rated Chinese cooking far ahead of the French in that period.

Early Chinatown bordered thus on Portsmouth Square, where San Francisco began and as the city expanded southward and thence up Market street, the Chinese found themselves squarely in the heart of a heated controversy. They owned some of the city's best property.

In July, 1877 a horde of men attempted to burn the Chinese quarter and failed. After the 1906 earthquake, the city supervisors discussed relocating the Chinese and now the city's towering financial skyscrapers loom ominously over Chinatown's shops and playgrounds. Chinatown's always unsettled past, appears to be the fate too, of its future. (WFH)

Chinese Cycle of Years

Twelve animals comprise the symbolic cycle of the Chinese lunar calendar. They are shown here, with the cycle of years of the lunar calendar, and the corresponding Western calendar year.

Western Calendar	Formal Celebration	Symbolic Animal	Lunar Calendar	Western Calendar	Formal Celebration	Symbolic Animal	Lunar Calendar
1973	*Feb. 3*	Ox	4671	1979	*Jan. 28*	Ram	4677
1974	*Jan. 23*	Tiger	4672	1980	*Feb. 16*	Monkey	4678
1975	*Feb. 11*	Hare	4673	1981	*Feb. 5*	Rooster	4679
1976	*Jan. 31*	Dragon	4674	1982	*Jan. 25*	Dog	4680
1977	*Feb. 18*	Serpent	4675	1983	*Feb. 13*	Boar	4681
1978	*Feb. 7*	Horse	4676	1984	*Feb. 2*	Rat	4682

Grant avenue–for over a century the heart of San Francisco's Chinatown.

Native Sons & Daughters

San Francisco is the birthplace of many notables, past & present, in the fields of politics, sports & the arts.

Abrams, Albert Physician
Adams, Ansel E. Photographer
Ahern, Francis J. Police Chief
Aiken, Ednah (Robinson) Writer
Aitken, Robert I. Sculptor
Alioto, Joseph L. Mayor
Alvarez, Luis W. Physicist
  (Nobel Prize 1968)
Arata, Raymond J. Judge
Arnstein, Flora J. Writer
Atherton, Mrs. Gertrude Writer
Barbagelata, John Supervisor
Beach, Chester Sculptor
Behan, Gary Football player

Beckett, Wheeler Conductor-composer
Belasco, David Actor, dramatist,
  producer
Bixby, Bill TV actor
Blanc, Mel Radio/TV actor
Blinn, Holbrook Actor
Bonnot, Theodore F. Writer
Brady, Loretta Ellen Writer
Bremer, Anne M. Artist
Brennan, Charles J. Fire Chief
Brewer, Wheaton Hale Writer
Brewer, William Augustus, Jr. Writer
Brown, Edmund G. Governor
Brown, Edmund G., Jr. Governor

Bruguiere, Emile Antoine Writer
Buckley, Nancy Writer
Burbank, William Freeman Writer
Burnett, Sarah Constantia Writer
Cahill, Arthur Artist
Cailleau, Relda Marie Writer
Calden, Keith Fire Chief
Camilli, Dolph Louis Baseball player
Campbell, John Beyard Taylor Writer
Carrigan, William L. Artist
Casey, Edmund Terence Writer
Casey, James Patrick Writer
Chamberlin, F. Tolles Sculptor
Chandler, Katherine Agnes Writer
Charles, Frances Asa Writer
Cleary, Alfred J. City administrator
Clift, Dennison Halley Writer
Coblentz, Edmond D. Newspaper editor
Coblentz, Stanton Arthur Writer
Coghill, Stanly Writer
Cole, George Townsend Artist
Conmy, Peter Thomas Oakland City
  Librarian
Connolly, Thomas A. Catholic Bishop of
  San Francisco
Conrad, Barnaby Writer
Corbett, James J. Boxer
Crocker, Charles Templeton Writer
Croudace, Lenore Maude Writer
Crum, Gertrude Bosworth Writer
Cucuel, Edward Artist
Cuneo, Rinaldo Artist
Dana, Julian Writer
De Guarre, Frank Harold Writer
Dickenson, Mary Freud Writer
Dillman, Bradford Actor
Dobie, Charles Caldwell Writer
Donohoe, Hugh A. Catholic Bishop of
  San Francisco
Dorn, Frank Brigadier General, U.S.A.
Dullea, Charles W. Police Chief
Duncan, Isadora Dancer
DuPen, Everett G. Educator, sculptor
Eastwood, Clint Actor
Edson, Charles F. Writer
Egan, Richard Screen actor

*Poet Robert Frost—an unexpected
San Franciscan.*

Elias, Solomon P. Writer
Ellert, Levi R. Mayor
Falk, Adrien J. President San Francisco
  Bay Rapid Transit
Fest, Mattie Lois Writer
Finn, Tom Political leader & sheriff
Fischer, Dr. Frank Writer
Fitzell, Lincoln Writer
Fitzpatrick, Timothy I. Judge
Flavin, Martin Writer
Fleishhacker, Herbert Capitalist
Foley, Thomas M. Judge
Foster, Maximillian Writer
Froelich, Maren M. Artist
Frost, Robert Lee Poet
Garnett, Porter Writer
Gaskin, William G. Artist
Giannini, Lawrence M. Banker
Gibbs, Ralph Erwin Writer
Girod, Julius L. Superintendent,
  Golden Gate Park
Goldberg, Rueben ("Rube") Cartoonist
Gray, Percy Artist
Groen, Mary Lauretta Writer

Green, Clay Meredith Writer
Gunnison, Charles A. Writer
Guthrie, William D. Lawyer
Hammond, John Hays Mining engineer
Hancock, George Allan Founder,
  United California Bank
Hansen, Armin C. Artist
Harris, George B. U.S. District Judge
Hart, Jerome A. Writer
Hartman, Paul Actor
Haslett, Harriet Writer
Hayes, Peter Lind Actor
Hearst, William Randolph Publisher
Hildebrand, George Baseball player
Hocht, Edith Writer
Holm, Dion Raphale City Attorney
Hotaling, Richard M. Writer
Iberg, Herman E. Baseball player
Irvine, James Capitalist
Jessop, George Henry Writer
Johnson, Gladys Etta Writer
Kahn, Florence Prag Congresswoman
Kanno, Gertrude B. Sculptor
Kelly, George Baseball player
Kenyon, Camilla E. Writer
Kenyon, Charles Arthur Writer
King, Walter Woolf Movie
  director/producer
Kyne, Peter Bernard Writer
Lange, Fred W. Baseball player
Lasson, May C. Writer
Lazzeri, Tony Baseball player
Lennon, Thomas J. Writer
LeRoy, Mervyn Movie producer
Lewis, George Baseball player
Lewis, Oscar Writer
London, Jack Writer
Loo, Brother Zachary F.S.C. Writer
Louderback, George D. Geology professor
Louderback, Harold Judge
Lundborg, Florence Artist
Lynch, Thomas C. California
  Attorney General
McAteer, J. Eugene State Senator
McCord, Tom Baseball player
McGaw, Blanche Evelyn Writer

McKuen, Rod Poet
McNamara, Robert S. Industrialist,
  government official
Mailliard, William S. Diplomat
Mancuso, Edward T. Attorney
Marion, Frances Writer
Marks, Milton State Senator
Martin, Tony Singer
Mason, Benjamin F. Writer
Mathews, Lucia K. Artist
Mathis, Johnny Singer
Meinecke, E. P. Botanist
Merle, Martin V. Writer
Meyer, George H. Writer
Miller, George Paul Congressman
Miller, Johnny Golfer
Mitchell, Ruth Comfort Writer
Montgomery, Regina Cleary Writer
Morabito, Anthony J. Owner, 49ers
  football team
Morgan, John Ainsworth Author/business
  executive
Moscone, George State Senator
Murphy, Dan C. Sheriff
Murray, Elinor Nell Writer
Nahl, Perham W. Artist
Newhall, Scott Newspaper editor
Nolan, Lloyd Actor
Nolan, Mae Ella Hunt Congresswoman
Norris, Kathleen Writer
O'Doul, Frank (Lefty) Baseball player
Osbourne, Lloyd Writer
O'Sullivan, Elizabeth Writer
Page-Fredericks, Joseph R. Writer
Pages, Jules Artist
Pardee, George C. Governor
Parsons, Marion R. Writer
Phelan, James Duval Mayor
Pierce, Lucy V. Artist
Plaisted, Thais M. Author/lecturer
Quinn, William Joseph Police Chief
Rand, Ellen G. Artist
Ray, Milton Smith Writer
Reardon, Timothy A. Politician
Reilly, George R. State Board
  of Equalization

Reinhardt, Aurelia Henry Educator
Rising, Lawrence Writer
Robinson, Elmer E. Mayor
Rolph, James Jr. Mayor & Governor
Rothermell, Frederick C. Writer
Ruef, Abraham Labor leader
Salinger, Pierre Journalist
Samuels, Maurice Victor Writer
Sargeant, Geneve Rexford Artist
Scheffauer, Herman G. Writer
Schmitz, Eugene E. Mayor
Seawall, Harry W. Artist
Shelley, John Francis Mayor
Shoaff, Walter Romer Brigadier General U.S.A.
Silverman, Milton Scientist/author
Sonnichsen, Albert Writer
Sonntag, Lincoln Writer
Sproul, Robert Gordon President, University of California
Starr, Kevin O. City Librarian
Steffens, Joseph Lincoln Writer
Sterling, George Poet

Stone, Irving Writer
Strong, Austin Writer
Stuart, Charles Duff Writer
Suhr, August Richard Baseball player
Sullivan, Albert J. Fire Chief
Sullivan, James William Baseball player
Symmes, Harold S. Writer
Sweeney, James J. Catholic Bishop of Honolulu
Taylor, David Wooster Writer
Thompson, Joseph S. Writer
Tobriner, Mathew O. Judge
Townsend, Annie Lake Writer
Urmy, Clarence T. Writer
Watrous, Harry Willson Artist
Weinberger, Caspar W. Government official
White, Charles H. Writer
Whitman, Stuart Actor
Wolden, Russell Assessor
Wood, Natalie Actress
Zellerbach, James David Ambassador

Accolades

Admirers, Past and Present

"It is not a port, but a whole pocketful of ports." —JUAN MANUEL DE AYALA *(Spanish commander of ship that made first exploration of Bay of San Francisco in 1775.)*

"There, when this bay comes into our possession, will spring up the great rival of New York." —JOHN C. CALHOUN, *Secretary of State in 1844 (indicating on a map place where San Francisco now stands).*

"San Francisco is, by her position, by her energy and wisdom, to be the Elect Lady of the Coast, and nothing but earthquakes will interfere with her growth." —REV. JOHN TODD

"San Francisco is a City of Romance and Destiny; a composite of the three P's of Progress,—the Past, the Present and the Prospective. Most distinctive city of the United States, although a junior, Romance, not merely of yester-

day, but of today and tomorrow, is the very kernel of the shell of it. To pass
the portals of the Golden Gate is to cross the threshold of Adventure. Metropolitan as it is, San Francisco is still an outpost of the frontier line of the
Grand Army of Progress, with its citizens of today as redblooded, as full of
the joy of living and the triumph of achieving as their forebears and forerun-
ners, the Argonauts of '49." —ALLAN DUNN

"Few cities in the world can vie with San Francisco either in the beauty or
in the natural advantages of her situation; indeed, there are only two places
in Europe—Constantinople and Gibraltar—that combine an equally perfect
landscape with what may be called an equally imperial position. The city
itself is full of bold hills, rising steeply from the deep water. The air is keen
and dry and bright, like the air of Greece, and the waters not less blue.
Perhaps it is this light and air, recalling the cities of the Mediterranean, that
makes one involuntarily look up to the tops of those hills for the feudal castle,
or the ruins of the Acropolis, that must crown them." —HON. JAMES BRYCE

"San Francisco has no rival in the United States. We may contrast, but not
compare it with Eastern or even European cities. London is grand but not
beautiful. Paris is beautiful but not grand. Constantinople is picturesque,
but has not architectural splendor. But San Francisco has all these attri-
butes. It has been compared to Cleveland, city of beautiful avenues, Cleveland is charming; San Francisco is stupendous, romantic; Cleveland is
lovely; San Francisco is grand; Cleveland is American; San Francisco is

"The City of Romance and the Gateway to Adventure."

Cosmopolitan; Cleveland is a garden made by man; San Francisco looks as if it were built by the Gods." —IRA G. HOITT

"San Francisco is like Venice and Athens in having strange memories; she is unlike them in being lit from within by a large and luminous hope. Wonder and terror may pass over her spirit; still nothing changes her purpose, nothing weakens her courage." —EDWIN MARKHAM

"For this city is one of those which have souls; it is a spirit sitting on a height, taking to itself form and the offices of civilization. This a thing that we know, because we have seen the land shake it as a terrier shakes a rat, until the form of the city was broken; it dissolved in smoke and flame. And then as a polyp of the sea draws out of the fluent water form and perpetuity for itself, we saw our city draw back its shapes of wood and stone, and statelier, more befitting a spirit that has endured so much." —MARY AUSTIN

"Even now San Francisco will impress all her visitors deeply in many ways. They will see it as very new; yet they will feel it is very old. Civilization is better organized here in some respects than in any city out of Paris; some of its streets look as if transplanted from a city of Europe; others are in the first stages of rescue from the barbaric desert. Asia, Europe and America have here met and embraced each other; yet the strong mark of America is upon and in all; an America, in which the flavor of New England can be tasted above all other local elements; an America in which the flexibility, the adaptability, and the all-penetrating, all-subduing power of its own race, are everywhere and in everything manifest." —SAMUEL BOWLES

"San Francisco should be called City of Flowers."
—CHARLES LORING BLACK

"The City of Romance and the Gateway to Adventure."
—KATHERINE AMOS TAYLOR

"San Francisco is a city where people are never more abroad than when they are at home." —BENJAMIN F. TAYLOR

"Queen of the Pacific Coast! Fair city whose changing skies for half the year shower down mist and rain, and the other half sunbeams of molten brass! Metropolis of alternate sticky mud and blinding dust! In spite of these and more thou art a city of my heart, O Ciudad de San Francisco!"
—T. S. KENDERDINE

"It is impossible for one to live long in San Francisco, and become familiar with its business and business men, without becoming attached to the City and State. However much he may see to dislike, he will also find much that commands his attention and fastens on his sympathies." —JOHN S. HITTELL

"San Francisco is West as all hell." —BERNARD DE VOTO

"San Francisco is largely, more largely than many of our people are willing to confess, the child of the mines. They gave it its first start; they have generously, though not exclusively nourished it ever since. They have called into existence a very large manufacturing interest, giving employment to tens of thousands of men. They have stimulated every branch of trade and internal commerce, quickened every pulse of industrial life. Nearly all our finest buildings have been erected out of the profits of mining enterprises. Every pound of ore that is taken out of the earth, from Alaska to Arizona, pays tribute here. A man may make his fortune in the desert of Nevada or Idaho, but he is pretty sure to spend it in San Francisco."

—SAMUEL WILLIAMS

"San Francisco is the most sophisticated city in the country. From prize-fights to grand opera, it is nearly always in good taste, yes, and has delicacy. A San Francisco audience is a test of a good play. As a matter of fact, a New York audience is no test at all." —KATHERINE F. GEROULD

"San Francisco—her commercial standing is in the front rank of the leading commercial cities of the world. She is even now in her infancy—in the bud—the opening of the flower and the ripening of the fruit is in reserve for her. She lies directly in the line of the great thoroughfare of swift trade and travel which girdles the earth. And when a noble group of Pacific States shall encircle her as a nucleus, all alive with a busy population, and rich in all agricultural and manufacturing wealth, she will be the New York or the London of the Occident. There is a hopeful, grand, and glorious future before San Francisco." —JOHN J. POWELL

"San Francisco holds the same relation to the State of California that Paris does to France. It forms the head and heart of, and is the miniature of, the commonwealth. The Romans had an expression which showed the importance of their city 'urbis et orbis' implying that the world was ruled from Rome. The same may be said of San Francisco in regard to the State of California. The city rules the state; and though topographically its site is not pleasant, the uneven surface of the country being a succession of hills and valleys, swamps and sandy plains; yet geographically the site of San Francisco is unequalled in any part of the globe." —REV. HUGH QUIGLEY

"San Francisco looks as if it were built by the gods."

"To a traveler paying his first visit, it has the interest of a new planet. It ignores the meteorological laws which govern the rest of the world."
—FITZ HUGH LUDLOW

"The port of San Francisco is a marvel of nature and may be called the port of ports." —FATHER FONT

"The bay of San Francisco has been celebrated from the time of its first discovery as one of the finest in the world. It rises into an importance far above that of a mere harbor. . . its latitudinal position is that of Lisbon, its climate that of Southern Italy, settlements attest to its healthfulness, bold shores and mountains give it grandeur, the extent and fertility of its dependent country give it great resources for agriculture, commerce and population. . . To this gate I gave the name Chrysopylae or Golden Gate. . . "
—JOHN FRÉMONT

"San Francisco is unique—a thing without a parallel, one that admits of no comparisons, for there is nothing like it in the histories of cities."
—WILLIAM M'COLLUM, M.D.

". . . this marvelous city, bazaar of all the nations of the globe, [compares] with the fantastic creations of 'The Thousand and One Nights'."
—EDMOND AUGER (*French gold hunter seeing San Francisco in '49*)

"After some experience in many parts of the world, I freely venture the opinion, there is no sheet of water on the globe better adapted for great national and commercial purposes than the Bay of San Francisco and its vast tributaries." —COMMANDER CADWALADER RINGGOLD

"I can fancy that the Muse of Montgomery must, in some Olympian flight, have caught a glimpse of this golden land, and felt the soft influence of its evening charms, when he sang so sweetly his beautiful ode on 'Night'. Surely no person needs a talent for sleeping in San Francisco.
"San Francisco has, in its location and unrivalled harbor, elements of prosperity which cannot be overcome by any other point on the coast. It will inevitably become, on the Pacific, what New York is in the Atlantic."
—E. S. CAPRON

"Nature ordained this queen of the Pacific a great metropolis—the second city on the American continent. Burned to the ground six times within eighteen months, her growth was not stopped, nor her prosperity impaired; and if a new earthquake were to shake down every building, not leaving one stone upon another, the town would soon be as large and as vigorous as ever." —ALBERT RICHARDSON

"San Francisco—no well-bred American, unless he comes from Chicago, ever says 'Frisco'—is a delicious combination of wealth and wickedness, splendour and squalor, vice, virtue, villainy, beauty, ugliness, solitude and silence, rush and row—in short San Francisco is just San Francisco, and that's all there is to it, as they say there." —GEORGE GRIFFITH

"I am a citizen of no mean city, although it is in ashes. Almighty God has fixed this as the location of a great city. The past is gone, and there is no use of lamenting or moaning over it. Let us look to the future and without regard to creed or place of birth, work together in harmony for the upbuilding of a greater San Francisco." —ARCHBISHOP P. W. RIORDAN

"Of all the marvelous phases of the Present, San Francisco will most tax the belief of the Future. Its parallel was never known, and shall never be beheld again. I speak only of what I saw with my own eyes. Like the magic seed of the Indian juggler, which grew, blossomed and bore fruit before the eyes of his spectators, San Francisco seemed to have accomplished in a day the growth of half a century." —BAYARD TAYLOR

"The City of San Francisco (the metropolis of the State) considering its age, is by long odds the most wonderful city on the face of the earth."
—G. W. SULLIVAN

"It (California) is the land where the fabled Aladdin's Lamp lies buried —and she (San Francisco) is the new Aladdin who shall seize it from its obscurity and summon the genie and command him to crown her with power and greatness and bring to her feet the hoarded treasures of the earth.

"I am bidding the old city a kind, but not a sad, farewell, for I know that when I see this home again, the changes that will have been wrought upon it will suggest no sentiment of sadness; its estate will be bright, happier, and prouder a hundred-fold than it is this day. This is its destiny. . . "
—MARK TWAIN (*in the Alta California, upon leaving California in 1866.*)

"That City of Gold to which adventurers congregated out of all the winds of heaven. I wonder what enchantment of the 'Arabian Nights' can have equalled this evocation of a roaring city, in a few years of a man's life, from the marshes and the blowing sand." —ROBERT LOUIS STEVENSON

"It's an odd thing, but anyone who disappears is said to be seen in San Francisco. It must be a delightful city and possess all the attractions of the next world." —OSCAR WILDE

"San Francisco is a really beautiful city. China Town, peopled by Chinese labourers, is the most artistic town I have ever come across. The people —strange, melancholy Orientals, whom any people would call common, and they are certainly very poor—have determined that they will have nothing about them that is not beautiful. In the Chinese restaurant, where these navies meet to have supper in the evening, I found them drinking teas out of china cups as delicate as the petals of a rose-leaf, whereas at the gaudy hotels I was supplied with a delft cup an inch and a half thick. Then the Chinese bill was presented—it was made out on rice paper, the account being done in Indian ink as fantastically as if an artist had been etching little birds on a fan."
—IBID.

"Every man should be allowed to love two cities, his own and San Francisco." —GENE FOWLER

"San Francisco is a world to explore."

"The extreme geniality of San Francisco's economic, intellectual and political climate makes it the most varied and challenging city in the United States." —JAMES MICHENER

"San Francisco is the only populated area from the Canadian border to the Mexican border that is known as 'The City!' " —CHESTER MACPHEE

"Of all American cities of whatever size the most friendly on preliminary inspection, and on further acquaintance the most likeable. The happiest-hearted, the gayest, the most care-free city on this continent."
—IRWIN S. COBB

"San Francisco the capital of the Gaslight Tradition." —CARL HEPP

"Every port is my oyster but San Francisco is the coo-coo clam of them all." —WILSON MIZNER

"San Francisco takes strange hold on the hearts of man. Even the most insensitive individual is conscious at times of this attraction, but it appears most importunately to young people, newspapermen, poets, and other sub-varieties of lunacy. For them (to whom Paris seems a weary bawd, and Vienna a gay girl-widow, and Chicago the 'hog butcher to the world'), San Francisco is the grayeyed mistress of sea captains, not young, but youthful, not old, but wise, a comrade of youth, a lover of the vigorous and adventurous, always a gazer over blue water, with the salt upon her face."
—GEORGE DYER

"San Francisco, the city, where nobody thinks." —FRANK NORRIS

"Fancy a novel about Chicago or Buffalo, let us say, or Nashville, Tennessee. There are just three big cities in the United States that are 'story cities', New York, of course, New Orleans, and best of the lot, San Francisco."
—IBID.

"God took the beauty of the Bay of Naples, the Valley of the Nile, the Swiss Alps, the Hudson River Valley, rolled them into one and made San Francisco Bay." —FIORELLO LA GUARDIA, *mayor of New York City*.

". . . a wordly wise yet forever juvenile hoyden swinging on her Golden Gate. . . the bronze buckler of the mountains at her back, the silver lance of her bay aimed at the breast of the sea." —IRVING COBB

"Los Angeles may be California's diamond stomacher, but San Francisco is the poppies in her hair." —IBID.

"No city invites the heart to come to life as San Francisco does. Arrival in San Francisco is an experience in living. . . " —WILLIAM SAROYAN

"San Francisco is the genius of American cities. It is the wild-eyed, all-fired, hard-boiled, tender-hearted, white-haired boy of the American family of cities. It is the prodigal son. The city which does everything and is always forgiven, because of its great heart, its gentle smile, its roaring laughter, its mysterious and magnificent personality. It is not the easiest city in the world to like at first. It seems cold, hard, ugly, indifferent, and out of the world. It is not an easy city to know. It seems delirious with energy, incoherent because of the many things it has to say, broken-hearted with sorrowful memories. You walk through the streets of the city and feel its loneliness, and you wonder what memory is troubling its heart." —IBID.

"There are no end of ways of enduring time in San Francisco, pleasantly, beautifully, and with the romance of living in everything. Eat any kind of dish the races of the world know how to prepare. Drink any kind of wine you like. Play any game you care to play. Go to the opera. The symphony. The concert. Go to a movie or a stage play. Loaf around in the high-toned bars, or in the honky-tonks. Sail in the bay. Go down to Bay Meadows or Tanforan and bet the horses. Go to church. If you are alive, you can't be bored in San Francisco. If you're not alive, San Francisco will bring you to life. You may be a fool for a week or two, but nobody will notice that because everybody else has been a fool too, and is likely to be a fool again. San Francisco is a world to explore. It is a place where the heart can go on a delightful adventure. It is a city in which the spirit can know refreshment every day." —IBID.

"San Francisco! —one of my two favorite cities. There is more grace per square foot in San Francisco than any place on earth!"
—BISHOP FULTON J. SHEEN

"I love this city. If I am elected, I'll move the White House to San Francisco. Everybody's so friendly. I went down to Fisherman's Wharf and they even let me into Alioto's. It may be Baghdad-by-the-Bay to you, but to me it's Resurrection City." —ROBERT KENNEDY

"San Francisco is ambiente." —JAMES D. ZELLERBACH

"New York is getting dirtier by the minute. San Francisco is so clean. It's more beautiful than I had remembered. San Francisco people are more scrubbed than washed, but the styles sold here are no more conservative than the rest of the country." —NORMAN NORELL

"San Francisco is a city with the assets of a metropolis without the disadvantages of size and industry." —JACK KENNY

"There is a very healthy lack of cliche in San Francisco and a willingness to accept people for what they are as individuals. Nature has provided an ideal setting for a deep interaction between individuals." —WALTER LANDOR

"Frisco (as we saucy auslanders call this fair burg) is one of the few cities left in the world (and I should say the only English-speaking one) where the pleasures plainly outweigh the perfidies. I think it may be truly said, in this century, that if you are tired of Frisco you are tired of life."
—CHARLES MCCABE

"Cities, like people, have souls and that of San Francisco is beautiful."
—MAYOR JOSEPH ALIOTO

"The Athens of the U.S." —MR. & MRS. HERBERT HOOVER

"San Francisco is Beautiful People wearing a bracelet of bridges."
—HAL LIPSET

"San Francisco is poetry. Even the hills rhyme." —PAT MONTANDON

"It has been said that all great cities of history have been built on bodies of water—Rome on the Tiber, Paris on the Seine, London on the Thames, New York on the Hudson. If this is a criterion of a city's greatness, surely San Francisco ranks in the first magnitude among cities of the world. For never was a metropolis more dominated by any natural feature than San Francisco by its bay." —HAROLD GILLIAM

Film & Theatrical Personalities

"San Francisco is very close to my heart. I first visited as a small boy, when my father appeared there with Helen Modjeska. . . I played my last stage engagement in "Laugh, Clown, Laugh". I wedged it in between screen assignments. That was in 1925. I remember many of the grand oldtimers I met on other stage engagements: Frank Unger, Joe Redding, and a gentlemen named Maloney, on the waterfront, who drew the finest mug of steam beer extant—a nectar fit for the gods which I have never found anywhere but in San Francisco. . . I remember its great artists, like William Keith, Joe Strong, McComas, who used to come up from Carmel in later years; George Sterling, the poet, and others in the Bohemian set. I often think of them, and also, on hot days, with a little yearning, of Maloney's steam beer, which of course, I wouldn't be able to drink it now, even if it could be found."
—LIONEL BARRYMORE

"I never dreamed I could like any city as well as London. San Francisco is exciting, moody, exhilarating. I even love the muted fogs."
—JULIE CHRISTIE

"I like the fog that creeps over the whole city every night about five, and the warm protective feeling it gives. . . and lights of San Francisco at night, the fog horn, the bay at dusk and the little flower stands where spring flowers appear before anywhere else in the country. . . But, most of all, I like the view of the ocean from the Cliff House." —IRENE DUNNE

"San Francisco is one of the great cultural plateaus of the world. . . one of the really urbane communities in the United States. . . one of the truly cosmopolitan places—and for many, many years, it always has had a warm welcome for human beings from all over the world." —DUKE ELLINGTON

"I always see about six scuffles a night when I come to San Francisco. That's one of the town's charms." —ERROL FLYNN

"It's a marvelous city." —AVA GARDNER

"Three cities lie nearest to my affections. They are the London and Paris of before the war, and San Francisco. San Francisco, with its metropolitan air, its fine restaurants and its genial spirit, charmed me from the first. In fact, I bought my home at Pebble Beach, where I go between pictures, largely because it is so close to San Francisco." —GREER GARSON

"I like the way the wind whips your skirts when you go by cable car up Nob Hill. I like the salt spray in your face when the surf breaks on the rocks at Fort Point. I like the white waves the ferry boats leave as they ply the bay, to the Oakland mole. I like the seals barking on the rocks at the Cliff House. I like the fog rolling over St. Francis Wood. I like the trolleys racing each other down Market Street's four tracks. I like the Irish cops and the Italian flower vendors. I just like San Francisco, I guess." —RITA HAYWORTH

"We're crazy about this city. First time we came here, we walked the streets all day—all over town—and nobody hassled us. People smiled, friendly-like, and we knew we could live here. We'd like to keep our place in Greenwich Village and have an apartment here, God and the Immigration Service willing. Los Angeles? That's just a big parking lot where you buy a hamburger for the trip to San Francisco.

"The food in this city is fantastic. Better than London. You know, more variety. And the beautiful old houses and the strange light. We've never been in a city with light like this. We sit in our hotel room for hours, watching the fog come in, the light change." —JOHN & YOKO LENNON

"Your city is so very beautiful, I think more beautiful than Naples, but not so romantic." —SOPHIA LOREN

"I don't like San Francisco, I love it!"—DOROTHY LAMOUR

"San Francisco, you know, is our favorite city on earth, due, among many things, to its beautiful grocery stores. Indeed Lynn and I would like nothing

"San Francisco is one of the truly cosmopolitan places."

better than to settle down to live here—except, of course, that we already live in Wisconsin." —ALFRED LUNT & LYNN FONTANNE LUNT

"I shall always feel that San Francisco is the Pacific Coast's only cosmopolitan city. It has big business, is a good show town, and if you like superb food, there is nothing to compare with it in the West." —DENNIS MORGAN

"Cities are like gentlemen, they are born, not made. You are either a city, or you are not, size has nothing to do with it. I bet San Francisco was a city from the very first time it had a dozen settlers. New York is 'Yokel,' but San Francisco is 'City at Heart.' " —WILL ROGERS

"I love San Francisco. It would be a perfect place for a honeymoon."
—KIM NOVAK

"From vaudeville days to today, I've always looked forward to visits to San Francisco. It's one of the best 'show towns' in the world. . . It's like New York with a California climate. It's a city that's smart, without being 'upstage' as we actors call it. That's why I like to go there often." —WALTER PIDGEON

"It is beautiful, rain or no rain. My pet city, here I feel at home."
—LILY PONS

"Now there's a grown-up swinging town." —FRANK SINATRA

"This is the last irreverent, impudent city in the country. There's more going on here in one day than goes on in Hollywood in a year. Don't let anybody kid you about Hollywood—it's still all plastic and tinsel."
—TOM SMOTHERS

"Whenever I visit San Francisco, I can't help thinking of David Belasco, Warfield, and my dear old friend, Hobart Bosworth. San Francisco to me represents a sort of cradle of the American theater because of the San Franciscans who made fame on the stage. I love the waterfront and its interesting characters. It was on Fisherman's Wharf that I saw the character who proved so suggestive to me when I played Manuel, the fisherman, in 'Captains Courageous.' And, above all, I have always loved the restaurants."
—SPENCER TRACY

"This is the first place in the United States where I sang, and I like San Francisco better than any other city in the world.
"I love no city more than this one. Where else could I sing outdoors on Christmas Eve!" —LUISA TETRAZZINI

"I'm just mad for San Francisco. It looks like London and Paris all stacked on top of each other." —TWIGGY

Foreign Visitors

"This is such a lovely city, I think I'll retire here."
—PRINCESS ALEXANDRA OF ENGLAND

"One of the most beautiful cities in the world. When we came under that beautiful bridge I felt like the Queen of Sheba before Solomon. Everyone brags about San Francisco. It seems an exaggeration till one sees it. Now I don't doubt it any more."
—PRINCESS ALICE, COUNTESS OF ATHLONE, OF ENGLAND

"San Francisco is the greatest. . . the hills. . . fabulous food. . . most beautiful and civilized people."
—THE DUKE & DUCHESS OF BEDFORD, OF ENGLAND

"Friendly city, the city of happy memory, of beauty and hospitality."
—SIR CARL BERENDSEN, *New Zealand Ambassador to U.S.*

"The loveliest city in the world." —PRINCE BERTIL

"San Francisco has the quality of a fairy tale."
—ELIZABETH BOWEN, *British novelist*

"And if it were possible I would like to take Golden Gate Park home with me. True, we have lovely parks in Paris, but your Golden Gate has—how do you say?—extraordinary contours." —JEAN CHERIOUX

"San Francisco is so attractive that one visit is not enough. It merely makes you want to see it again."—VYACHESLAV ELUTIN, *Russia*

"San Francisco continues to be a spot symbolizing our best hope of peace . . . the first city of the world and the promised land of world unity."
—FERIDUN C. ERKIN, *Turkish Ambassador to U.S.*

"City of St. Francis where the roses are always flowering and never thorned." —OSCAR GANS, *Cuban Minister of State*

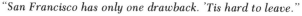

"San Francisco has only one drawback. 'Tis hard to leave."

"I've fallen in love with San Francisco. My friends told me that this city and Rome were outstanding for their character and beauty. I heartily agree with them." —SIR ALEC GUINESS, *England*

"Everybody told me that it was the most beautiful city in the country. It is better than I expected. The people here act quickly and think quickly, and they are more cosmopolitan than in most American cities."
—DR. INGEBORG HANACK, *Germany*

"San Francisco is the best city in the United States. It does not need to make this claim—America accepts it . . . It is blessed with beauty, an aristocrat among cities—this city of the Golden Gate and the golden heart . . . San Francisco today fears nothing except another earthquake. But this is a word you must never mention, for San Francisco would be offended—and anyone who offends San Francisco is a clod." —DON IDDON, *London columnist*

"To this day the city of San Francisco remains to the Chinese the Great City of the Golden Mountains." —KAI FU SHAH, *Chinese Minister to U.S.*

"This is a place where people seem to be waiting for the next movie company to arrive. Almost without trying, San Francisco is a delight to the eye." —RICHARD LESTER, *British film producer*

"San Francisco has only one drawback. 'Tis hard to leave."
—RUDYARD KIPLING

"It is a mad city, inhabited by perfectly insane people whose women are of remarkable beauty." —IBID.

"Really I am delighted with what I've seen of San Francisco. A most picturesque city, indeed, and quite remarkable for the many opportunities for enjoyment if offers the traveler. You will excuse my preference for Madras, Bombay, and a few other cities of India, but residing there for so many years I'm rather disposed in their favor." —IBID.

"Yes there is no doubt about the greatness of this city, en passant as we say in Bengal, I'll freely admit that your institutions charm me. There is geniality about your policemen that appeals irresistibly to politest instincts, and I have no hesitation in stating that your Mayor is a brick, I may say a pressed brick." —IBID.

"The cable cars have for all practical purposes made San Francisco a dead level. They take no count of rise or fall, but slide equally on their appointed courses from one end to the other of a six-mile street. They turn corners almost at right angles, cross other lines and for ought I know may turn up the sides of houses. There is no visible agency of their flight, but once in a while you shall pass a five story building humming with machinery that winds everlasting wire cable and the initiated will tell you that here is the mechanism. If it pleases Providence to make a car run up and down a slit in the ground for many miles and if for two pence half penny I can ride in that car, why shall I ask the reason for the miracle."

—IBID (*American Notes*, 1891)

"I like California, but best of all I am charmed by this beautiful City of San Francisco." —NIKITA KHRUSHCHEV, *Russian Premier*

"Selection of San Francisco as the Peace Conference city was made with fitness and propriety."

—MOHAMMED ZAFRULLA KHAN, *Foreign Minister of Pakistan*

"It's the grandest city I saw in America. If everyone acted as the San Franciscans did, there would be hope for settlement of the world's difficulties." —FROL ZOZLOV, *First Deputy Premier of Russia*

"San Francisco is a sympathetic city. It reminds me of Tangiers—but bigger." —PRINCESS LALLA, *of Morocco*

"I had heard so much about San Francisco that I was afraid I would be disappointed—but it lived up to my expectations!"

—PRINCESS MARGARET, *of England*

"Two days in this city is worth two months in New York."

—ROBERT MENZIES, *Prime Minister of New Zealand*

"I have never seen such fuchsias. All of our best flower seeds come from California. And Golden Gate Park is the most beautiful I've ever visited."

—MRS. TERENCE O'NEIL, *wife of Prime Minister of Northern Ireland*

"San Francisco is the loveliest city in the world."

—ANTOINE PINAY, *French Foreign Minister*

"A very pretty place. . . San Francisco. . . prettier than a lot of places. . . but not prettier than Monaco." —PRINCE RAINIER, *of Monaco*

"Queen of the Pacific, the city that saw the birth of the United Nations Charter and to which from now on all treaties and pacts to restore or consolidate peace will be linked." —ROBERT SCHUMAN, *French Foreign Minister*

"No visit to the United States would be complete without San Francisco—this beautiful city, center of the West, very well known for its beauty and the place where the United Nations were born."
—QUEEN SIRIKIT, *of Thailand*

"I am deeply moved by the cordial friendship of the citizens of San Francisco." —CEVDET SUNAY, *President of Turkey*

"The most beautiful city in the world. When our countries become friendlier again, what I want to be is the Soviet Consul in San Francisco."
—GHERMAN TITOV, *Soviet Cosmonaut*

"Noel Coward told me in New York that whatever I do, I must see San Francisco. I saw San Francisco first on Saturday, a lovely spring day. This Easter day I see it in the rain. I love it both ways. The two things that have impressed me most in America are the Lincoln Memorial in Washington and San Francisco." —GODFREY WINN, *British author & lecturer*

"It is a city of ever-fresh memories that will remain with me as long as I live." —SHIGERU YOSHIDA, *of Japan*

Chronology

1776
June 29 Presidio of San Francisco founded
Oct. 9 Mission Dolores founded
1835
June 25 Pueblo founded with erection of first building by Wm. Richardson
1846
July 9 American flag raised at Yerba Buena
Nov. 18 First "Thanksgiving Day" celebration observed
1847
Jan. 9 San Francisco's first newspaper, *The California Star*, publishes first issue

Jan. 30 Yerba Buena renamed San Francisco
1848
Jan. 9 First commercial bank established in San Francisco
Jan. 24 Gold discovered in Coloma, Calif.
Feb. 2 Brig *Eagle* brings first shipload of Chinese to San Francisco
Apr. 3 First American public school opened in San Francisco
Nov. 9 Post office opens at Clay & Pike streets
1849
Feb. 18 First regular steamboat service to California inaugurated by the arri-

May 4, 1850. Fire destroys part of The City.

val of the Pacific Mail's *California*

July 28 First clipper ship, the *Memnon*, arrives in San Francisco, 120 days from New York

Nov. 19 Public sale of pueblo land held

Dec. 24 Fire destroys part of the city

1850

Jan 3 Great sale of beach and water property

Jan. 5 California Exchange opens

Jan. 16 Eagle Theater and Washington Hall open

Jan. 19 National Theater dedicated

Jan. 21 French newspaper *Le Californien* established

Jan. 22 The *Alta California* is metamorphosed to a daily newspaper, the first in California.

Jan. 23. San Francisco's second daily journal, *The Journal of Commerce*, established by Washington Bartlett

Feb. 18. Legislature creates Bay region counties: San Francisco, Contra Costa, Marin, Santa Clara, Sonoma, Solano, and Napa

Feb. 19. National Theater opens

Mar. 18. Town Council rules that all titles to land made by grants or sales in any form, by any person or persons whatever, other than the legally elected Alcalde or Town Council are illegal

Mar. 23. Phoenix Theater opens, on Pacific near Montgomery

Apr. 1. San Francisco County government established

Apr. 15. City of San Francisco incorporated

May 4. Fire destroys part of city bounded by Montgomery, Kearny, Clay, Jackson, Washington and Dupont streets

May 7. Foley's Olympic Ampitheater opens

May 9. Two Boards of Aldermen met at the new City Hall, corner of Kearny and Pacific

May 11. Construction begins on first brick building (Naglee) at corner of Montgomery and Merchant streets

June 1. *San Francisco Daily Herald* begins publishing

June 4. Empire Engine Co. No. 1 organized

June 14. Fire destroys part of city; St. Francis Hook & Ladder Co. No. 1, Howard Engine Co. No. 3 and Sansome Hook & Ladder Co. No. 3 organized

July 1. The *California Courier* established by James M. Crane and F. W. Rice

July 1. At this time there were some 626 vessels lying in the Bay of San Francisco and contiguous harbors

July 4. Dramatic Museum, California Street between Montgomery and Kearny, opens; Independence Day celebrated and a flag-pole, 111 ft. high, is erected on the Plaza

Aug. 3. *Evening Picayune* established by Dr. J. H. Gihon

Aug. 13. Athenaeum I Theater opens, Commercial between Kearny and Montgomery

Aug. 14. Rowe's New Olympic Ampitheater, Montgomery between Sacramento and California, opens

Sept. First San Francisco City Directory published by Charles P. Kimball

Sept. 7. Bank runs occur

Sept. 9. California admitted to the Union

Sept. 12. First issue of Octavian Hoogs' paper *La Gazette Républicaine*

appears; Italian Theater, Jackson & Kearny, opens

Sept. 17. Fire destroys part of city bounded by Dupont, Montgomery, Washington and Pacific Streets

Sept. 30. Foley's Ampitheater, west side of Portsmouth Plaza, re-opens

Oct. 16. Adelphi I Theater, Clay between Montgomery and Kearny, opens

Oct. 17. Knickerbocker Engine Co. No. 5 organized

Oct. 29. Day devoted to celebrating the admission of California into the Union as the 31st State

Oct. 30. Jenny Lind Theater opens

Nov. 6. Yerba Buena and Angel Islands reserved by executive order for military purposes

Nov. 9. Adelphi Theater opens, south side, between Montgomery and Kearny

Nov. 18. Col. Chas. L. Wilson granted concession to build a plank-road from San Francisco to Mission Dolores on a toll basis

Nov. 30. Day set apart as Thanksgiving Day for the admission of California into the Union

Dec. 8. Newspaper *Public Balance* established by Benjamin R. Buckelew and Eugene Casserly

Dec. 14. Foley's New Amphitheater, west side of Portsmouth Plaza, opens

1851

Jan 12. Foley's Amphitheater closes

Jan. 18. California Circus Theater opens

Jan. 31. First orphan asylum in California, the San Francisco Orphan Asylum, founded by the Protestants

Mar. 26. Legislature of the State of California enacts law by which the State relinquishes title to all lots below high water mark within the city limits to the City of San Francisco

May 4. Fire destroys almost entire city

May 6. Chamber of Commerce organized

May 19. Theater of Arts, Jackson Street near Dupont, opens

May 24. Shepard & Company commences publishing the *Morning Post*

June 9. First Committee of Vigilance organized

June 13. Jenny Lind Theater re-opens, Kearny near Washington Streets

June 22. Fire destroys part of the city

Aug. 1. Adelphi II Theater opens

Oct. 4. Jenny Lind Theater re-opens

Oct. 20. American Theater, Sansome Street between California and Sacramento Streets, opens

1852

Jan 15. Charles E. Pickett begins publishing the *Western American*, a daily newspaper

Feb. 17. Publication of the *San Francisco Shipping List and Prices Current* commenced by S. O. Johnson & Co.

Apr. 8. Vigilant Engine Co. No. 9 organized

Apr. 19. California Historical Society incorporated

May 14. James King of William, editor of the *Evening Bulletin*, shot and killed

May 25. *The Evening Journal* begins publication by Pinkham Gee & Co.

June 1. The French newspaper *L' Echo du Pacifique* established

July 23. First interment in U.S. National Cemetary at Presidio

Aug. 1. Colored Methodists organize Zion M.E. Church

Nov. 4. Crescent Engine Co. No. 10, Columbian Engine Co. No. 11 and Pennsylvania Engine Co. No. 12 organized

Nov. 23. Shortly before midnight, after a shock like that of an earthquake, the waters of Lake Merced sink about 30 feet

Dec. 19. *The Golden Era*, a literary weekly, established

Dec. 23. The Chinese Theater, Dupont Street near Green, opens

Dec. 24. San Francisco Hall, Washington between Kearny and Montgomery, opens

1853

Jan. 2. The U.S. Land Commission begins its sittings in San Francisco to decide on the validity of claims of those holding or attempting to hold land under the old "Spanish grants"

Jan. 16. The weekly *California Farmer*, an agricultural paper, begun by J.L.L. Warren

Jan. 27. *The Pioneer*, a monthly magazine, published by Lecount & Strong, is established

Feb. 13. Chinese Mission House organized by Rev. William Speer

Feb. 15. *The Curiosity Shop*, a humorous illustrated weekly, established

Mar. 17. *The Wide West*, a Sunday literary newspaper, established by Bonestill & Williston

Apr. 1. Ladies' Protection & Relief Society founded

Apr. 17. U.S. Marine Hospital established at the Presidio

Apr. 28. The *Golden Hill News*, published in Chinese, established by Howard & Hudson

May 1, Emma Jane Swasey crowned first Queen of May; Russ Gardens, Harrison & Sixth Streets, opens

June 1. Lafayette Hook & Ladder Co. No. 2, Broadway between Dupont & Stockton, organized

June 16. Daily newspaper *Present and Future* established by Dr. E. Theller

July 17. Construction starts on St. Mary's Church, California & Dupont Streets

July 26. Musical Hall, Bush between Montgomery and Sansome, opens

Sept. 9. Pacific Engine Co. No. 8 organized

Sept. 11. First electric telegraph opened for use, connecting the Merchant's Exchange with Point Lobos

Sept. 16. Money appropriated for building fence around Yerba Buena Cemetary

Sept. 19. Lafayette Hook & Ladder Co. No. 2 organized

Oct. 1. Olympic Theater, Washington & Sansome Streets, opens; California State Telegraph Co. line opened between San Francisco and San Jose

Oct. 22. St. Francis Hotel, corner Dupont & Clay streets, destroyed by fire

Oct. 30. Olympic Theater closes

Nov. 17. Street signs authorized to be affixed at the various crossings

Dec. 24. Guillot's Theater, Pacific between Stockton and Dupont, opens

Dec. 25. Metropolitan Theater opens, first theater to be lit by gas

1854

Jan. 1. Young America Engine Co. No. 13 organized

Feb. 11. Principal streets lighted with coal gas for first time

Mar. 1. California Steam Navigation Co. organized

Apr. 12. Walls of the U.S. Bonded Warehouse at Battery and Union collapse

May 6. The Catholic Church organ, the *Weekly Catholic Standard*, established

May 11. The *Star of the West*, formerly the *California Temperance Organ*, begins publication

May 19. F. A. Bonnard's *Daily Sun* appears as a weekly

May 27. Marine telegraph from Fort Point to San Francisco completed

May 30. Lone Mountain Cemetery dedicated

June 20. Volunteer Engine Co. No. 7 organized

June 22. San Francisco Accumulating Fund Association incorporated

June 28. First interment in Laurel Hill Cemetery

July 17. Calvary Presbyterian Church organized

Aug. 5. People's Theater, Commercial between Kearny and Dupont, opens

Sept. 25. The German newspaper *Abend Zeitung* established by A. J. Lafontaine

Nov. 2. Cobblestone paving of Washington street between Dupont & Kearny commences

Nov. 4. Lighthouse on Alcatraz established

Nov. 12. William H. Mantz & Co. begin publishing *Town Talk*

Dec. 4. American II Theater opens

Dec. 25. Old St. Mary's Church dedicated

1855

Jan. 4. *The Oriental*, a Chinese newspaper, established by Rev. William Speer

Mar. 26. Paving of Washington Street between Dupont & Kearny completed

Apr. 7. *The Fireman's Journal*, devoted to the interests of the fire department, established by C. M. Chase & Co.

June 20. Commissioners appointed to lay out streets and blocks west of Larkin, extending to the city charter line of 1851.

July 15. St. Ignatius Church, Market between 4th & 5th, dedicated

July 22. French semi-weekly paper *Le Phare* established by P. Hertzberg, A. H. Rapp, and Wm. M. Hinton

Oct. 8. *Daily Evening Bulletin* begins publication

Oct. 15. St. Ignatius Academy on Market Street opens to students

Dec. 24. James P. Casey establishes the *Weekly Sunday Times*

Dec. 25. The first German Protestant Church build on the Pacific Coast the German Evangelical Lutheran

Church on Sutter between Dupont and Stockton, dedicated

Dec. 28. Tiger Engine Co. No. 14 organized

1856

Jan. Coal from Coos Bay, Ore., first introduced to the San Francisco market

Jan. 22. M. Derbec starts publication of the *Eco del Pacifico*, a daily Spanish paper

Mar. 13. Moody & Co. begin publication of the *Daily Globe*

Mar. 26. Ladies' Seamen's Friend Society founded

May 4. Notre Dame des Victoires Church dedicated

May 15. Second Vigilance Committee organized

May 22. Execution of James P. Casey and Charles Cora by the Vigilance Committee.

Nov. 29. Maguire's Opera House opens

Dec. 1. The *Daily Morning Call* established

1857

Jan. 16. Concert Hall, corner Clay & Sansome, opens

Apr. 29. Headquarters for Army's Division of the Pacific permanently established at the Presidio

June 15. San Francisco Water Works organized

Aug. 15. Metropolitan Theater burns

Sept. 8. Mechanics Pavilion, west side Montgomery between Post and Sutter opens

Dec. 15. Johnson's Melodeon opens

1858

Jan. 1. Drs. J. B. Trask & David Wooster establish the monthly *Pacific Medical Journal*

May 15, 1856. The second Vigilance Committee is organized.

May 22, 1856. The execution of Casey and Cora.

Jan. 2. New German Hospital opens at Steamboat Point

Mar. 6. The *Weekly Monitor*, an organ of the Catholic Church, established by Marks Thomas & Co.

Mar. 13. Lyceum Theater, northwest corner of Washington & Montgomery, opens

Mar. 15. French Hospital on Brannan Street opens

June 2. Adelphi Theater burns

Oct. 1. W. H. Mantz & Co. begin publishing the *Daily Evening Telegram*

Oct. 3. J. C. Duncan commences publication of the *Weekly California Home Journal*

Oct. 24. Clock completed on St. Mary's Cathedral tower

Dec. 23. *The Telegraph Hill*, a weekly newspaper, begins publication

1859

Mar. 1. Present seal of the City of San Francisco adopted

Apr. 12. Hibernia Savings & Loan Society of San Francisco incorporated

Oct. 2. Cornerstone of St. Francis Church on Vallejo laid

Dec. 5. Gilbert's Melodeon, northeast corner Kearny and Clay, opens

Dec. 19. Grading commenced for Market Street Railroad

1860

Feb. 1. French Savings & Loan Society incorporated

Mar. 17. Japanese Embassy arrives in San Francisco aboard the Japanese steamer *Candinmarruh*

Mar. 24. Clipper ship *Andrew Jackson* arrives from New York in 89 days

Apr. 14. First Pony Express rider arrives in San Francisco from St. Joseph, Missouri

May 1. First school for the deaf founded on Tehama Street

June 7. Workmen laying track on Market Street Railroad

July 1. Single track of the San Francisco and Mission Railroad completed, a distance of three miles from the foot of Market street to the Mission

July 4. Service commences on city's first street railway

July 9. Olympic Theater, formerly Athenaeum II, closes

Aug. 6. Musical Hall, Montgomery & Bush, opens after being rebuilt

Aug. 16. Archbishop Alemany purchases 60 acres of Lone Mountain properties and consecrates the greater portion as Calvary Cemetery

Sept. 3. Exempt Fire Co. organized

Oct. 4. Prince Kamehameha arrives on his private yacht

Oct. 8. Telegraph line opened between San Francisco and Los Angeles

Nov. 8. Calvary Cemetery dedicated

Nov. 27. Lyceum Theater destroyed by fire

Dec. 22. New Rincon Hill Schoolhouse dedicated

1861

Feb. 15. Fort Point completed and garrisoned by two companies of 3rd Artillery

Apr. 4. Spring Valley Water Company celebrates the filling of the Potrero Hill reservoir

Apr. 11. Metropolitan Theater opens after being rebuilt

May 11. Union demonstration at Market & Post Streets following the news of the firing on Fort Sumter

June 1. Banking house of Donohoe, Ralston & Co. established

June 14. Howard Engine Company opens new firehouse with a banquet

July 1. New public schoolhouse, corner Washington and Mason Streets, opened

July 3. Arrival of the Pony Express with overland letters from New York, etc.

Aug. 1. Well-attended mass meeting is held at Mechanics' Hall and an association, the Mechanics' League, is formed to carry on the fight against convict labor

Aug. 27. The *Daily Times* suspends publication

Sept. 9. Military organization called the McClellan Guard organized

Sept. 25. Military organization called the Siegel Rifles organized

Nov. 16. Completion of the new St. Mary's Hospital on Rincon Hill

Dec. 8. St. Joseph's Catholic Church dedicated

Dec. 31. Incorporation of the California Powder Works with a capital of $100,000

1862

Jan. 11. Fire destroys the boarding house known as Sarsfield Hall, Pacific & Montgomery Streets

June 18. San Francisco Savings Union incorporated

July 11. Grand torchlight demonstration of firemen in honor of passage of the Pacific Railroad Bill

Aug. 17. Calvary Cemetery consecrated by Archbishop Alemany with the rites of the Catholic Church

Sept. 4. North Beach & Mission Railway Co. organized

Sept. 6. Illumination, firing of guns, and other manifestations of joy at San Francisco in honor of supposed victory of Union forces at Manassas. Subscription started for the relief of the sick and wounded soldiers of the Union Army

Sept. 15. Citizens of San Francisco propose to raise a regiment of infantry for service in the East

Sept. 20. The sum of $100,000 sent East, as a contribution for the relief of the sick and wounded soldiers to be disbursed by the National Sanitary Commission

Nov. 6. Direct telegraphic communication established between New York and San Francisco

Dec. 11. Company of cavalry, known as the "California Hundred," intended for service in the East, sails in the *Golden Age* for Panama

1863

Jan. 28. Society of California Pioneers incorporated

Feb. 22. Gov. Stanford lays cornerstone for the Broderick monument in Lone Mountain Cemetery

Mar. 15. Schooner *J. M. Chapman* seized in the Bay and five men arrested as privateers

June 4. Fight at the Farallone Islands between the Farallone Egg Company and a party of Italians; one killed and five wounded

July 2. Water of the Spring Valley Water Works first brought to the city from Lake Honda

Sept. 1. Railroad and ferry connection with Oakland inaugurated

Oct. 15. The Cliff House opens

Oct. 15. San Francisco and San Jose Railroad formally opened

Oct. 20. First number of *Democratic Press* issued

Oct. 28. Telegraph cable laid across heads from Fort Point to Lime Point

Nov. 1. Troops begin erecting fortifications on Angel Island

Nov. 21. Harbor Commissioners take possession of Vallejo, Jackson, Clay, Washington, & Mission wharfs

Nov. 27. Count di Castiglione and Major Devecchi, Commissioners of Exploration, feted by the Italian merchants of the city

Dec. 2. Irataba, Chief of the Mohave Indians, arrives in town

1864

Jan. 5. More's Wharf caves in

Jan. 11. Strike for higher wages by stable grooms

Jan. 16. San Francisco-San Jose Railroad celebrates completion of their road with a grand dinner and speeches at San Jose

Feb. 24. Meeting of German citizens regarding Holstein-Schleswig war question

Mar. 4. Rev. Thomas Starr King dies

Apr. 2. Rincon Hose Co. No. 6 goes into service

Apr. 15. General Wright issues order forbidding vessels entering the harbor of San Francisco to pass north of Alcatraz on penalty of being fired upon

Apr. 28. Officers quarters at Black Point Battery destroyed by fire

May 18. Maguire's Academy of Music opens

June 11. 300 feet of Meigg's Wharf washed away in gale

Aug. 31. Cosmopolitan Hotel opens

Nov. 14. The *Comanche*, an iron-clad monitor of the U.S. Navy, launched

Dec. 29. Fire Department celebrates with the first annual ball

1865

Jan. 16. First issue of *San Francisco Dramatic Chronicle* published by Charles and Michael deYoung

Mar. 1. City Hall bell removed to the Old Union Hotel building where it hereafter will sound the alarm in case of fire

Apr. 24. Fire alarm and police telegraph system inaugurated

May 1. Olympic Melodeon, formerly Gilbert's Melodeon, opens

June 29. Olympic Melodeon closes

Sept. 24. James Cooke performs ropewalking feat from the Cliff House to Seal Rocks

Sept. 25. Ground broken for the track of the Front Street, Mission and Ocean Railroad

Oct. 8. Earthquake in San Francisco

Nov. 19. Odd Fellows' Cemetery on Point Lobos Road dedicated

Dec. 12. Hostlers strike for higher wages

1866

Mar. 23. New Synagogue Emanu-El on Sutter Street consecrated

Apr. 16. Nitroglycerine explosion at Wells Fargo & Co. Express Office

Apr. 24. Steamer *Continental* arrives with 75 of Mercer's female immigrants for Washington Territory

May 4. Woodward's Gardens in the Mission opened to the public

Aug. 1. Union State Central Committee meets in San Francisco and adopts resolutions in favor of equal rights to all men, without distinction as to color

Aug. 6. Journeymen plasterers strike and demand the 8-hour system of work

Sept. 20. $1,000 for the best design of a seawall awarded to Lewis & Allardt

Oct. 13. Odd Fellows Savings Bank incorporated

Nov. 9. Cornerstone of the new Trinity Church at the corner of Post & Powell Streets, laid with the ceremonies of the Episcopal Church

Dec. 3. Paid Fire Department goes into active operation

Dec. 31. China and Japan Steamship Line inaugurated with grand banquet at the Occidental Hotel

1867

Feb. 1. Bricklayers begin work under the 8-hour rule

Feb. 12. Chinese laborers employed in excavating a lot on Townsend Street driven from their work. Their shanties and provisions destroyed by a mob of disaffected laborers, who afterwards proceeded to the Potrero and drove off the Chinese employed at the rope works of Tubbs & Co., setting fire to their homes

Feb. 20. Mass meeting held and an organization formed to establish anti-coolie clubs

Mar. 29. Workingmen's Convention opens

Apr. 23 Cosmopolitan Hotel fire; $150,000 damages

June 3. More than 2,000 men march through the streets carrying flags and banners heralding the 8-hour work day

June 27. Bank of California opens

July 14. Three noted Indian chiefs from the northern portion of the State visit in company with B. C. Whiting, Supt. of Indian Affairs for California

July 15. The Merchant's Exchange opens

July 21. The City Gardens on Folsom Street opened for the first time

July 31. The new California Market opens

Aug. 16. North wall of the old Chinese Hospital on Pine Street falls to the ground

Sept. 9. Work commenced on the first section of the seawall

Sept. 12. The Almshouse opens

Sept. 22. Trinity Church consecrated by Bishop Kip

Sept. 27. The *John L. Stephens*, first steamer to sail between California and Alaska, sails

Oct. 11. The *Pacific Hygenist*, a monthly journal, issued for the first time

Nov. 4. Blast of 90 kegs of powder exploded at Telegraph Hill to obtain section of the seawall

1868

Jan. 18. New Idea Theater, Commercial between Kearny and Dupont, opens

Jan. 27. Chinese Theater on Jackson Street opens

Feb. 10. German Savings and Loan Society incorporated

Feb. 13. Cornerstone laid for the Alhambra Theater on Bush Street

Mar. 1. The *Alaska Herald* founded by A. Honcharenko

Mar. 31. Chinese Embassy and suite arrive in San Francisco on the steamship *China*

Apr. 18. San Francisco Society for Prevention of Cruelty to Animals formed

Apr. 28. Grand banquet given at Lick House by merchants of San Francisco to the Chinese Embassy

Apr. 29. Chinese Embassy in company with General Halleck, Admiral Fletcher and others visit fortifications in the harbor of San Francisco

May 22. Alhambra Theater opens on Bush Street

Sept. 1. First *Morning Chronicle* issued with declarations of policy

The earthquake of 1868

Oct 21. A severe earthquake rocked San Francisco

Nov. 26. First baseball game played in enclosed field at 25th and Folsom Streets

1869

Jan. 18. California Theater opens

Apr. 18. First International Cricket Match held in the city won by the Californians

May 8. Celebration in honor of the completion of the Central Pacific Railroad across the continent, with civic and military processions

May 16. The new Calvary Presbyterian Church on Powell Street dedicated

Aug. 23. First carload of freight (boots and shoes) arrives from Boston after 16-day rail trip

Aug. 30. First shipment of tea overland (90 baskets) sent to Williams, Butters & Co., Chicago

Sept. 6. Steamer *Alameda* is first vessel to connect with the overland passenger train to reach San Francisco Bay.

Sept. 12. The new Italian Hospital formally opened

Sept. 22. Red Stocking Club of Cincinnati, famous baseball club, arrives overland

Sept. 26. Cornerstone of St. Patrick's Church laid by Archbishop Alemany

Oct. 9. San Francisco Yacht Club formally opens new club house on Long Bridge

Oct. 21. First shipment of fresh oysters arrives overland from Baltimore

Nov. 4. Masonic Savings & Loan Society incorporated

Nov. 15. Free Postal Delivery formally inaugurated

Nov. 24. Humboldt Savings & Loan Society incorporated

1870

Feb. 22. Anti-Chinese association, the Industrial Reformers, established

Mar. 14. Legislative act making Golden Gate Park possible is approved

Apr. 4. Golden Gate Park established by Order 800: an act to provide for the improvement of public parks in the City of San Francisco

Apr. 8. Serious fight between rival Chinese cigar makers occurs on Battery Street

June 1. Excursion party from Boston arrives overland

July 25. Board of Supervisors issues order forbidding any person to hire or let rooms for sleeping purposes in which there is less than 500 cubic feet of air per person

Aug. 8. William Hammond Hall awarded contract to make a minute topographical survey of Golden Gate Park for the sum of $4,860

Dec. 25. Chinese Mission Institute, corner Washington and Stone Streets, dedicated

1871

Jan. 14. Aerial steamer successfully tested by an association at the City Gardens

Jan. 25-27. First annual meeting of the California Woman Suffrage Society

Jan. 31. Birds pass over western part of city in such numbers as to darken the sky

Mar. 28. San Francisco Art Association holds opening reception in rooms at 430 Pine Street

Apr. 10. William Hammond Hall's surveys and maps of Golden Gate Park officially adopted by the first Board of Park Commissioners

Apr. 23. Blossom Rock (discovered and named by Capt. Beechey in 1826) in San Francisco Bay blown up

Sept. 23. The *Enterprise*, a workingmen's journal, makes its first appearance

Oct. 5. Occidental Skating Rink, Post and Stockton Streets, destroyed by fire

Oct. 11. Large and enthusiastic meeting held at the Merchant's Exchange for the relief of sufferers of the Chicago Fire; approximately $25,000 contributed on the spot

Nov. 3. "California Rifles" mustered out of service by order of Governor Haight

Nov. 4. First number of *The West* appears

Nov. 11. California Olympic Club organized

Dec. 28. First stone of the new City Hall laid with appropriate ceremonies

1872

Jan. 20. California Stock Exchange Board organized

Jan. 20. "Committee of One Hundred," organized to oppose cession of Goat Island to the railroad companies, holds its first meeting

Feb. 22. City Hall cornerstone laid

Apr. 20. Bar Association of San Francisco organized

May 16. Lamps of the Metropolitan Gas Company lit for the first time

May 17. Bohemian Club incorporated

June 18. Woman's Suffrage Convention held at Mercantile Library Hall

July 2. National Guard of Virginia arrive to participate in the celebration of the Fourth of July

Aug. 23. First Japanese commercial vessel ever in the port arrives with a cargo of tea

Nov. 15. Telegraphic courtesies exchanged between the Mayor of San Francisco and the Mayor of Adelaide, Australia, on the completion of the telegraphic route to Australia via Europe

Nov. 29. Hayes Park Pavilion destroyed by fire

Dec. 21. Hercules Powder Works blows up

1873

Apr. 20. Central Presbyterian Tabernacle on Tyler Street and the Church of the Holy Cross on Eddy Street are dedicated

May 8. Bodies of Captain Thomas and Lt. Howe, killed in the Modoc War, arrive en route to the East

May 9. Grand Chapter, Order of the Eastern Star, organized

May 23. Postal cards sold for the first time in this city

May 28. Chinese Six Companies telegraph to Hong Kong to have emigration to this port stopped

June 2. Ground broken for world's first cable street railroad on Clay Street

June 24. California Savings & Loan Society incorporated

June 29. St. Dominic's Church, Bush and Steiner Streets, dedicated

July 4. Aquarium in Woodward's Gardens opens

July 16. Baby show at Pacific Hall

Aug. 2. Trial run of Andrew Hallidie's cable car on Clay Street hill between Kearny and Jones, a grade of 307 feet

Nov. 12. Bay District Race Track opens

1874

Jan. 7. Conductors and drivers on the Bay View and Potrero Railroad strike claiming to be overworked

Jan. 8. Meeting of property holders to consider proposition to tunnel Russian Hill under Broadway, from Mason to Hyde

Feb. 21. Professor Allen and several citizens make ascensions in a balloon from Woodward's Gardens

Mar. 20. Captain Barbiere, the aeronaut, arrives with the French Mail balloon, Le Secours

Mar. 28. Captain Barbiere makes his first ascension from Woodward's Gardens in the balloon Le Secours

Apr. 19. The balloon America ascends from Woodward's Gardens with several passengers, who in descending from an altitude of 3,000 feet narrowly escape with their lives; Alcatraz Island barracks destroyed by fire

Sept. 4. Brewer's Protective Association incorporated

Nov. 5. The new U.S. Mint is formally transferred to Gen. O. H. La Grange, the superintendent, with befitting ceremony

Nov. 29. King Kalakaua of Hawaii pays a visit

1875

Jan. 7. Inauguration of the Northern Pacific Coast Railroad, from San Francisco to Tomales, via Sausalito

Feb. 21. Immense meeting of Catholics to protest against the expulsion of Sisters of Charity from Mexico

Mar. 2. Underwriter's Fire Patrol is organized

Mar. 30. The painting "Elaine" by Toby Rosenthal goes on exhibit at the galleries of Snow & May

May 24. Fire Insurance Patrol begins active duty

May 28. Chinese purchase church north side Washington and Stockton for mercantile and lodging use

June 5. Pacific Stock Exchange formally opens

June 19. Formal opening of the new U.S. Marine Hospital

July 11. First parlor of the Native Sons of the Golden West organized

Sept. 9. Lotta's Fountain, located at Kearny and Market Streets, dedicated; gift of Miss Lotta Crabtree to the people of San Francisco

Oct. 5. Palace Hotel on Market Street opens

Dec. 24. The Commercial Bank suspends business

Dec. 26. Spanish American Church dedicated

1876

Jan. 17. Wade's Opera House, Mission and 3rd Streets, opens

Mar. 6. Baldwin Hotel, Market Ellis and Powell Streets, opens

Apr. 3. Chinese Six Companies petition Board of Supervisors for protection

Apr. 11. Senatorial Chinese Investigation Commission convened at San Francisco; Benevolent and Protective Order of Elks organized

Apr. 25. Pedro II, Emperor of Brazil, arrives for visit

May 2. District Judge S. B. McKee rules that ordinance imposing special tax upon Chinese laundries is unconstitutional

June 3. Ordinance providing for cutting off hair of county jail prisoners enforced by cutting off queue of Chinese convict

July 4. San Francisco's first public exhibition of electric light, from roof of St. Ignatius College, Market Street between Fourth and Fifth, by Father Joseph M. Neri, S.J.

Sept. 2. Society for the Prevention of Cruelty to Children incorporated

Sept. 4. The first California Council of the Sovereigns of Industry established

Sept. 6. Southern Pacific line connecting Los Angeles and San Francisco completed

Oct. 31. Fire at the Chinese Theater on Jackson Street kills 19 Chinese

Nov. Diphtheria epidemic in San Francisco in the closing days of month

1877

Apr. 17. Ariel Rowing Club organized

July 5. Anti-Coolie convention assembled

July 15. Work begun on the California Street Railroad

July 23. An estimated 8,000 people gather at open-air mass meeting called in support of the Eastern Railroad strikers

July 24. Anti-Chinese sentiment results in first of San Francisco's "sandlot riots"

July 25. James d'Arcy speaks to jobless workers at Fifth and Mission Streets

July 29. Baptist Church, Eddy near Jones, dedicated

Aug. 3. Attempts made to burn the residence of William T. Coleman

Sept. 18. Clement Grammar School opens, named for Joseph Clement

Oct. 5. Denis Kearney organizes his sandlot party, called the "Workingmen's Party of California"

Nov. 12. Fidelity Bank closes its doors

1878

Jan. 3. Approximately 500 unemployed men march to City Hall and demand that the mayor give them work

Jan. 14. Baby contest in Platt's Hall

Jan. 21. First state convention of the Workingmen's Party of California begins

Mar. 26. Hastings College of Law founded by S. Clinton Hastings

Apr. 10. Sutro Railroad opens

Apr. 14. Convent of St. Rose dedicated

Apr. 29. Judge Lorenzo Sawyer, of the U.S. District Court, holds the Chinese not eligible for citizenship

May 4. Phonograph exhibited at the Grand Opera House for first time

June 1. San Francisco's first telephone book issued by the American Speaking Telephone Company of San Francisco and Butchertown

July 1. Principal municipal offices moved into new City Hall at McAllister and Larkin

July 8. Construction starts on the new St. Ignatius Church, Van Ness and Hayes Street

July 26. Chen Lan Pan, Chinese Ambassador, arrives on visit

Sept. 12. General John C. Frémont, newly appointed Governor of Arizona, arrives for visit

Sept. 22. Independent Order of B'nai B'rith lays cornerstone of new building on Eddy Street

Oct. 20. Cornerstone of the new St. Ignatius Church on Van Ness Ave. laid

Nov. 10. Baseball championship won by the Athletics

1879

Jan. 25. Seawall between Montgomery and Sansome to Battery begun

Feb. 10. First electric arc light used in California Theater

Feb. 18. Ferryboats *Alameda* and *El Capitan* collide in dense fog on the Bay

May 24. First annual regatta of the Pacific Amateur Rowing Association off Long Bridge

June 3. State convention of the Workingmen's Party of California meets to nominate candidates, for State, Legislative, and Congressional offices

June 7. Public Library opened in rented quarters Bush Street between Kearny and Dupont

July 8. Steam yacht *Jeanette* leaves on Arctic exploration voyage

July 13. Dedication of new B'nai B'rith building

Aug. 23. Charles de Young shoots and seriously wounds Isaac Kalloch

Oct. 6. Golden Gate Kindergarten Association organized

January 8, 1880. Demise of Norton I, Emperor of the U.S. and Defender of Mexico.

1880

Jan. 8. Emperor Norton dies

Feb. 1. St. Ignatius Church dedicated

Feb. 7. Crowd of 1,000 men gather on the sandlots and listen to speech by Thomas Allen

Feb. 15. Geary Street Railroad opened

Feb. 16. 1,200 Chinese discharged by wool and jute factories in San Francisco and Oakland

Mar. 11. Denis Kearney arrested on charge of using incendiary language

Mar. 15. Local branches of the Workingmen's Party hold convention and nominate 15 freeholders for places on Board which is to draft a new city charter

Mar. 17. Ferdinand de Lesseps, French engineer who built Suez Canal, visits

Mar. 27. Seawall from Battery between Front and Davis begun

Apr. 23. Charles de Young shot and killed by Isaac M. Kalloch

July 19. Public Library opened to book borrowers

Aug. 12. Seawall completed between Front and Davis on Battery

Sept. 4. Seamen's Protective Union formed

Sept. 9. President Rutherford B. Hayes visits

1881

Jan. 10. New 75-foot long flagstaff placed over Point Lobos Signal Station

Mar. 2. Security Savings Bank incorporated

Apr. 8. Seawall completed between Montgomery and Sansome to Battery

Aug. 1. U.S. Quarantine Station authorized for Angel Island

Sept. 1. Second annual convention of Woman's Temperance Union held at Young Men's Christian Association Hall

1882

Mar. 28. Oscar Wilde visits

Apr. 12. California Safe Deposit & Trust Co. of San Francisco incorporated

Apr. 24. Trades Assembly State Convention of labor and anti-Chinese organizations meet

May 9. Telegraph Hill Railroad Company organized

July 4. Telegraph Hill Observatory opens

Sept. 1. Carpenters demand and obtain the 8-hour day for Saturday only

Nov. 25. Fort Point renamed Fort Winfield Scott

1883

June 18. Representatives of the carpenters, painters, metal roofers, bricklayers, and stair-builders meet to form Confederation of Building Trades

Aug. 24. Laying of the cornerstone of the Garfield monument in Golden Gate Park

Sept. 5. Fourth annual convention of the Woman's Temperance Union held at the Y.M.C.A. Hall

Oct. 29. Merchants' and Manufacturers' Association organized

1884

Feb. 20. Seawall begun between Front and Davis to Drumm

Mar. 5. First National Gold Bank of San Francisco drops the word "gold" from its title and becomes the First National Bank

June 3. Bear cub found at Pacific and Baker Streets turned over to Cooper Medical College

June 12. Ocean Beach Pavilion at the terminus of the Park & Ocean Railroad opened

Sept. 2. Drygoods Men's Association of San Francisco organized

Oct. 6. Golden Gate Kindergarten Association incorporated

Oct. 19. D. F. Riehl swims from the cave on the north of the Cliff House to the central one of the Seal Rocks and back

Nov. 27. Central Park at Market and Eighth Streets opens to the public

Dec. 18. Moulder School at the corner of Page and Gough Streets dedicated

Dec. 19. Cleveland School on Harrison between 10th and 11th Streets dedicated

1885

Jan. 6. Seawall from Drumm to Pacific begun

Feb. 25. First Pacific Coast broadsword contest takes place on Telegraph Hill

Mar. 13. Seawall between Front and Davis to Drumm completed

Sept. 5. Sutro Heights Park opened

Nov. 16. Alcazar Theater, O'Farrell Street between Stockton and Powell, opens

1886

Feb. 11. Plasterers', plumbers' and gas fitters', and painters' unions, and the Laborers' Protective Benevolent Association (hodcarriers) meet and form a Building Trades Council

Apr. 3. Seawall from Drumm to Pacific completed

May 11. An estimated 10,000 union members march in the largest workers' parade the city has witnessed

Aug. 31. Crocker-Woolworth National Bank organized

Nov. 27. California's first Arbor Day, promoted by Joaquin Miller, celebrated with ceremonies on Yerba Buena Island; Adolph Sutro plants first tree

1887

Jan. 16. Schooner *Parallel*, carrying a cargo of powder, blows up below the Cliff House, badly damaging it

Jan. 30. Thomas S. Baldwin makes record-breaking parachute jump from a balloon

Feb. 5. Snow covers San Francisco

Feb. 23. Congress grants Seal Rocks to the City and County of San Francisco

Apr. 20. Queen Lilioukalani of Hawaii pays a visit

May 12. Seawall from Pacific to Clay begun

June 30. Orpheum Theater, 147 O'Farrell Street, opens

1888

Feb. 28. Explosion of ferry in San Pablo Bay

July 2. Market Street cable road known as the Fairmont Line, via Market and Castro, opens

Aug. 2. Incandescent lamps used for first time at the Bijou Theater, 726 Market Street

1889

Feb. 10. First Unitarian Church, at the corner of Gough and Franklin Streets, dedicated

Mar. 17. Olivet Congregational Church, 17th and Noe Streets, dedicated

May 13. California Theater (new) opens at Bush, between Kearny and Dupont

May 31. Seawall from Pacific to Clay completed

Nov. 21. Mutual Savings Bank of San Francisco incorporated

1890

Jan. 30. King Kalakau of Hawaii visits

May 31. Butchertown destroyed by fire

Sept. 22. Construction on seawall at foot of Powell Street begun

Nov. 27. Police Department's first signal box goes into operation

1891

Feb. 9. First shipment of asparagus from Sacramento arrives

Mar. 1. Donohoe-Kelly Banking Company incorporated

Apr. 25. President Benjamin Harrison visits

Oct. 8. Post Office site, 7th and Mission Streets, selected

Dec. 10. Sequoia Chapter, D.A.R. organized

1892

Apr. 21. First buffalo born in Golden Gate Park

May 1. U.S. Quarantine Station opens on Angel Island

Dec. 1. Army post at Alcatraz Island designated "saluting station" to return salutes of foreign vessels of war

1893

Jan. 18. Columbus Savings & Loan Society incorporated

Jan. 23. Site of Fort Miley awarded to U.S. Army under condemnation proceedings

May 22. Seawall Powell to Taylor Streets completed

July 8. Mayor Ellert appoints Midwinter Fair Finance Committee

Aug. 24. Groundbreaking for Midwinter Fair in Golden Gate Park

1894

Jan. 27. Midwinter Fair in Golden Gate Park opens

July 4. Midwinter Fair closes

Dec. 25. Cliff House, owned by Adolph Sutro, destroyed by fire

1895

July 1. Alcatraz Island designated as U.S. Disciplinary Barracks

Nov. 2. The Chutes, Haight Street between Clayton and Cole, opened

1896

Mar. 14. Sutro Baths opened

Apr. 1. Building Trades Council proclaims that after this date no union member will work on jobs with men without union working cards

May 27. Bay District Race Track closes

June 28. Corbett-Sharkey fight

July 9. Harbor Commissioners approve use of Colusa sandstone in the construction of the new union ferry depot (Ferry Building)

Aug. 30. Postal Station D moves into the new temporary postoffice building at the foot of Market Street

Oct. 19. Trees planted by Daughters of the American Revolution in Golden Gate Park

1897

July 8. Harbor Hospital formally opened

November 23, 1898. Fire destroys Baldwin's Hotel & Theater.

1898

Jan. 1. Lightship replaces whistling buoy at entrance to Bay

Apr. 12. Army transfers Yerba Buena Island to Navy, retaining small plot as base port for mine-layers

May 3. Camp Merriman established in Presidio

May 17. Camp Merritt established in Presidio

May 23. First Philippine Expeditionary Troops sail from San Francisco

May 25. The First California Regiment, Oregon Volunteers, and the 14th U.S. Infantry leave San Francisco for the Philippines

May 26. San Francisco electorate accepts new city charter, authorizing municipal acquisition and ownership of public utilities (put into effect Jan. 1, 1900)

June 16. Naval authorities request the time ball atop the Ferry Building flagstaff be painted black, as the gold painted ball cannot be seen

July 13. Ferry Building opens

Nov. 23. Baldwin Hotel and Theater destroyed by fire

1899

Feb. 18. San Francisco named as one of two ports for dispatch of Army transports

Apr. 16. Riot of 1,000 soldiers at the Presidio, 300 arrested

July 1. New City Hall turned over to City after 29 years of building

Aug. 23. Wireless telegraph message sent from the San Francisco lightship to a station in the Cliff House restaurant building: first ship-to-shore wireless transmission to be received in the United States

Aug. 24. First regiment, California Volunteers, returns from the Philippines

Oct. 17. Sutro Railroad sold to Robert F. Morrow for $215,000

Nov. 15. Bush Street Theater (formerly the Alhambra) burns

1900

Jan. 8. City flag requested by Mayor Phelan of Board of Supervisors

Feb. 23. Steamer *Rio de Janiero* sunk in Bay

Mar. Bubonic plague hits San Francisco

Apr. 14. Veteran's Hospital established at Fort Miley

Apr. 24. Andrew Hallidie, cable car builder, dies

Apr. 30. Shag Rock in Bay blown up

April 30, 1900. Blowing up Shag Rock, a navigation hazard.

Sept. 19. Ringling Bros. Circus makes its first appearance in San Francisco at 16th and Folsom Streets

1901

Jan. 1. Department stores observe 6 p.m. closing every weekday but Saturday

Apr. 19. United Railroads employees strike

May 1. Recently-formed union of cooks and waiters calls industry-wide restaurant strike

May 12. President William McKinley visits

May 20. International Association of Machinists call strike

July 30. Waterfront strike called

Aug. 1. Burials within city limits prohibited

Aug. 15. Arch Rock in the Bay blown up with 30 tons of nitrogelatin

Nov. 2. Captive balloon bursts its bonds at Market, Eleventh, Mission and Twelfth Streets; lands near Pescadero

1902

Jan. 6. Derrick crashes down upon the sidewalk from the 12th story of the new Mutual Savings Bank building under construction at Geary & Market Streets

Jan. 8. Mayor Eugene Schmitz assumes office

Jan. 28. Lumber schooner *Mary E. Russ* runs aground off Baker's Beach

Feb. 10. Board of Supervisors vote down ordinance permitting racing at the Ingleside Track

Feb. 20. Heavy waves break over Seal Rocks and damage Sutro Baths

Feb. 22. Giant elk shot in Golden Gate Park Paddock, on orders of Park Commissioners, for presentation to San Francisco Lodge No. 2, P.P.O.E.

Nov. 18. Junction issued by Judge Carroll Cook against Gray Brothers to stop further blasting or excavating on Telegraph Hill

Nov. 27. First religious service held in new First Presbyterian Church at Jackson & Fillmore streets

1903

Jan. 6. French American Bank incorporated

Jan. 29. Central Trust Company of California incorporated

Feb. 7. Mission Bank, first bank in the Mission District, incorporated with James Rolph as president

Mar. 3. Golden State Bank incorporated

Mar. 4. Bay Counties Bank, Central Exchange Bank, Seal Rocks Bank, United Bank & Trust Company, incorporated

Mar. 5. Standard Bank, Federal Savings Bank, Oriental Bank, State Savings & Commercial Bank, Japanese Bank incorporated

May 14. President Theodore Roosevelt visits

June 7. Republic Theater fire

June 29. Keys to the convenience station beneath the sidewalk on the east side of Union Square presented to the city by the Merchants Association

July 4. The Pacific cable from San Francisco by way of Hawaii and Guam to the Philippines opened as President Theodore Roosevelt sends, first, a message to the Philippines, and then a message around the world in 12-minutes time

July 25. Castle atop Telegraph Hill destroyed by fire

Aug. 14. Jim Jeffries defeats Jim Corbett in fight

Aug. 18. Dirigible of Dr. August Greth makes its first flight in San Francisco

Aug. 31. A Winton automobile completes a 63-day journey from San Francisco to New York City; first time an automobile has crossed the continent under its own power

Oct. 26. The *Yerba Buena* is the first Key System ferry to cross Bay

Nov. 23. Tivoli Opera House closes

Dec. 30. Seawall, foot of King to South of Berry, begun

1904

June 23. Several hundred electrical linemen strike against the Pacific States Telephone & Telegraph Company

Sept. 4. Odd Fellows Conclave opens

Oct. 17. Bank of America (Italy) established

Dec. End of first bubonic plague epidemic

1905

Apr. 9. Teatro Appolo, 810 Pacific, opens

Apr. 27. Seawall, foot of King to south of Berry, completed

July 8. Secretary of War allots land on Angel Island to Dept. of Commerce and Labor for Immigration Detention Station

Sept. 27. Burnham Plan for city reconstruction submitted to Board of Supervisors

1906

Apr. 18. Earthquake starts fire which destroys a large part of San Francisco

Apr. 19. 176 prisoners moved from city jail to Alcatraz

May 20. Orpheum Theater, formerly the Chutes at Haight, between Clayton and Cole, opens

June 30. Davis Theater, McAllister near Fillmore, opens; Park Theater, Market at 8th, opens

July 30. United Railroads employees strike for higher wages and the 8-hour day

Aug. 3. Stockholders of the Mission Bank organize the Mission Savings Bank

Aug. 26. Strike of carmen

Sept. 17. Colonial Theater, McAllister Street near Leavenworth, opens

Ferry boats on the Bay, 1906.

Nov. 3. Auditorium Skating Palace, corner Fillmore and Page Street, opens

Dec. 17. Novelty Theater opens

1907

Jan. 22. American Theater, Market above Seventh, opens

Mar. 11. Van Ness Theater, 259 Van Ness Ave., opens

Mar. 18. 16 grafting supervisors, including 10 labor leaders, brought before the Grand Jury

Mar. 21. Union State Bank incorporated

Apr. 1. Laundry workers strike for wage increases and the 8-hour day

Apr. 18. Fairmont Hotel opens

May 1. Bay Area metal trades unions begin their first general strike since 1901

May 3. Approximately 500 women and girls of the Telephone Operators' Union begin their strike

May 5. 1,500 members of the Carmen's Union vote to strike for the 8-hour day

May 11. The Bank of San Francisco incorporated

May 15. Abe Ruef pleads guilty to extortion charge

May 27. Bubonic plague again appears in San Francisco

June 13. Seawall between Brannan and Townsend to foot of King begun

June 18. Imperial Bank incorporated

July 4. Pioneer Park atop Telegraph Hill has a flag-raising

July 9. Mayor Eugene Schmitz sentenced to five years in San Quentin for corruption in office

Aug. 21. First Federal Trust Company incorporated

Aug. 26. Harry Houdini escapes from chains underwater at Aquatic Park in 57 seconds

Sept. 1. Temple Emanu-El re-dedicated

Sept. 6. Dr. Rupert Blue ordered by Federal Government to take charge of San Francisco's plague campaign.

Sept. 7. Sutro's ornate Cliff House destroyed by fire

Oct. 1. Canton Bank incorporated

Oct. 30. California Safe Deposit & Trust Co. with four branches forced into liquidation by bank commissioners

Nov. 3. Banca Popolare Operaia Italiana incorporated

Dec. 18. Citizens State Bank forced into liquidation by bank commissioners

1908

Jan. 30. Last case of bubonic plague reported

Feb. 21. The Market Street Bank forced into liquidation by bank commissioners

Feb. 28. Bank of Greater San Francisco forced into liquidation by bank commissioners

Mar. 21. Commission men hold Fruit Banquet in Front Street to celebrate their sanitary campaign

Mar. 24. The Thomas Flyer arrives in San Francisco participating in the New York-to-Paris auto race

May 6. Swedish-American Bank incorporated

May 7. Great White Fleet arrives in Bay

May 23. C. A. Morrell's 450-foot, six-engine dirigible explodes over San Francisco Bay; 16 passengers fall from the airship but are not killed

June 4. Seawall between Brannan and Townsend to foot of King completed

July 7. The Great White Fleet leaves

Aug. 27. The Imperial Bank (Japanese) forced into liquidation by bank commissioners

Oct. 23. Last infected rat of the bubonic plague caught

Dec. 11. Abe Ruef sentenced to 14 years in jail

1909

Apr. 9. Anglo-California Trust Company incorporated

Apr. 19. Orpheum Theater, O'Farrell between Stockton and Powell Streets, opens

May 22. *David Scannell*, city's first fire boat, launched

May 23. Yerba Buena School, Filbert near Fillmore Street, dedicated

June 5. John Jules Jusserand, French Ambassador to Washington, presents a gold medal to San Francisco, commemorative of her rise from the ashes and ruins of the earthquake of 1906

June 15. Fireboat *Dennis T. Sullivan* launched

June 16. *Gjoa* presented to the City of San Francisco at ceremonies at the foot of Howard Street, Pier 1

June 17. Excavation work for Hall of Justice completed

July 1. Golden Gate Bank closes

July 5. *Gjoa* towed through the Golden Gate and beached south of Cliff House

July 6. Excavation for San Francisco General Hospital completed

July 17. State Savings, Commercial Bank of San Francisco, and Union State Bank of San Francisco close

Aug. 18. Pacific Aero Club of San Francisco holds its first annual exhibition at Dreamland Rink

Aug. 29. Seawall begun at point between Bryant and Brannan to foot of Main

Sept. 9. First annual parade of the San Francisco Work Horse Association

Oct. 18. Japanese American Bank of San Francisco closes

Oct. 19. Portola Festival opens to celebrate San Francisco's recovery from the earthquake and fire

Dec. 6. Seawall foot of Mission Street begun

1910

Jan. 10. Columbia Theater, Geary at Mason, opens

Jan. 12. Cornerstone of American Music Hall Theater, Ellis Street between Stockton and Powell, laid

Jan. 14. The Chutes, Fillmore and Eddy, opens

Mar. 10. The Seawall, foot of Mission, completed

Mar. 22. Panama Pacific International Exposition Company incorporated

Mar. 29. Seawall begun at foot of Harrison to between Bryant and Brannan

Aug. 22. First load of passengers for the Western Pacific was carried by the ferry *Telephone* from the San Francisco Ferry Building to the Oakland Terminal

Oct. 9. Mount St. Joseph's Orphanage destroyed by fire

Oct. 31. The International Banking Corporation purchases the Swedish-American Bank of San Francisco

Nov. 21. Ground broken for the temporary City Hall (later called the Whitcomb Hotel and now called the San Franciscan)

Dec. 24. Luisa Tetrazzini sings to 250,000 at Lotta's Fountain

1911

Jan. 5. San Francisco has its first air meet

Jan. 7. Hubert Latham pilots the French monoplane *Antionetta* through the Golden Gate at 2:45 p.m.

Jan. 18. Eugene Ely lands on deck of the U.S.S. *Pennsylvania* in San Francisco Bay

Jan. 31. Congress passes a resolution naming San Francisco the exposition city to celebrate the opening of the Panama Canal

Feb. 25. The International Banking Corporation purchases the Bank of Commerce of San Francisco

Feb. 28. The City and County Bank of San Francisco sold to the Western Metropolis National Bank

July 4. Hermon Lee Ensign Memorial Fountain at Mission, Otis and Duboce presented to city by National Humane Alliance of New York

Sept. 7. Seawall completed between Bryant and Brannan to foot of Main

Oct. 13. President William Howard Taft visits

Nov. 23. Post Hospital at Presidio renamed Letterman General Hospital in honor of Major Jonathan Letterman

Dec. 23. Alcazar Theater, O'Farrell near Powell, opens

Dec. 29. San Francisco Symphony Orchestra formed

Dec. 30. Pantages Theater opens

1912

Jan. 3. Southern Pacific Railroad Company offers to carry the Liberty Bell across the continent without expense to the Exposition

Jan. 24. Bank of Daniel Meyer incorporated

Mar. 2. Poppies planted in the hills surrounding Noe Valley

Mar. 14. Fire breaks out in the Officers Club in the Presidio; Engine 23 responding turns over

June 15. Olympic Club's new Post Street building opens

Dec. 28. Mayor Rolph runs Street Car No. 1 up Geary Street to open Muni Railroad service

1913

Jan. 1. Thousands take part in celebration of breaking ground for Machinery Hall at Harbor View

Jan. 4. Seawall begun at foot of Folsom to foot of Harrison

Feb. 22. Lowell High, Hayes and Masonic, dedicated

Mar. 12. Tivoli Opera House opens

June 3. Last trip of a horse-drawn car,

from the Ferry up to 8th Street, with Mayor Rolph at the brake

June 15. The first Loughead design, a hydroplane called Model G is flown by Allan Loughead

Oct. 22. Portola Festival begins

Oct. 25. Cornerstone of the new City Hall laid

Dec. 8. Construction begins on Palace of Fine Arts for 1915 Exposition

Dec. 18. First district pavement dance held at Clement between 5th and 6th Avenues to the music of the Muni Band

1914

Jan. 6. Board of Supervisors passes ordinance providing for removal of all human remains in the cemeteries within the city

Jan. 15. Travelers Aid organized

Feb. 7. Steel work completed for the Civic Auditorium

Feb. 16. Silas Christofferson makes first airplane flight from San Francisco to Los Angeles

Feb. 23. "Year Before Opening Celebration" is held on the Exposition site; 20,000 people attend

Feb. 26. City Engineer O'Shaughnessy discusses plans for movable sidewalk on the Fillmore Street hill

Feb. 28. Erection of the Exposition's Tower of Jewels begun

May 12. Representatives from clearing houses in the 12th Federal Reserve District assemble in the rooms of the San Francisco Chamber of Commerce to discuss plans to establish the Federal Reserve Bank of San Francisco

May 16. Ewing Field, off Masonic Ave., opens

Aug. 15. The Van Ness Ave. line of the Municipal railway system commences operation

Aug. 29. First vessel, the steamship *Arizonan*, arrives via Panama Canal

Sept. 7. Potrero Avenue line of the Municipal Railroad system commences operation

Nov. 1. Fort Mason tunnel completed, connecting the Belt Line Railroad with government transport docks

Nov. 8. Richmond Branch Library dedicated

Nov. 30. Ground broken for Twin Peaks Tunnel

Dec. 11. Stockton Street Tunnel completed

Dec. 28. Completion of the Stockton Street Tunnel celebrated

Dec. 29. The Stockton Street line of the Municipal Railway system commences operation

1915

Jan. 9. Masked ball celebrates dedication of the Exposition Auditorium (Civic Auditorium)

Jan. 25. First transcontinental talk by phone; Alexander Graham Bell speaks from New York to Thomas Watson in San Francisco

Feb. 20. Panama Pacific International Exposition opens

May 6. Seawall foot of Folsom to foot of Harrison completed

Aug. 27. General Pershing's wife and three children die in Presidio home fire

Sept. 14. Dedication ceremonies at the western terminus of the Lincoln Highway in Lincoln Park

Sept. 20. Laying of the submarine cable across the Golden Gate commenced

Sept. 26. Boulevard El Camino Del Mar opens

Dec. 4. Panama Pacific International Exposition closes

Dec. 28. Dedication of City Hall by Mayor James Rolph

1916

Apr. 29. Artists Ball held to raise funds to keep Palace of Fine Arts open another year

July 10. The Law & Order Committee formed to bring industrial peace to the city

July 22. Preparedness Day Parade and bombing

Sept. 22. Dedication of North American Hall, California Academy of Sciences, in Golden Gate Park

Oct. 4. Market Street's "Path of Gold" lit for first time

1917

Feb. 15. San Francisco Public Library building in the Civic Center dedicated

Apr. 8. Public dedication of the Municipal Auditorium organ

May 18. San Franciscans inducted into Army by passage of Selective Military Conscription Bill

June 26. Fort Funston named in honor of Major-General Frederick Funston

July 15. Celebration for the completion of Twin Peaks Tunnel held at the westerly portal

Aug. 11. United Railroads employees strike against the open shop

Sept. 17. 30,000 men called out to strike, shutting down shipyards, foundries, machine shops, etc.

Nov. 1. California Theater opens

Nov. 22. Carmen's Union votes to call off its strike

Dec. 11. Katherine Stinson sets nonstop distance flight record of 610 miles by flying from San Diego to San Francisco; the flight took 9 hours, 10 minutes

1918

Feb. 3. Street cars begin to operate through Twin Peaks Tunnel

Mar. 14. First seagoing concrete ship built by San Francisco Shipbuilding Company launched

Oct. 26. Great flu epidemic

Dec. 31. Ferry Building siren sounded for first time at 5 p.m.

1919

Sept. 5. Bank of Montreal incorporated

Sept. 17. President Woodrow Wilson visits

Sept. 22. Maitland Theater opens

Oct. 14. Albert, King of the Belgians, visits

Nov. 3. Crissy Field, Presidio of San Francisco airport, dedicated

Nov. 30. James Lick Baths, at 10th and Howard, erected in 1889, closed

Dec. 8-31. Army transcontinental group flight from New York to San Francisco and return; 10 planes complete the round-trip

1920

Apr. 20. Asia Banking Corporation incorporated

May 5. Captive Army balloon sent up from Pier 32 to take aerial photographs of San Francisco and the waterfront; project sponsored by the San Francisco Chamber of Commerce, the U.S. Army, and the State Board of Harbor Commissioners.

June 28. Democratic Convention begins at Civic Auditorium

July 29. First transcontinental airmail flight from New York completed at San Francisco

Aug. 1. Panama Pacific International Exposition Corporation dissolved in Superior Court

Oct. 26. Ocean Shore Railroad closes

1921

Jan. 2. De Young Museum, Golden Gate Park, opens

Jan. 24. Asia Banking Corporation opens for business

Feb. 22-23. Jack Knight and E. M. Allison, civilian mail pilots, fly mail from San Francisco to New York in 33 hours, 20 minutes

July 4. Photos of Carpentier-Dempsey fight delivered by plane to San Francisco just 48 hours and 45 minutes after leaving Hoboken, New Jersey

July 2, 1924. First transcontinental airmail plane lands.

Aug. 8. Bank of Italy interests organize the Liberty Bank of San Francisco as a day-and-night bank on Market Street

Dec. 31. Last firehorses leave the Department's stables and they are officially closed

1922

April 15. The Poodle Dog Restaurant closes

Apr. 22. Radio Station KPO established

Nov. 8. Municipal Popular Symphony Concerts begin

Dec. 19. Excavation begun for the new Spring Valley Water Company building, Mason Street between Geary and Post

1923

Jan. 31. Merchants National Bank of San Francisco purchased by the Sacramento-San Joaquin Bank

July 29. President Warren Harding arrives

Aug. 2. President Harding dies at the Palace Hotel

Sept. 29. Steinhart Aquarium, Golden Gate Park, opens to the public

Dec. 10. The *Illustrated Daily Herald* begins publication

Dec. 30. Thousands of walnuts are cast up by waves near Fort Point, part of a shipment condemned and thrown from a passing ship by Federal inspectors

1924

Apr. 15. The Huntington Apartments, Taylor and California Streets, open

June 23. First "Dawn to Dusk" flight across continent, by Lt. Russell A. Maughan, successfully completed at Crissy Field

July 2. First airmail plane, inaugurating the Transcontinental Air Mail Service from New York to San Francisco, lands at Crissy Field

Nov. 11. Palace of Legion of Honor dedicated

Dec.. 22. Columbia Theater, formerly Tivoli Opera House, Eddy near Mason, opens

Dec. 25. Geary Playhouse, formerly the Columbia, opens

1925

Jan. 3. Geary Playhouse closes

Jan. 12. Wilkes Theater, Geary at Mason, opens

Apr. 30. Fleishhacker Playground opened

May 2. Kezar Stadium in Golden Gate Park opens

May 2. Embarcadero subway opens

July 18. Harding Memorial Park opens

Sept. 6-12. Diamond Jubilee celebration (75th anniversary of California's admittance to the Union)

Dec. 26. First East-West football game played in Ewing Field to a crowd of 25,000

1926

Apr. 7. Golden Gate Ballroom, Eddy and Jones, opens

Apr. 15. Visitacion Valley branch of the San Francisco Boy's Club gymnasium dedicated

July 19. The Canton Bank closes

1927

May 7. San Francisco Municipal Airport (Mills Field) dedicated

Sept. 17. Charles Lindbergh in San Francisco

1928

April 14. Maddux Air Lines starts daily passenger service between Los Angeles and San Francisco

May 26. Western Air Express starts daily passenger and express service between Los Angeles and San Francisco

Oct. 21. Duboce (or Sunset) Tunnel opened

Nov. 19. Egyptian Building of De Young Museum, Golden Gate Park, being demolished by Symon Brothers Wrecking Company

1929

June 9. Seawall at Ocean Beach completed

June 27. Orpheum Theater, O'Farrell Street, closes

June 28. Fox Theater opens

Aug. 22. Pantages Theater closes

Aug. 25. Graf Zeppelin (airship) arrives from Tokyo, Japan, sailing over San Francisco on its way to Los Angeles

Sept. 6. Orpheum Theater, formerly Pantages, Market opposite 8th, opens

Sept. 11. Mayor Rolph inaugurates city's new pedestrian traffic signal system

Oct. 20. Bayshore Highway opened

Dec. 4. Southside Playground renamed Father Crowley Playground

Dec. 20. Mt. Davidson dedicated as a city park

1930

Mar. 3. Communist parade

Mar. 3. San Francisco Water Department takes over operation of system bought from the Spring Valley Water Company

March 30. Columbia Theater, O'Farrell near Stockton, opens

Aug. 11. War Department establishes the minimum clear height of the future Golden Gate Bridge above mean higher high water, at 210 feet at the piers and 220 feet at the center of the main span

1931

Feb. 20. Congress grants the State of California the right to construct a bridge from Rincon Hill, San Francisco, to Yerba Buena Island, to Oakland

Feb. 25. Celebration marks the completion of the Newark-San Lorenzo Pipe Line connection between the San Francisco Water System and that of the East Bay Municipal Utility District

Apr. 7. Seals Stadium opens

June 3. Goat Island's old Spanish name Yerba Buena (good herb) is restored by the U.S. Geographic Board

June 17. First construction contracts for Golden Gate Bridge awarded

Nov. 11. Cornerstones for Opera House and Veteran's Building laid

1932

Jan. 8. Ratification of present City Charter

Feb. 10. James Lick Junior High accepted from builders by Board of Education

Apr. 10. Anza Branch Library dedicated

Apr. 30. Market Street parade and gala inaugural ball in Civic Auditorium to celebrate the 200th anniversary of the birth of George Washington

June 4. Dedication of Sigmund Stern Grove

June 19. First symphony concert in Stern Grove with G. Merola directing

Oct. 15. Opera House dedicated with performance of "La Tosca"

March 3, 1930. Communist parade up Market street.

1934. Golden Gate Bridge piers constructed by Fort Point.

Nov. 8. President Herbert Hoover visits

1933

Jan. 5. Construction begun on Golden Gate Bridge with the digging of a pit for the Marin County anchorage

Feb. 26. Ground-breaking ceremony at Crissy Field for the Golden Gate Bridge

Apr. 27. Fremont Elementary School, McAllister near Baker, destroyed by fire

May 21. Mt. Davidson Cross lit by President Roosevelt at the White House via telegraph

Oct. 8. Coit Tower on Telegraph Hill dedicated

Oct. 12. Alcatraz Island made a Federal Prison

1934

Jan. 1. U.S. officially takes over Alcatraz Island as a Federal Prison

Jan. 10-11. Lt. Cmdr. Kneffler McGinnis leads six Consolidated flying boats on a flight from San Francisco to Pearl Harbor in 24 hours, 45 minutes, breaking three world records

Mar. 4. Easter Cross on Mt. Davidson dedicated

May 9. Longshoremen strike

May 25. General strike ties up city

June 30. Emperor Norton reburied in Woodlawn Cemetary by citizens of San Francisco

July 1. New $850,000 jail in San Mateo County dedicated

July 5. "Bloody Thursday" clash be-

tween police and strikers on waterfront; two die

July 12. United States Disciplinary Barracks abandoned at Alcatraz Island

July 19. Longshoremen end strike

Oct. 24. Water flows into Crystal Spring
Reservoir for first time

Dec. 14. Simson African Hall, California Academy of Sciences, opens

1935

Mar. 14. The Folsom Street Line (36)
becomes the first line in the city to
use one-man trolley cars

Apr. 4. Wrecking crews begin de-
molishing the Odd Fellows Cemetery
Office Building, built in 1865

Apr. 16-17. Pan American Clipper flies
from San Francisco to Honolulu in 18
hours, 39 minutes, for a test flight

May 10. South Park is set aside today by
the Park Commission for "soap box
speeches"

Oct. 6. Trackless trolleys are put into
service by the Market Street Railway

Nov. 22-29. Pan American Airways
starts transpacific air-mail service
from San Francisco to Manila, stop-
ping at Honolulu, Midway, Wake,
and Guam

1936

Feb. 10. Father Damien's body (famed
leper priest) lies in state at St. Mary's
Cathedral

Feb. 11. Pumping begins to build
Treasure Island

Mar. 4. George Bernard Shaw visits

Mar. 31. Lurline Baths, Bush and Larkin Streets, closes

Apr. 18. The "Clipper" establishes regular passenger air transportation from
San Francisco to Honolulu

June 30. Crissy Field abandoned as
Army airport

Oct. 28. Cardinal Eugenio Pacelli (later
Pope Pius XII) blesses the San Francisco—Oakland Bay Bridge

Oct. 29. Waterfront strike begins

Nov. 12. San Francisco and Oakland
Bay Bridge Fiesta begins with the
opening of the bridge to traffic.

Nov. 18. Main span of the Golden Gate
Bridge joined

1937

Feb. 4. Waterfront strike ends

Feb. 17. 10 men die when scaffolds fall
from beneath Golden Gate Bridge

May 27. Golden Gate Bridge dedicated

July 1. Time ball atop the Fairmont
Hotel discontinued

Aug. 2. Furniture Mart on Market
Street opens

Aug. 26. Treasure Island pumping ends

Dec. 29. Pan American begins service
between San Francisco and Auck-
land, New Zealand, with Honolulu,
Kingman Reef, and Samoa as step-
ping stones

1938

Feb. 15. Frank Fuller, Jr. flies from San
Francisco to Los Angeles in one hour,
7 minutes, 7 seconds

May 25. Frank Fuller, Jr. flies from San
Francisco to Seattle in two hours, 31
minutes, 41 seconds

June 1. Earl Ortman flies from San
Francisco to San Diego in one hour,
48 minutes, one second

July 14. President Franklin Delano
Roosevelt visits

Sept. 7. Mormon crickets invade all districts of San Francisco

Sept. 16. Spanish newspaper *Eco His-
pano* established

Oct. 1. Horse "Blackie" swims the Golden Gate in 23½ minutes

1939

Jan. 7. Governor Olson pardons Tom
Mooney

Jan. 22. Aquatic Park dedicated

Feb. 14. Beginning of Fiesta Week

Feb. 18. Golden Gate International Exposition opens on Treasure Island

May 21. Beginning of Golden Forties Fiesta

June 7. 1894 Bell Tower in Golden Gate Park burns to the ground

July 30. Municipal Railroad bus #11 established to carry people from Union and Powell to Coit Tower

Oct. 2. Birdbaths installed in Union Square

Oct. 29. Closing day, Golden Gate International Exposition

1940

April 16. Ferryboat *Yosemite* (now *Argentina*) sails for Montevideo

April 21. $1,350,000 Funston Ave. approach and Park-Presidio Tunnel opened to Golden Gate Bridge traffic

May 25. Golden Gate International Exposition reopened

Sept. 29. Golden Gate International Exposition closes a second time

Oct. 6. Zoological Gardens, Sloat and Sunset Blvd., opens

Oct. 28. Post office at Ferry Building vacated; moved to Mission and Spear Streets

Dec. 1. Tait's-At-The-Beach destroyed by fire

1941

Mar. 1. Northwestern Pacific (San Francisco to Sausalito) ferries discontinued

Mar. 31. Ground broken for Union Square Garage

Apr. 1. Navy takes over Treasure Island

Apr. 5. Castro and Fillmore street cars replaced by buses

Aug. 9. Civic Center Hospitality House opens

Sept. 3. Land's End slide wrecks home and business of the "Mayor" of Land's End, Charles L. Harris

Sept. 7. Bronze tablet commemorating the site of the Old Yerba Buena Cemetary unveiled by the California Genealogical Society

Oct. 18. President Rafael Larco Herrera of Peru visits

Nov. 15. Cow Palace opens

Dec. 8. With declaration of war against Japan, San Francisco experiences first blackout at 6:15 p.m.

1942

Apr. 6. First San Francisco Japanese evacuation set today

Aug. 20. Dimout regulations effective in San Francisco

Sept. 8. Wool auction held at Palace Hotel

Sept. 28. First scrap metal drive

Oct. 1. Red Mass celebrated for first time by Catholics

Oct. 4. Second scrap metal drive

1943

Jan. 17. Tin can drive day

Mar. 5. Pepsi Cola Center, 948 Market Street, opens for servicemen

Mar. 29. Charlotte, Grand Duchess of Luxembourg, visits

June 3. Fillmore Street arches removed. Free Farmer's Market opens at Market Street & Duboce

Aug. 18. Construction begins on barracks in Civic Center for servicemen

Aug. 30. City of Paris department store purchases their building, quarters previously rented

Nov. 1. Dimout ban lifted

1944

Aug. 1. City and County of San Francisco assumes management of the Farmer's Market

Oct. 5. Mayfair Heights Corporation purchases the Catholic Calvary Cemetery, bounded by Geary and Turk Streets, and St. Joseph's and Masonic Avenues for homes

Dec. 9. Fleet Hospital, No. 113, Crocker Amazon Playground, commissioned

1945

Feb. 12. San Francisco selected as site

of the United Nations Conference

Mar. 8. Bataan prisoners of war welcomed

Apr. 25. United Nations Conference begins

June 25. President Harry S. Truman visits

June 26. United Nations Conference ends

Aug. 15. Riot in San Francisco celebrating the end of World War II

Sept. 9. General Wainwright welcomed

1946

Jan. 9. Mission Rock burned off so that the rock can become the base for extension of Pier 50

Apr. 4. Pix Theater, Market near Mason, opens

May 2-4. Alcatraz Island revolt by prisoners; two guards, three prisoners die

June 30. Civic Center Hospitality House closes

July 16. Attempt made to recall Mayor Lapham, first in San Francisco history

Aug. 26. Sailors Union of the Pacific votes to strike and tie up port

Sept. 8. Notre Dame Hospital opens

Oct. 17-20. First annual Municipal Art Exhibition by Bay Region artists held in Civic Center Plaza

Dec. 7. Carbarn built in the 1870's at Haight and Stanyan closes

Dec. 19. Civic Center barracks demolished

1947

Feb. 8. Bal Tabarin night club on Columbus Ave. closes

June 26, 1945. Pres. Truman addresses U.N. Conference.

Apr. 3. Campaign started by Market Street Association to rid Civic Center of pigeons

Apr. 10. Galley K and the Treasure Island Mess Hall on Treasure Island destroyed by fire

June 6. Guild Theater, Market between Sixth and Seventh, opens

June 21. The Queen Mother of Egypt, Queen Nazli, visits

Sept. 1. The Humphreys home, built in 1852, at Chestnut and Hyde Street demolished

Sept. 2. Parking meters installed in the Polk Street District

Oct. 10. First arrival of Pacific Area dead on the ship the *Honda Knot*

Oct. 16. O'Connor Moffat & Co., Stockton and O'Farrell, sold to Macy's

1948

Jan 13. Lewis Reece attempts to harness tide at Point Lobos; fails after three attempts

Feb. 12. Second arrival of Pacific Area war dead on the U.S. Army transport *Cardinal O'Connell*

Mar. 14. Freedom Train arrives in San Francisco

Mar. 23. Third arrival of Pacific Area war dead on ship *Walter W. Schwenk*

May 25. City gets its first telecast

June 22. City's first mailomat device goes into service

June 27. Funston Playground returned to city by Army

July 2. Industrial Exposition opens in Civic Auditorium

July 3. The last No. 7 streetcar to make the 65-year-old run along Haight Street is retired and replaced by trackless trolleys

July 28. Milton Van Noland climbs up 50-foot flagpole at a used car lot on Van Ness Ave. and begins flagpole sitting

Sept. 28. Ground breaking for Youth Guidance Center

Oct. 17. Portola Festival begins

Nov. 25. Fort Funston's 16-inch coastal guns dismantled

Dec. 9. "Winged Victory" statue moved from Turk, Market and Mason Streets to Golden Gate Park

1949

Jan. 22. Chinatown telephone exchange closed

Feb. 12. Car barn at beach destroyed by fire

Apr. 15. Robert L. Niles first person to make a stunt leap from the Golden Gate Bridge

Apr. 23. Courtesy mail boxes for motorists initiated

May 15. Ground breaking for U.S.F.'s Gleeson Memorial Library

July 3. Old streetcars on the Nos. 5, 6, 7, and 21 lines replaced by trolley coaches

Nov. 21. Hastings Store at 135 Post Street opens

Dec. 11. Mohammad Reza Shah Pahlavi of Iran visits

1950

Feb. 15. Demolition of the Chutes at the Beach commences

Aug. 25. Hospital ship U.S.S. *Benevolence* sinks after colliding with the freighter *Luckenbach* in heavy fog off the Golden Gate

Sept. 20. Golden Gate Park burros replaced by ponies in the Children's area

Dec. 3. U.S.F.'s Gleeson Memorial Library dedicated

1951

Jan. 22. The Queen Mother of Egypt, Queen Nazli, visits

Feb. 16. City Hall dome fire

Mar. 11. John P. Murphy Playground, 9th Ave. and Ortega, dedicated

Apr. 18. General Douglas MacArthur visits

April 18, 1951. Gen. MacArthur returns from Korea.

May 27. Maritime Museum, foot of Polk Street, opens

June 10. Goat Island officially rechristened Yerba Buena Island

June 29. President Galo Plaza of Ecuador visits

June 29. Land's End scenic drive reopens after being closed for nine years due to slides

July 25. California Legislature creates special commission to study Bay Area transportation problems

Sept. 8. Prime Minister Yoshida of Japan signs treaty ending World War II at Opera House

Sept. 23. Josephine D. Randall Junior Museum opens

Oct. 21. Ping Yuen, Chinatown housing project, dedicated

Dec. 1. Golden Gate Bridge closed to traffic due to high winds

1952

Feb. 8. Mission Dolores designated first minor Basilica in the West

April 18. Queen Juliana of the Netherlands visits

Aug. 24. Faisal II, King of Iraq, visits

Aug. 26. Fluoridation of city's water begins

Sept. 1. Sutro Baths purchased by George Whitney

Oct. 8. Pres. Dwight D. Eisenhower visits

Oct. 16. Woolworth's, corner Powell and Market, opens

Dec. 21. Broadway Tunnel opens

1953

Feb. 23. Downtown Theater, Mason and Ellis Streets, demolished

Mar. 26. Hastings College of Law dedication of new building, northeast corner of McAllister and Hyde

Apr. 19. Norodom Shianouk, Prince of Cambodia, visits

Apr. 30. Rent control abolished

Aug. 26. President Elpidio Quirino of the Philippines visits

Dec. 1. U.S. House Committee on Un-American activities opens hearings

1954

Feb. 7. Celal Bayar, President of Turkey, visits

Mar. 24. First meeting of the Telegraph Hill Dwellers held at Schaeffer School of Design

Apr. 21. Rally on Market Street at the new Equitable Life Insurance Company building to celebrate the end of the noisy pile driver called "the monster"

June 9. Miraloma Playground dedicated

June 13. Emperor Haile Selassie visits

July 6. Golden Pheasant Restaurant on Powell Street closes

Aug. 7. President Syngman Rhee of Republic of Korea visits

Aug. 29. San Francisco International Airport opens

Dec. 17. Mohammad Reza Shah Pahlavi of Iran visits

1955

Jan. 18. Mayor Elmer Robinson dedicates new Junipero Serra Playground on Stonecrest Drive near 19th Ave.

Jan. 27. Land's End scenic drive closed due to slide

Apr. 9. United Nations Charter hearing

May 3. Sky Tram begins operation from the Cliff House Terrace to Point Lobos

June 1. President Dwight D. Eisenhower visits

July 11. Four-alarm fire destroys the Italian Village nightclub

July 19. The *Balclutha* ties up at Pier 43 and becomes a floating museum

Aug. 3. Chinatown police squad disbanded

Aug. 9. Portuguese bull fight at Cow Palace, first time held in the United States

Aug. 27. Beniamino Bufano's 18-foot black Swedish granite statue of St. Francis set in place at the entry steps of the Church of St. Francis of Assisi

Oct. 11. "Big Dipper" at Playland-at-the-Beach demolished

Oct. 12. Ground broken for Town School building

Oct. 16. Dick Pee, 9-year-old boy swims Golden Gate

Dec. 1. The Lilliput Theater, 3110 Fillmore Street, opens

1956

Mar. 8. Giovanni Gronchi, President of Italy, visits

Apr. 12. The California Academy of Sciences unveils its new seismograph

Apr. 19. First Black & White Ball held at the Palace, St. Francis, Mark Hopkins and Fairmont Hotels

May 5. William G. Irwin home (Blood Bank) at Washington and Laguna destroyed by fire

May 13. Turnabout Theater, Polk and Turk Streets, opens

May 23. World Trade Center in the Ferry Building dedicated

June 2. President Sukarno of Indonesia visits

Aug. 1. Tommy, San Francisco's last workhorse, retired to a Los Altos ranch

Aug. 20. Republican Convention begins at the Cow Palace

Aug. 21. President Dwight D. Eisenhower visits

Sept. 2. Washington-Jackson cable line replaced by bus service

Oct. 25. Port facility dedicated, conversion of Piers 15 and 17 into a modern terminal

Oct. 29. San Francisco Conservatory of

Music moves from 3400 block of Sacramento Street to 19th Ave. and Ortega

Nov. 13. Martin Hanson's Twin Peaks monolith, erected in 1925, demolished in the Market Street widening project.

Nov. 19. Postmaster's Wharf in Presidio demolished

Dec. 3. Helicopter taxi service begins from heliport at Ferry Building

Dec. 7. Site for new Lowell High dedicated at Eucalyptus and Meadowbrook Drives

Dec. 29. Geary Street cars replaced by full time bus service

1957

Jan. 13. P.G.&E. smokestack in the Marina District demolished

Jan. 17. Nine-county Commission recommends legislation to create Bay Area Rapid Transit District

Feb. 8. Public Library's bookmobile formally unveiled and dedicated at City Hall

Mar. 22. Earthquake rocks San Francisco and vicinity

Apr. 7. Hyde Street cable runs again after absence of three years

May 6. Ngo Dinh Diem, President of Vietnam, visits

June 4. California Legislature approves creation of five-county Bay Area Rapid Transit District

June 5. Jackson Square celebrates its new role as San Francisco's interior design center

June 11. Governor Goodwin J. Knight signs law establishing a five-county Bay Area Rapid Transit District

Sept. 22. Rossi Swimming Pool at Arguello and Anza Streets dedicated

Oct. 1. Equitable Life Insurance Company time and temperature indicator atop the Sutter and Montgomery Street building lit for first time

Oct. 12. Statue of Christopher Columbus by Italian sculptor Vittorio de

Colbertaldo dedicated. Boeing Stratoclipper with 40 persons leaves San Francisco for Antarctica, via Hawaii and New Zealand; first commercial flight between California and Antarctica

Nov. 11. Demolition of cable car barn at California and Hyde Streets begins

Nov. 14. BART District officially established with formal meeting of board of directors

Dec. 5. Mohammed V, King of Morocco, visits

1958

Jan. 1. Bay Area Rapid Transit District offices established in Flood Building, later moved to 814 Mission Street

Feb. 23. City's last arch light (erected in 1913) over the intersection of Mission and 25th Streets razed

Mar. 27. Mayor Christopher breaks ground for new North Beach Branch Library

Apr. 11. Brooks Hall in Civic Center dedicated

Apr. 20. Buses replace the Key System's trains at 3:00 a.m.

May 8. Crystal Plunge at Lombard and Taylor Streets demolished

May 9. Last run of the Municipal Railway's two-man street cars, replaced by one-man cars

May 26. Union Square made an official State Historical Landmark with dedication of a plaque honoring John W. Geary, first mayor of San Francisco

June 12. President Theodore Heuss of West Germany visits

June 22. Mohammad Reza Shah Pahlavi of Iran visits

July 29. Southern Pacific Bay Ferries discontinued

Oct. 21. President Dwight D. Eisenhower visits

Nov. 24. Queen Frederika of Greece visits

1959

Mar. 11. Peter II of Yugoslavia visits

Mar. 23. King Hussein of Jordan visits

Mar. 28. H.R.H. The Duke of Windsor visits

May 14. Parsons-Brinckerhoof-Tudor-Bechtel retained as engineering consultants for BART's system design and construction

May 21. Baudouin, King of the Belgians, visits

May 31. Jefferson Elementary School, 19th Ave. and Irving Street, destroyed by fire

July 10. State legislation authorizes use of Bay Bridge tolls to finance construction of Trans-Bay Rapid Transit Tube

July 25. Storyland at Fleishhacker Zoo opens

Aug. 1. Crystal Palace Market on Market Street closes

Sept. 21. Premier Nikita Khrushchev of U.S.S.R. visits

Nov. 11. Seals Stadium demolished

Nov. 29. Prince Karim, Aga Khan IV, visits

1960

Jan. 5. Crown Zellerbach Building dedicated

Mar. 1. Civic Center Garage opens

Apr. 27. President Charles De Gaulle of France visits

May 7. Mahendra Bir Birkram Shan Deva of Nepal visits

May 9. Brundage Collection of Oriental Art in Golden Gate Park opens

May 13. Riot at City Hall over Red Hearing protest

May 14. 3,000 join in peace march

May 22. President Sukarno of Indonesia visits

July 1. The office of Public Administrator is created under authority of Section 5175 of the Welfare Institutions Code

July 13. King Bhumibol Adulyadez of Thailand visits

Sept. 12. Grace Cathedral tower lighted for first time

Oct. 6. King Frederick of Denmark visits

Oct. 20. President Dwight D. Eisenhower visits

1961

Mar. 16. Statue of St. Francis of Assisi removed from steps of St. Francis Church and moved to Oakland

May 5. Outsen Milling Company, last San Francisco grain mill, closes

June 1. Blyth-Zellerbach Committee report on Municipal Management submitted to the Mayor and Board of Supervisors

July 8. Peace rally in Golden Gate Park

July 20. P. & O. liner *Canberra* arrives in San Francisco on her maiden voyage

July 25. Public Utilities Commission votes to purchase 12 acres of Islais Creek property for Water Department maintenance yard

Aug. 1. New Hall of Justice opens

Sept. 5. Huge SP sign (installed in 1954) atop 65 Market Street removed

Sept. 14. Yerba Buena Plaza, apartment building and senior citizens recreation center, dedicated

Oct. 7. Family Rosary Rally held in Golden Gate Park

Oct. 21. Midtown Terrace Reservoir Playground dedicated

Oct. 28. Helen Wills Playground dedicated

Nov. 20. Chung Hee Park, President of Korea, visits

1962

Mar. 1. Alcazar Theater demolished

Mar. 23. President John F. Kennedy visits

Apr. 12. San Mateo County withdraws from BART district

Apr. 29. State Theater on Market Street demolished

May 17. Marin County withdraws from BART district

June 13. First police dog joins Police Department

Aug. 30. Ground broken for Golden Gateway Project

Sept. 7. Fire destroys St. Mary's Cathedral on Van Ness Ave.

Sept. 8. Statue of Father Miguel Hidalgo unveiled in Mission Park, 19th & Dolores Streets

Oct. 23. First boxing ring set up in Candlestick Park for the Gene Fulmer-Dick Tiger middleweight fight

Nov. 6. BART's bond issue approved by a 66.9% favorable vote

Dec. 10. Hunter's Point jitney stops running after 50 years service

Dec. 19. Street signs voted by Park Commission for Golden Gate Park

1963

Jan. 4. Statue of St. Francis of Assisi by Bufano set in place at Beach and Taylor Streets

Jan. 31. Navy closes its San Francisco oceanographic office in the Appraisers Building

Feb. 28. Fox Theater demolition begins

Mar. 22. Alcatraz evacuated as a prison

Mar. 31. Pelton Water Wheel Company at 2929 - 19th Street closes after being in business since 1889

Apr. 16. *Sakura Maru* arrives, first Japanese liner into the Bay since World War II

June 25. San Francisco has a new day: Flower Day

Sept. 5. President Theater, on McAllister Street, San Francisco's last burlesque house, closes

Sept. 13. King of Afghanistan visits

Sept. 27. Dedication of new Produce Terminal at Islais Creek

Oct. 5. Hyde Street Pier re-opens as a State Historical Park

Oct. 12. Bay Bridge traffic changeover

to one-way operation on each deck goes into effect at 4 a.m.

1964

Feb. 20. Mayor's South of Market Redevelopment Committee adopts San Francisco Redevelopment Agency proposal that the South of Market Redevelopment Area D-1 be called Yerba Buena

Mar. 8. Band of Sioux Indians stake claim to Alcatraz Island

Apr. 27. King Hussein of Jordan visits

May 23. Fire at All Hallows Church in the Bayview District kills 17

May 29. Mwami Mwambusta IV, King of Burundi, visits

June 18. President Lyndon B. Johnson visits

June 19. Republican Convention begins at Cow Palace

July 29. Human Rights Commission established

Oct. 1. Cable cars declared a National Landmark

Oct. 5. Fire Department Museum dedicated

Oct. 11. President Diosado Macapagal of Philippines visits

Oct. 12. President Lyndon B. Johnson visits

1965

Jan. 27. Ground broken for "Dragon Gateway" to Grant Ave.

Jan. 27. Alcoa Building dedicated

Apr. 3. St. Nicholas Antiochian Orthodox Church on Diamond Heights dedicated

Apr. 20. Paramount Theater on Market Street closes

June 14. Walton Square, Golden Gateway, dedicated

June 26. President Lyndon B. Johnson visits

Aug. 19. Crew leaves Mile Rock Lighthouse so that demolition can commence

June 26, 1966. Sutro Baths destroyed by fire.

Nov. 4.   Princess Margaret of Great Britain visits

1966

Mar. 12.   Pioneer Plaza dedicated

June 16.   Allyne Park, Vallejo and Gough, opens to the public

June 26.   Sutro Baths destroyed by fire

Aug. 6.   Vietnam war peace march up Market Street

Sept. 22.   President Ferdinand E. Marcos of Philippines visits

Sept. 26.   The ship *Staten Island* is the first icebreaker to enter San Francisco Bay

Oct. 3.   Leopold Sedar Senghor of Senegal visits

1967

Jan. 19.   Autos banned from band concourse area in Golden Gate Park on Sundays

Feb. 2.   King Lupou of Tonga visits

Mar. 18.   Lurline Pier at Ocean Beach demolished by wrecking crews

Apr. 8.   President Cevdat Sunay of Turkey visits

Apr. 15.   Vietnam War peace march from 2nd and Market to Kezar Stadium

June 26.   North Point Theater opens

July 1.   BART construction teams begin tearing up Market Street

July 4.   Fireworks at Candlestick Park for first time; moved from the Marina Green due to weather

July 22.   President Adams of Anguilla visits

July 25. Construction begins on Market Street subway

Aug. 5. H.S.H. Rainier of Monaco visits

Aug. 9. Peace torch arrives from Hiroshima

Aug. 15. San Francisco Mining Exchange closes

Aug. 18. Fire Dept. Headquarters at 260 Golden Gate Ave. dedicated

Aug. 27. Peace torch begins its journey to Washington, D.C. for a demonstration against the Vietnam War

Aug. 28. Colonel Stewart Evans swims from the Farallon Islands to San Francisco

Sept. 30. Palace of Fine Arts reopens

Oct. 5. President Diori of Niger visits

1968

Feb. 22. Pres. Summerskill of San Francisco State College resigns

Mar. 22. President's daughter Lynda Johnson ordered off cable car for eating ice cream cone

Mar. 27. Japanese Trade & Cultural Center dedicated

Apr. 18. Old Hall of Justice demolished

Apr. 27. Peace march and rally

Apr. 30. Olav V of Norway visits

Aug. 31. President Nagush Arutyanyan of Armenia visits

Sept. 19. Baby born to Marin County couple on the Golden Gate Bridge

Oct. 12. GI's and vets march for peace from Golden Gate Park to Civic Center

Oct. 19. Tolls collected southbound only on Golden Gate Bridge

Nov. 6. First day of San Francisco State College strike

Nov. 26. Robert R. Smith, President of San Francisco State College, resigns

Nov. 26. S. I. Hayakawa made acting President, San Francisco State College

Dec. 13. Playland at the Beach reopens

1969

Mar. 18. Bank of California Building, 400 California Street, dedicated

Apr. 6. Peace march

May 16. Cowell Hall, California Academy of Sciences, in Golden Gate Park opens

June 19. Bike route, Lake Merced through Golden Gate Park, dedicated

July 23. President Richard M. Nixon visits

Aug. 21. President Richard M. Nixon visits

Nov. 15. Thousands march for peace

Nov. 20. Indians seize and occupy Alcatraz Island

Dec. 15. Fire Department replaces leather helmets with plastic helmets to test their suitability

Dec. 22. Radio Free Alcatraz broadcasts for first time on radio station KPFA-FM

November 15, 1969. Anti-Vietnam march by thousands.

1970

Jan. 21. Harbor Advisory Radar, a new monitoring system for ship traffic begins operation

Feb. 26. President Pompidou of France arrives for a visit

Feb. 28. Bicycles permitted for first time to cross Golden Gate Bridge

Mar. 13. 4-day strike by city employees begins

Mar. 24. The S.S. *Eppleton Hall*, a steam paddleboat, arrives from Newcastle-upon-Tyne, England

Mar. 26. Golden Gate Park Conservatory made a City landmark

May 15. Five-alarm fire at the Furniture Mart on Market Street

May 15. Teamster strike ends

May 31. Indians on Alcatraz Island celebrate "Liberation Day"

May 31. President Suharto of Indonesia visits

June 1. Five buildings on Alcatraz destroyed by fire

July 20. Baby born to Mrs. Trudell, first baby to be born on Alcatraz

Oct. 15. First mass said in St. Mary's Cathedral

Nov. 18. "Black Wednesday" protest by Police Dept.

Nov. 19. Golden Gate Park Conservatory made a California State Historical Landmark

1971

Jan. 19. Standard Oil freighters collide beneath Golden Gate Bridge and release millions of gallons of oil into Bay

Jan. 27. Last subway tunnel link on BART system, the Montgomery Street Station subway "holed through."

May 31, 1970. Indian "Liberation Day" on Alcatraz.

Apr. 14. Fort Point dedicated as the first National Park site in the San Francisco Bay Area

Apr. 24. Militants cut peace rally short

Apr. 26. San Francisco Lightship replaced by automatic buoy

May 5. Many arrested in financial district during anti-war demonstration aimed at halting business

June 11. United States marshals recapture Alcatraz Island from the Indians

June 22. "Enchanted World" on Fisherman's Wharf opens

July 1. The Golden Gate Bridge pays off its $35-million bond debt. ILWU closes all Coast ports

July 7. New portable swimming pool set up for first time in the Chinese playground at Sacramento and Waverly Streets

Sept. 13. School Dept. begins busing students

Sept. 29. H.R.H. Princess Alexandra arrives at San Francisco International Airport for the start of British Week

Oct. 1. City of London Treasures open, City Hall

Oct. 7. ILWU strike ends on waterfront

Oct. 16. McLaren Park Amphitheater dedicated

Dec. 14. Golden Gate Bridge lights out all night due to power failure

1972

Jan. 22. Howard-Langton mini-park, Howard between 7th and·8th Streets, dedicated by Mayor Alioto

Feb. 21. Longshoreman's strike ends

Mar. 4. Sultan of Selangor and family visit

Mar. 18. "Flying Scotsman," a steam train that served for 40 years on the express run between Edinburgh and London, begins weekend runs along the waterfront

Mar. 23. The City of Paris taken over by Amfac, an Hawaiian based corporation. To reopen June 1st as City of Paris by Liberty House

May 4. The sloop *Gjoa*, famous for its Northwest Passage, returned to Norway

Aug. 26. Clinton's Cafeteria on Market Street closes

Nov. 9. Golden Gate Bridge closed for two hours to install new scaffolding

Nov. 14. Westbury Hotel, Sutter and Powell Streets, opens

Nov. 30. Five-alarm fire destroys Pier 20

Dec. 1. Last Coast Guardsman to tend the light on the Southeast Farallon Island leaves as light is automated

Dec. 8. Alaska Commercial Building at Sansome and California Streets (6885 feet) sold to the Bank of Tokyo for $2,500,000; highest known price paid for land in California history

Dec. 18. Ferry Building siren replaced by electronic Westminster type chimes

1973

Jan. 16. Hyatt Hotel on Union Square opens

Feb. 13. The Sumitomo Bank of California, celebrating its 20th anniversary, presents 50 Kanzan cherry trees to the people of San Francisco to be planted at the Palace of Fine Arts, and 50 to be planted around the Chain of Lakes in Golden Gate Park

Mar. 21. Pier 7 destroyed by fire

May 8. Hyatt Regency Hotel in Embarcadero Center opens

Aug. 10. First train travels through transbay tube to Montgomery Street Station

Oct. 26. The National Park Service begins guided tours of Alcatraz Island with ferry service departing from Pier 43

Nov. 20. Abba Eban visits

1974

May 1. Muni's "Fast Pass" initiated

June 20. Vice President Gerald Ford visits

July 29. Vice President Gerald Ford visits

Aug. 23. Grant School, Pacific Ave. between Broderick and Baker demolished

Sept. 16. BART starts regular transbay service

Sept. 28. Liberty House, 120 Stockton Street at O'Farrell, opens new building to public

Nov. 11. Olga Korbut, Russian gymnast visits

Nov. 20. One Hundred Van Ness Ave., new 29-story public office building opens

Dec. 18. Visitors Center, City Hall, opens

City Government & Departments

Alcaldes & Mayors

Before May 1, 1850, the title of the Chief Executive Officer was Alcalde; from that day until July 1, 1856, Mayor; then for six years, President of the Board of Supervisors; and since July 1, 1862, Mayor.

Mayors

The mayor is the chief executive of San Francisco in both name and power. He is elected directly by the people for a term of four years. He has the general duty of enforcing all of the laws of the city. He appoints numerous city officers, commission members, and board members. He prepares the annual budget for submission to the Board of Supervisors. He is responsible for the administration of all city departments that have been placed under his control by the charter. He has the power to veto any ordinance passed by the Board of Supervisors, and he may compel the board to reconsider rejected measures.

Mexican Alcaldes

Alcalde—a word derived from the Turkish term *cadi*. In Spain and Portugal, an *alcalde* was a sheriff, or justice of the peace; in early California, however, his functions were often broader, including that of mayor and judge.

Francisco de Haro 1834
José Joaquin Estudillo 1835

Francisco Guerrero 1836
Ignacio Martinez 1837
Francisco de Haro 1838-1839
Francisco Guerrero 1839-1841
Francisco Sanchez 1842-1843
William Hinckley 1844
Juan N. Padilla 1845
Jésus de la Cruz Sanchez 1845
José de Jésus Noe 1846

American Alcaldes

Lt. Washington Allon Bartlett
         July 1846-Feb. 1847
Edwin Bryant
         Feb. 22, 1847-June 1847
George Hyde
         June 1, 1847-April, 1848

Dr. John Townsend
         April 1848-Sept. 1848
Thaddeus M. Leavenworth
         Oct. 1848-Aug. 1849

Date of Office	Date of Office
John White Geary . . . . May 1, 1850	Edward B. Pond . . . . Jan. 3, 1887
Charles James Brenham . . . May 5, 1851	George Henry Sanderson . . Jan. 5, 1891
Stephen Randall Harris . . . Jan. 1, 1852	Levi Richard Ellert . . . . . . Jan. 3, 1893
Charles James Brenham . Nov. 10, 1852	Adolph H.J. Sutro . . . . Jan. 7, 1895
Cornelius K. Garrison . . . . . Oct. 3, 1853	James Duval Phelan . . . . . . Jan. 4, 1897
Stephen Palfrey Webb . . . . Oct. 2, 1854	Eugene E. Schmitz† . . . . . . Jan. 8, 1902
James Van Ness . . . . July 1, 1855	Charles Boxton** . . . . July 9, 1907
George J. Whelan . . . . July 8, 1856	Edward Robeson Taylor**† July 16, 1907
Ephriam Willard Burr . . . Nov. 15, 1856	Patrick Henry McCarthy . . Jan. 8, 1910
Henry F. Teschemacher Oct. 3, 1859	James Rolph, Jr. . . . . Jan. 8, 1912
Henry Perrin Coon . . . . . . July 1, 1863	Angelo Joseph Rossi . . . . . Jan. 7, 1931
Frank McCoppin . . . . Dec. 2, 1867	Roger Dearborn Lapham . . Jan. 8, 1944
Thomas Henry Selby . . . . . Dec. 6, 1869	Elmer Edwin Robinson . . . Jan. 8, 1948
William Alvord . . . . Dec. 4, 1871	George Christopher . . . . . . Jan. 8, 1956
James Otis* . . . . Dec. 1, 1873	John Francis Shelley . . . . . Jan. 8, 1964
George Hewston** . . . . . . Nov. 4, 1875	Joseph Lawrence Alioto . . . Jan. 8, 1968
Andrew Jackson Bryant . . . Dec. 6, 1875	
Isaac Smith Kalloch . . . . . . Dec. 1, 1879	*Died in office
Maurice Carey Blake . . . . . Dec. 5, 1881	**Appointed to fill term
Washington Bartlett . . . . . . Jan. 8, 1883	†Resigned

Alcaldes

Francisco de Haro

Accompanied the San Blas Infantry to California after the Hippolyte Bouchard attack on Monterey in 1818. He served twice as alcalde, living and maintaining his office at Mission Dolores. He died January 1, 1849.

José Joaquin Estudillo

Born in Monterey in 1798. On January 1, 1836 he took office as alcalde with Gregario Briones and Jose C. Sanchez as regidores. He died in 1852.

Francisco Guerrero

Mexican by birth, came to California from Tepic in 1834 as a member of the Hijar-Padres colonizing venture. He was a justice of the peace at Mission Dolores where he lived with his family and had his office. He died in 1851.

Ignacio Martinez

Born in Mexico City. He entered military service at an early age, retiring in 1831 as a Lieutenant, after 41 years of service. In 1837 he was appointed alcalde. He was the owner of Rancho Pinole in Contra Costa County where he lived until his death in the early 1850's.

Francisco Sanchez

First municipal elector to choose members to the Departmental Assembly at Monterey in 1836. In 1835 and 1836 he was secretary to the Ayuntamiento. From 1837 to 1840, military commandant at the Presidio, and justice of the peace for the years 1842-1843. His office was at Mission Dolores.

William Sturges Hinckley

Born in Hington, Massachusetts about 1807. He became a prominent merchant in Honolulu before coming to California in 1829. In the early 1840's he became a naturalized Mexican citizen and settled in Yerba Buena. Hinckley was elected alcalde January 9, 1844. He died in June, 1846.

Juan Nepomuceno Padilla

A barber and saloon keeper, elected alcalde December 22, 1844. He resigned from office March 15, 1845 but was persuaded to continue as alcalde until replaced by José de la Cruz Sanchez. He later commanded a party of Californians against the Bear Flaggers.

José de la Cruz Sanchez

Second alcalde elected in 1845. He had his office at Mission Dolores, afterwards moving to his farm in the country. He died in 1878.

José de Jésus Noe

Arrived in California as a member of the Hijar-Padres colony. He served as the last Mexican alcalde from his office in back of Dupont Street.

Lt. Washington Allon Bartlett

Appointed Chief Magistrate, or alcalde, by Capt. John B. Montgomery, commander of the U.S. sloop-of-war *Portsmouth*, who formally took possession of Yerba Buena on July 8, 1846. This appointment was subsequently ratified by a formal election by citizens. He held the office until February, 1847.

Edwin Bryant

Native of Massachusetts, came to Yerba Buena after leaving Frémont's battalion. He served as alcalde from February 22 to June, 1847. He left San Francisco June 2, 1847 for the East and returned in 1849. He died in Louisville, Kentucky, in 1869.

George Hyde

Born in Pennsylvania on August 22, 1819. He was educated at Mount St. Mary's College in Maryland, studied law in Philadelphia, and was admitted to the bar in June, 1842. He arrived in Yerba Buena August 10, 1846 on the U.S. frigate *Congress* having served as clerk to Commodore Stockton. He was appointed alcalde June 1, 1847, and served until April 1, 1848. He died August 16, 1890.

Dr. John Townsend

Born in Fayette County, Pennsylvania, in the early nineteenth century. He received his medical degree from Lexington Medical College and headed West, arriving in California with the Stevens-Murphy overland party in 1844. He settled in Yerba Buena in 1845. In April, 1848, he was appointed alcalde, serving until October, 1848. He died of cholera in December, 1850.

Thaddeus M. Leavenworth

Born in Connecticut and educated in medicine and theology. He came to California with Stevenson's Regiment as chaplain, and in September, 1848 became the alcalde, serving until August, 1849. In 1850 he went to Sonoma County where he was claimant for part of Agua Caliente rancho. He died in Santa Rosa, January 30, 1893.

Mayors
John White Geary

Born December 20, 1819 in a loghouse, situated near Mount Pleasant, Westmoreland County, Pennsylvania. On January 22, 1849, President Polk appointed him Postmaster of San Francisco, with powers to create post-offices, appoint postmasters, establish mail routes, and make contracts for carrying the mails throughout California. Geary was elected alcalde in August, 1849 and became the city's first mayor on May 1, 1850. He returned to Pennsylvania in 1852 where he served as Governor from 1867 to 1873. He died February 8, 1873 in Harrisburg, Pennsylvania.

Charles James Brenham

Born in Frankfort, Kentucky, November 6, 1817. He was well-known on the Mississippi as a steamboat captain. He arrived in San Francisco August 18, 1849 and took command of the steamer *McKim*, which ran between San Francisco and Sacramento. In 1850 he received the unsolicited nomination of the Whig Party for the mayoralty, but the nomination went to Geary. He was elected mayor in 1851 and again in 1852, serving unconnected terms. In 1852 President Fillmore appointed him Treasurer of the Mint and Assistant Treasurer of the United States but Brenham declined the appointments. He later served as agent for the California, Oregon and Mexico Steamship Company. He died in San Francisco, May 10, 1875.

Stephen Randall Harris

Born in Poughkeepsie, New York, in 1802. He was a graduate of the College of Physicians and Surgeons, Columbia University, New York, and for six consecutive years a New York health commissioner. He arrived in San Francisco in June, 1849, and founded the city's first real drug store at the corner of Clay and Montgomery streets. He became mayor in 1852, but continued to carry on his practice. From September 19, 1864 to December 2, 1867 he served as coroner of San Francisco. He died at Napa, California, April 27, 1879.

Cornelius Kingland Garrison

Also known as Commodore Garrison, because of the large shipping interests he controlled. He was born March 1, 1809 at Fort Montgomery, New York. He began his career in Canada, and afterward engaged in various enterprises on the lower Mississippi, near New Orleans. The discovery of gold in California led to his acceptance of the San Francisco agency of the Nicaragua Steamship Line. Within six months of his arrival in 1853 he was elected mayor. He returned to New York in 1859. During the Civil War he rendered great assistance to the government and received formal acknowledgment from President Lincoln. At a time when the U.S. merchant marine had almost entirely disappeared from the high seas he founded the only mail steamship line carrying the American flag on the Atlantic Ocean. He died in New York City, May 1, 1855.

Stephen Palfrey Webb

Born in Salem, Mass., on March 20, 1804. He graduated from Harvard in 1824 after which he studied law with the Honorable John Glen King and was admitted to the Essex Bar. He practiced law in Salem, served as Representative and Senator in the Massachusetts State Legislature, and was elected mayor of Salem in 1842, serving three years. He was also treasurer of the Essex Railroad Company in the late 'forties. About 1853 Webb arrived in San Francisco and served as Mayor from 1854 to 1855. He returned to Massachusetts and was again elected mayor of Salem for the period 1860-1862, later becoming city clerk for the years 1863-1870. He died there on September 29, 1879.

James Van Ness

Born in Burlington, Vermont in 1808.

He arrived in San Francisco in 1851 and served as alderman for many years before being elected mayor in 1855. He moved to San Luis Obispo in later years and became a farmer. He was elected Joint-Senator from San Luis Obispo and Santa Barbara counties in 1871. He died at San Luis Obispo, California, December 28, 1872.

George J. Whelan

On Tuesday, November 12, 1974, the Board of Supervisors adopted Resolution No. 882-74, declaring official recognition of the Honorable George J. Whelan as the eighth mayor of the City of San Francisco.

Up to this time Whelan had never been officially credited for such service, undoubtedly because he was not an elected official. However, city records clearly show that he was installed as the legally appointed President, of the Board of Supervisors, on July 8, 1856, and that he served until November 15, 1856. Whelan had come into office under the new city charter which was known as the Consolidation Act. This act empowered four sitting Justices of the Peace to serve as the Supervisory Board and to appoint an interim president to govern San Francisco.

This temporary government met much opposition in the papers and they were asked to resign. When they did not, newspapers continued to report in detail each week the meeting of the Board and its president. The San Francisco *Daily Evening Bulletin* for July 1, 1856 stated: "God help the City of San Francisco. She has in time past, been the worst governed and best plundered city that it was ever our fortune to live in. We have had one charter a year for several years past; and this last and crowning act of absurdity, the famous Consolidation Act, is the cap-stone. It is said it will go into operation today, but its provisions are so covered up in mystery and

contradiction, that neither Judge, Jury, its framers nor the people are able to discern its objects, or declare its legality."

Little is known of Whelan's background. His name first appears in the 1861 city directory as an attorney. The last listing is 1861. Wherever he came from, and wherever he went is unknown at this time.

Ephraim Willard Burr

Born in Rhode Island, March 7, 1809. He came to California in 1850 to secure crews for whaling ships; however, realizing he could no longer provide men to man the ships, he turned his attention to new business enterprises. He became a commission merchant in partnership with J. Mattoon and later established the San Francisco Accumulating Fund, later called the Savings and Loan Society, but more popularly known as the Clay Street Bank. This was the first savings bank on the Pacific Coast. The People's Party elected him mayor in 1856 and he officially took office Nov. 15th. After his three-year term as mayor he returned to the Clay Street Bank as its president and remained there until forced to resign in 1878 because of charges that he had accepted a five percent commission for granting loans on Navy Paymaster's Certificates. He died in San Francisco, on July 20, 1894.

Henry Fredrick Teschemacher

Arrived in California in 1842 representing the Boston firm of Wm. Appleton & Co., hide and fur traders. He settled in San Francisco after 1849 and was elected mayor in 1859. He died November 29, 1904, at Territet, Switzerland.

Henry Perrin Coon

Born in Columbia County, New York, September 30, 1822. He received his degree in medicine, and established himself as a physician upon his arrival in San Francisco in 1853. He purchased a drug business and in February, 1854 founded the San Francisco Chemical Company. He was elected Police Judge November 15, 1856 and served two terms. On July 1, 1863 he took over the office of mayor after being elected by the People's Party. He was re-elected May 16, 1865. He was an elder, trustee, and one of the founders of Calvary Presbyterian Church. After leaving the office of mayor he was engaged in the real estate and life insurance business until 1870. He died in San Francisco at the Palace Hotel, December 4, 1884.

Frank McCoppin

Born in the city of Longford, Ireland, on July 4, 1834. He arrived in San Francisco in 1858 and was engaged as superintendent of construction of the Market Street City Railroad. He was elected Supervisor for four terms commencing in 1860, and was elected mayor in 1867. He became a naturalized citizen of the United States on December 12, 1864. He was elected to the State Senate from the 13th Senatorial District in 1875. He died in San Francisco, May 26, 1897.

Thomas Henry Selby

Born in New York City, May 14, 1820. He landed in San Francisco in August 1849. In the summer of 1850 he erected a brick building at California and Montgomery streets in which he established the business of Thomas H. Selby & Co., and commenced the importation of metals and merchandise. In April, 1851, he was elected Assistant Alderman of the fifth ward and re-elected in 1852. He took the office of mayor on December 6, 1869, and served the city free, donating the salary of his office to various charitable institutions. He declined to accept renomination. He served as President of the Merchant's Exchange and as the first President of the Industrial School Association, President of the Board of Trustees of Calvary Church and of City College, and as a life director of the Mercantile Library Association. He died in San Francisco, June 9, 1875.

William Alvord

Born in Albany, New York, on January 3, 1833 and educated at the Albany Academy. He arrived in California in 1853, settled at Marysville and established the hardware store of Alvord & Haviland. After two years of successful business at Marysville he came to San Francisco and opened the large wholesale and importing house of William Alvord & Co. In 1871 he was nominated and elected Mayor of San Francisco. He later served as Police Commissioner, Park Commissioner, President of the San Francisco Art Association and President of the California Academy of Sciences. He also served as president of: the Alaska-Treadwell Gold Mining Company, the Alaska-United Gold Mining Company, the San Francisco Clearing House, the Spring Valley Water Company, the Pacific Club, the Loring Club, and the Astronomical Society of the Pacific, also as director of the Selby Smelting & Lead Works, the United Railroads of San Francisco, Spreckels and Western Sugar Refining Companies, the Security Savings Bank and the California Title Insurance Company. He died in San Francisco on December 21, 1904.

James Otis

Born August 11, 1826 in Boston. In 1849, at the age of 23, he sailed for San Francisco by way of the Isthmus. He worked three years as a partner in Macondray &

Co., before returning to Boston. After a year's absence he returned to California and re-entered the firm, which he headed for many years prior to his death. He took a prominent part in all civic work, and also in politics. He was twice President of the Chamber of Commerce, twice President of the Mercantile Library Association, and twice elected to the Board of Supervisors. During the Civil War he was chosen Secretary of the Pacific Branch of the United States Sanitary Commission. He was also delegated to cast the electoral votes of California for Abraham Lincoln and General Grant. He became mayor in 1873 and died in office on October 30, 1875, of diptheria.

George Hewston

Born in Philadelphia, Pennsylvania, in 1826. He graduated from the Philadelphia College of Medicine in 1850, receiving his degree as Doctor of Medicine. In 1851 he commenced his private practice, continuing until coming to California in 1861. He was for seven years Surgeon on the Staff of Major General Allen, commanding the State Militia from 1863 to 1870. Dr. Hewston was elected to the Board of Supervisors in 1873 and in 1875 was chosen by the Board to fill the unexpired term of Mayor Otis, the first Mayor of San Francisco to die in office.

Andrew Jackson Bryant

Born in Ettingham, Carroll County, New Hampshire in 1831. In April, 1850 he arrived in California after coming around the Horn on the brig Ark. He went directly to the northern mines but soon found he was better suited to business and established himself in Benicia, where he was twice elected City Marshal. He later moved to Sacramento and engaged in merchandising liquor, afterwards moving to San Francisco. In 1866 he was appointed Naval Officer by

President Andrew Johnson and held the office until 1870 when he was made general agent on the Pacific Coast for the Brooklyn Life Insurance Company. He later became manager of the State Investment and Insurance Company. He served two terms as Mayor, from 1875 to 1879. From 1882 until his death he served as president of the California Light Company. On May 11, 1888, he fell from the ferry *Encinal* on San Francisco Bay and was drowned.

Isaac Smith Kalloch

Nicknamed "Golden Voice." He was born in East Thomaston (now Rockland) Maine, on July 10, 1832. He attended Colby College, Maine, a Baptist institution, from which he was expelled in his freshman year. Because he was a brilliant pulpit and platform orator, he was later awarded an honorary Master of Arts degree from Colby and Colgate Universities and became the Rev. Dr. Kalloch. In 1875 he left Leavenworth, Kansas for San Francisco, giving as his reason: "there are more wicked people of both sexes in San Francisco and he felt compelled of God to go and convert them." He built the Metropolitan Temple at the corner of Fifth and Jessie streets, and it was in front of this temple on August 23, 1879 that he was shot twice by *The Chronicle*'s Charles deYoung. From these wounds, and with the help of the Workingman's Party, he gained the office of Mayor. "I am not going to steal any money from the city, get drunk, or do any other dishonorable act," he stated before he took office. During his administration (1879-1881), he was continually opposed by the Board of Supervisors and in 1880 an attempt was made to impeach him. He resigned as pastor of the Metropolitan Temple in July, 1883, and moved to Whatcom (Bellingham) Washington, where he died on December 9, 1887.

Maurice Carey Blake

Born in Otisfield, Maine, on October 20, 1815. He graduated from Bowdoin College in 1838. He was admitted to the bar and began the practice of law in Camden, Maine. He was a Whig in politics and in 1846 was elected his party's representative to the Legislature. Under President Taylor's administration he was appointed Collector of the Belfast Customs District, an office he held for four years. He arrived in San Francisco in 1853 and continued to practice law. He was a member of the Vigilance Committee and in 1857 was elected a member of the Legislature from San Francisco. The following year he was elected Judge of San Francisco County by the People's Party, subsequently serving as Probate Judge and Judge of the Municipal Criminal Court. In 1881 Judge Blake was elected Mayor. Following his one year term of office he returned to his legal practice and in 1884 was a delegate to the Republican Convention. He died in San Francisco on September 26, 1897.

Washington Bartlett

Born at Savannah, Georgia, February 29, 1824. He sailed around Cape Horn from Charleston, South Carolina in January, 1849, arriving in San Francisco in November. Being a trained printer he soon opened a printing shop and was responsible for printing the first English language book in California, *California As It Is And As It May Be Or A Guide To The Gold Country*. He was appointed deputy county clerk for San Francisco County in 1857. In 1859 he won election as County Clerk, a position he was re-elected to in 1867. He was admitted to the bar in 1863. Governor Haight appointed him State Harbor Commissioner in 1870 and in 1873 he was nominated by the Citizen's Independent Party and the People's Union Party as one of the State Senators from San Francisco. He was elected Mayor of San Francisco in 1882 and re-elected in 1884. In 1886 he

won the gubernatorial election and was inaugurated on January 8, 1887. Governor Bartlett died September 12, 1887, in Oakland, California.

Edward B. Pond

Born December 7, 1833 at Bellville, New York. He crossed the plains and settled in Chico, California, in 1855. After many years in Chico he moved to San Francisco where he was the head of the wholesale house of Pond & Reynolds. He was elected to the Board of Supervisors in 1882 and served two terms. He assumed the office of Mayor beginning January 3, 1887, and was re-elected in 1888. Following his second term of office he returned to private business. He was director of the San Francisco Savings Union for 19 years, vice-president for five years, and president for 11 years, retiring in 1909. He died in San Francisco at the Granada Hotel on April 22, 1910.

George Henry Sanderson

Born in Boston, Massachusetts in 1824. He came to California during the height of the gold fever in 1849. In 1865 he moved to San Francisco where he was employed by the grocery firms of Weaver, Wooster & Co., and Jones & Co. In 1878 he became a member of the wholesale grocery firm known as Root & Sanderson. He served two terms as president of the Board of Trade and was Mayor from January 5, 1891 to January 3, 1893. He died very suddenly of acute pneumonia on February 1, 1893 in San Francisco, just one month after retiring from office.

Levi Richard Ellert

San Francisco's first native-son Mayor, born in the city on October 20, 1857. He established the druggist firm, L. R. Ellert & Co., at the corner of California and Kearny in 1883. His first venture into the political field was an unsuccessful attempt for election as School Director. In 1888 he was elected Supervisor on the Republican ticket and re-elected in 1890. He was elected Mayor in 1892 on the Non-Partisan ticket. During his incumbency he appeared before the Supreme Court, passed the bar examination, and was admitted to the Bar. He served as director of the California Title Insurance & Trust Company and the Continental Salt & Chemical Company, and as president and general manager of the Sanitary Reduction Works, a position he held until October, 1899. Ellert died July 21, 1901, in San Francisco.

Adolph Heinrich Joseph Sutro

Born in Aachen (Aix-la-Chapelle), Prussia, on April 29, 1830. He was well educated in the field of mining engineering. He arrived in San Francisco aboard the steamship *California* on November 21, 1850, and immediately engaged in trade, first in San Francisco and later in Stockton. In 1859, when the Comstock Lode made headlines, he was again attracted to mining. He established a small mill, called the Sutro Metallurgical Works, in East Dayton, Nevada, for the reduction of ores by an improved process of amalgamation and was responsible for the planning and building of the Sutro Tunnel. This tunnel made it possible to drain and ventilate the many mines in the Comstock Lode and permit the miners to bring out the rich silver ore. In 1879 Sutro sold his tunnel to the McCalmont Brothers and countless lesser investors and returned to San Francisco. in 1894 he ran for Mayor on the Populist ticket and served one term. At one time he owned one-twelfth of the acreage in San Francisco. He purchased the Cliff House in the early 'eighties and a thousand acres of land facing the ocean, now called Sutro Heights. He built the Sutro salt water baths and planted Sutro Forest. He owned the finest private library in America most of which was destroyed in the 1906 earthquake and fire. Sutro died in San Francisco on August 8, 1898.

James Duval Phelan

Born in San Francisco, April 20, 1861. He was educated at Saint Ignatius High School and graduated with an A.B. degree from the University of San Francisco in 1881, followed by a degree in law from the University of California. However, he did not pursue a law career but became a partner in the banking firm of Phelan & Son, assuming responsibility of the First National Bank, the Mutual Savings and the Bank of Santa Cruz County upon the death of his father in 1892. Without any previous political experience Phelan was elected Mayor for three terms beginning in 1897. Following the earthquake of 1906, Phelan became President of the Relief & Red Cross Funds, and was designated by President Theodore Roosevelt as custodian of the Relief Funds, amounting to $9,000,000. He was elected United States Senator in 1913 and served six years. Senator Phelan died at his country estate Villa Montalvo, Montalvo, California, August 7, 1930.

Eugene E. Schmitz

Born in San Francisco on August 22, 1864. A musician and occasional orchestra conductor, he rose to the presidency of the Musicians Union, a position giving him entree into society along with nominal membership in the labor movement. Perhaps it was because of this unique position that "Handsome Gene" came under the appraising eye of Abraham "Boss" Ruef, who, with minimal delay, installed the handsome and popular Schmitz as his newly formed Union Labor Party's mayoral candidate. To the considerable surprise of all concerned, 1901 saw him elected Mayor of San Francisco, the first Union Labor mayor in United States history. 1906 brought San Francisco two shocks: (1) the Earthquake and Fire, and (2) the arrest of Mayor Schmitz on 27 counts of graft and bribery. Convicted and given the maximum penalty, he appealed and the conviction was reversed by both the Appelate Court and the State Supreme Court. Thus freed of the legal stigma, he returned to politics and, after an unsuccessful bid for the Mayor's chair in 1915, was elected to the Board of Supervisors where he remained until 1925 (running again for Mayor in 1919). He was engaged in private business until he died in San Francisco on November 20, 1928.

Charles Boxton

Born in Shasta County, California, on April 24, 1860. He studied dentistry and reportedly left a flourishing practice to join the California Volunteers on their way to participate in the quelling of the Philippine Insurrection. He returned from the wars covered with glory and decided to enter politics, winning election to the Board of Supervisors in 1899. Along with his rising political halo, his professional status increased and he became the Dean of the Dental Department of the College of Physicians and Surgeons. Although involved in considerable scandal generated by the Schmitz-Ruef trials, the Board of Supervisors selected him to fulfill the remainder of the term of the convicted Mayor. The new chief executive was not terribly pleased with their choice and stated upon his appointment, "It is with great feeling of sadness that I take this office." He did not suffer too long, however, for he resigned and was replaced upon the seventh day of his administration. He returned to the practice of dentistry and died in San Mateo on August 29, 1927.

Edward Robeson Taylor

Born in Springfield, Illinois, September 24, 1838. He arrived in California on February 4, 1862. He received the degree of Doctor of Medicine from the Toland Medical College in San Francisco in 1865. While acting as private secretary to Governor Haight of California (1867-1871) he studied law and was admitted to the Bar of the Supreme Court in January, 1872. Seven years later he was admitted to

practice in the Supreme Court of the United States. He also served as a Public Library and Law Library trustee, vice-president of Cooper Medical College, president of the San Francisco Bar Association, president of the Bohemian Club and dean of Hastings College of Law. He was appointed Mayor by the Board of Supervisors to replace Charles Boxton on July 16, 1907. His position had to be officially confirmed by the State Supreme Court on August 19, due to the Schmitz trial. In November of the same year he was elected by the people as their Democratic mayor for a two-year term. He was also the author of numerous volumes of verse which won him world-wide acclaim. His *To Arms* written in 1920 following World War I, was responsible for his decoration with the cross of the Legion of Honor from the French government. He died in San Francisco on July 5, 1923.

Patrick Henry McCarthy

Born in County Limerick, Ireland, on March 17, 1863. He came to America in 1880 and to San Francisco in 1886. He became president of the San Francisco Building Trades Council in 1894, and served as its head for 29 years, also serving 22 years as president of the State Building Trades Council. He was responsible for the eight-hour law for city labor, and the $2 minimum wage clause in the charter. He served as civil service commissioner for four years under Mayor Phelan. He was defeated in his first campaign for mayor by Edward Robeson Taylor. His second attempt was more successful, he was elected on November 2, 1911, carrying almost the entire Union Labor ticket into office with him, and for one term was the last symbol of Union Labor's complete control of San Francisco government. In 1915 he served as a director of the Panama Pacific International Exposition. Upon retiring from active participation in the Building Trades

Council in 1923, he engaged in the investment banking business. He died in San Francisco on July 1, 1933.

James Rolph, Jr.

Born August 23, 1869 in San Francisco. He was educated in Mission District schools and began his business career as an office boy in the commission house of Kittle & Co. In 1900 he formed a partnership with George Hind and engaged in the shipping and commission business. In 1903 he helped found the Mission Bank, of which he became president, also serving as president of the Mission Savings Bank. He founded the Rolph Navigation & Coal Company, the Rolph Shipbuilding Company, and the James Rolph Company. he was asked to run for mayor in June, 1909, but declined, choosing to run in the 1911 election. For the next 19 years Rolph was "Sunny Jim" to San Franciscans with "There Are Smiles That Make You Happy" as his theme song. Along with his job as mayor and his private shipping interests he also served as director of the Ship Owners & Merchants Tugboat Company, the San Francisco Chamber of Commerce, president of the Merchants Exchange, and vice president of the 1915 Panama Pacific International Exposition. In November, 1930, James Rolph Jr. won the California gubernatorial election, with his resignation as mayor effective simultaneously with his inauguration as Governor, on Tuesday, January 6, 1931. On November 9, 1933, Brooke Hart, son of a wealthy San Jose merchant was kidnapped. The two men responsible were caught, later forcibly removed from jail and hung by a vigilante committee. Governor Rolph by condoning the lynching was given the name "Governor Lynch" and received extremely bad publicity across the nation. Following this episode he suffered several heart attacks and died at Riverside Farm, Santa Clara County, on June 2, 1934.

Angelo Joseph Rossi

Born January 22, 1878 in Volcano, Amador County, California. In 1890 his family moved to San Francisco where he attended the North Cosmopolitan School. He began work as an errand boy for the florist firm of Carbone & Manti, eventually heading the firm as president and manager. He served as director of the Downtown Association of San Francisco for many years and as its president during 1920 and 1921. Mayor James Rolph Jr. appointed him a member of the playground commission and he served on this board from 1914 to 1921. He was elected to the Board of Supervisors in 1925 and again in 1929. Upon the election of Mayor James Rolph Jr. as Governor of California, Rossi was elected Mayor by the Board of Supervisors on January 7, 1931 and re-elected by the people in 1935 and 1939. He died in San Francisco on April 5, 1948.

Roger Dearborn Lapham

Born in New York City on December 6, 1883. He attended Harvard University, then entered his family-founded American Hawaiian Steamship Company as a clerk, and rose to its presidency in 1925. He was appointed a member of the National Defense Mediation Board in 1941 by President Franklin Roosevelt. Returning to San Francisco in 1943 he ran for Mayor as an independent candidate, pledging he would accept the office for one term only. "I know nothing about city administration but I think I can learn," were his campaigning words. He later survived a recall movement in 1946 opposing his consolidation of the private Market Street Railway with the Municipal Railway. After leaving office in 1948 Lapham headed the U.S. Economic Cooperation Administration's mission to China and in 1950-1951 headed the E.C.A.'s mission to Greece. He died in San Francisco on April 16, 1966.

Elmer Edwin Robinson

Born in San Francisco on October 3, 1894. After graduating from night law school, he was admitted to the California Bar in 1915. As a young lawyer, he worked as a deputy in the District Attorney's office from 1915 to 1921, then branched out on his own. After 15 years before the bench, he was appointed Municipal Judge in January, 1935, and Superior Judge nine months later. He was elected to a six-year Superior Court term in 1936 and re-elected in 1942. In 1933, under appointment by Franklin Roosevelt, at the request of the Disabled American Veterans, he directed adjustment of compensation claims for veterans of World War I. During World War II, Judge Robinson served as State Chairman of a national salvage committee. He resigned his place on the Superior Court Bench in 1947 to run for the office of Mayor, winning this election and the following one in 1951. Upon his retirement from office in January, 1956 he returned to his law practice and to the position of president and general manager of Woodlawn Memorial Park.

George Christopher (Christopheles)

Born in Arcadia, Greece, December 8, 1907. He was brought to San Francisco at the age of two and educated in the public schools, later graduating with a degree in accounting from the Golden Gate Night College. In 1930 after becoming a citizen of the United States, he changed his name to Christopher. The Excelsior Dairy made him an official in 1937, followed by a partnership in the Meadow Glen Dairy, which eventually became the Christopher Dairy. In 1945 he began his political career by election to the board of Supervisors, with re-election in 1949 when he served as President of the Board. He was elected Mayor in 1955 and served two terms. In the 1966 primary election George Christopher ran against Ronald Reagan for the office of governor but was defeated.

John Francis Shelley

Born September 3, 1905 in San Francisco. He graduated from the University of San Francisco Law School in 1932, and was elected president of the San Francisco Labor Council in 1937. From 1948 to his election to Congress in 1949, he was secretary-treasurer of the Council and from 1947 to 1950 was also president of the California State Federation of Labor. He was elected in 1938 to the State Senate, and in 1949 began the first of his eight terms in Congress. Jack Shelley was elected Mayor on Tuesday, November 5, 1963, defeating Supervisor Harold Dobbs by 120,560 votes to 92,627. Due to ill health he declined to run for a second term saying, "The job of Mayor is an endless, impossible and exhausting drain, trying not only to keep a City intact, but on the right track." Shelley served as San Francisco's lobbyist in Sacramento until his death September 1, 1974.

Joseph Lawrence Alioto

Born in San Francisco on February 12, 1916. He is a graduate of St. Mary's College, and the Catholic University of America Law School in Washington, D.C. He has also received Honorary Doctor of Law degrees from St. Mary's College, Santa Clara University and the Catholic University of America. From law school, Alioto joined the Department of Justice where he worked five years in the anti-trust division under Judge Thurman Arnold and Justice Tom Clark. In the 1950's he served as president of the Board of Education and was then appointed to the Redevelopment Agency. In 1959, Alioto became general manager and president of the Rice Growers Association and rapidly expanded its annual sales from $25- to $70-million. He revolutionized production methods and pioneered the use of ships as seagoing silos for the transportation of edible bulk rice. He was elected Mayor on November 7, 1967, defeating Harold Dobbs and re-elected to a second term in 1971.

City Charter

"On April 15th, 1850, San Francisco was incorporated as a City, by act of the Legislature. By that act it became the legal successor of the Pueblo of San Francisco, vested with all its property, and that same statute took away all the power of the Prefect. The title to the Pueblo Lands was therefore vested in the City of San Francisco. This charter was subsequently repealed by the Charter of 1851, which, in its turn was repealed by that of 1854; but the charter of 1850 authorized the city to 'hold, lease, sell and dispose of property for the benefit of the city.' The charter of 1851 empowered the city to purchase, receive, and hold property, real and personal, and sell or otherwise dispose of the same for their common benefit; the charter of 1855, continue the power in the city to 'purchase, receive, hold and enjoy real and personal property, and sell, convey, mortgage and dispose of the same for the common benefit.' "

(John W. Dwinelle, *The Colonial History of the City of San Francisco.* 1866)

"The 1856 Charter was not efficient; it was said that nobody knew what it meant except the city clerk and one or two lawyers. The California Constitution of 1879 provided for the city to pass a freeholder's charter, but attempts to do so were defeated four times until, finally in 1900, a strong-mayor-council type was adopted. However, under the 1900 Charter, the Mayor was not so strong as was expected and his executive powers were weakened by boards and commissions which chose their own executives."

(Martin W. Judnich, *San Francisco Government.* 1967)

The city's present Charter was ratified by vote of the people on March 26, 1931: ratified by the Legislature of the State April 13, 1931; in effect January 8, 1932.

It has been amended nearly 400 times since its adoption in 1931, and has more than 110,000 words.

The San Francisco Citizens Charter Revision Committee was appointed by the Mayor in February, 1968, pursuant to a resolution of the Board of Supervisors unanimously adopted in October, 1967. The Committee consisted of 21 members selected to be broadly representative of the citizenry of San Francisco.

In the November 4, 1969 election, the voters were asked to revise their Charter for the first time since 1931. 63 percent of the voters rejected Proposition E.

Later the Committee decided to restructure, but not change, the present charter and received voter approval of Proposition R on November 2, 1971.

Fire Department

Soon after the December 24, 1849 fire, some six volunteer fire companies were organized by the citizenry of San Francisco. Many of these men had been active firemen in New York, Boston, Philadelphia, and other eastern cities before coming to this gold rush city.

The city was constructed, at this time, mostly of combustible materials in the form of wood, cloth and canvas, which accounted for the large amount of property destroyed by the following fires:

Dec. 24, 1849	$ 1,000,000
May 4, 1850	$ 3,500,000
June 14, 1850	$ 3,000,000
Sept. 17, 1850	$ 450,000
May 3, 1851	$12,000,000
June 22, 1851	$ 3,000,000

The first election for Chief Engineer (Fire Chief) took place on October 19, 1850, when Frederick D. Kohler was elected to that office.

The Paid Fire Department (148 members) went into active operation on December 3, 1866. It stemmed from legislation approved by the State Legislature on March 2, 1866.

Fire Chiefs

Frederick D. Kohler
    Jan. 28, 1850-Nov. 3, 1851
Franklin E.R. Whitney
    Nov. 3, 1851;
        resigned Nov. 17, 1851
George H. Hossefross
    Dec. 6, 1851;
        resigned Oct. 1, 1853
Charles P. Duane
    Acting chief from Oct. 1, 1853
    Chief Dec. 5, 1853-Dec. 3, 1855
James E. Nuttman
    Dec. 3, 1855-Dec. 1, 1856
Franklin E.R. Whitney
    Dec. 1, 1856-Dec. 3, 1860
David Scannell
    Dec. 3, 1860-Dec. 3, 1866
Franklin E.R. Whitney
    Dec. 3, 1866-July 20, 1870
Charles H. Ackerson
    July 20, 1870-Apr. 4, 1871
David Scannell
    Apr. 4, 1871-April 22, 1873
Franklin E.R. Whitney
    April 22, 1873-Dec. 1, 1873
David Scannell
    Dec. 1, 1873-March 30, 1893
Dennis T. Sullivan
    April 4, 1893-April 22, 1906

Patrick H. Shaughnessy
    June 15, 1906-March 16, 1910
Thomas R. Murphy
    March 16, 1910-May 1929
Charles J. Brennan*
    Acting chief July 2, 1929
    Chief Nov. 11, 1929-Mar. 16, 1943
Albert J. Sullivan
    March 17, 1943-Jan. 21, 1948

Officers of Tiger Engine Co., S.F. Volunteer Fire Department, in 1864.

Engine No. 10, S.F. Fire Department, in 1900.

Edward P. Walsh
>Jan. 21, 1948-Aug. 20, 1953

Frank P. Kelly
>Aug. 21, 1953-Nov. 13, 1956

William Murray
>Acting chief Nov. 13, 1956
>Chief Dec. 16, 1956

Keith Calden
>Jan. 4, 1971

*When ill-health forced his retirement he was appointed "Fire Chief Emeritus"—the first award of its kind in United States fire fighting circles—receiving a gold badge and scroll and title of "chief emeritus."

Home of San Francisco Fire Chiefs:
Dennis Sullivan Memorial

Some time after Chief Sullivan's death (April 22, 1906) a fund of more than $15,000 was raised by subscription to build a memorial to his memory. The building of the home was delayed until 1922 owing to differences of opinion as to a location, and the great advance in the cost of building materials. The home is situated on the north side of Bush Street near Taylor. There is a bronze tablet in the center of the building with a picture of Chief Sullivan, and the following words by famed San

Francisco poet George Sterling:

"By fire shall heroes be proven
Lest virtue's gold grow dim.
And his by fire was tested,
In life's ordeal of him,
Now California renders
The laurels that he won—

Dead on the field of honor,
Her hero and her son."

The Department Museum, recalling the city's flaming past, is located next to Truck 10 - Engine 26 Station at Euclid and Presidio avenues.

Municipal Flag & Motto

Mayor James Phelan in his message to the Supervisors on January 8, 1900 recommended the Board adopt a flag for the City of San Francisco and appointed a committee to request designs.

Over 100 drawings were submit-

ted and on April 14, 1900 the design of John M. Gamble was adopted.

The Phoenix, the crest of the city, taken from its seal, is used to symbolize the municipality. It is shown arising from the ashes of the old Consolidation Act to renewed power

The official flag, as adopted in 1900.

under the New Charter, and may be taken as an emblem of the era of prosperity in store for the city under improved conditions. This was the designer's idea, but now it is generally interpreted as meaning the rebirth after the fire of 1906.

A white flag bordered in gold with the crest of a Phoenix bird arising from a ring of fire, the motto, "Oro en Paz, Fierro en Guerra" (Gold in Peace, Iron in War) in gold on a black banner and the words, "San Francisco" printed in blue across the lower portion of the white body of the flag.

In 1952 the original flag of handwoven heavy silk with gold filigree edges was located in the Hall of Justice. It had been entrusted to Police Chief William P. Sullivan in a May 1, 1900 ceremony. The flag was carried to safety in 1906.

Mayor Elmer Robinson presented the flag to the Society of California Pioneers "in order that historical value of the flag be preserved and it be displayed for the benefit of the people of San Francisco and of California."

City Flower

The dahlia, long regarded as the city flower, was officially designated as such on October 4, 1926.

The Board of Supervisors in their resolution Number 26244 said, "The dahlia partakes essentially of the character of our beloved city, in birth, breeding and habit, for it was originally Mexican, carried thence to Spain, to France and England in turn, being changed in the process from a simple daisylike wild flower to a cosmopolitan beauty."

Official Landmarks

On February 9, 1966 Mayor John F. Shelley requested that the City Planning Commission study, evaluate, and develop the framework for public policy on historical landmarks in San Francisco. Out of the request Article 10 of the City Planning Code was initiated. It provided administrative tools by which actions may be taken to insure that the city will continue to be enhanced by the presence of the works of many periods and styles.

The legislation assigns primary responsibility for landmarks preservation to the City Planning Commission. Administration is threefold: (1) identification and designation of landmarks; (2) protection of landmarks from improper remodeling of exterior façades; (3) imposition of a moratorium on demolition to allow time for the community at large to make efforts to save the landmark.

The legislation also creates a nine-member citizens advisory group called the Landmarks Preservation Advisory Board. This board, made up of both the lay public and experts in historic preservation, is appointed by the Mayor to provide the City Planning Commission with the expertise required in the administration of such a code.

Landmarks Officially Designated by the Board of Supervisors

Mission Dolores - Dolores Street near 16th Street

Old Saint Mary's Church - California Street and Grant Avenue

Bank of California - California and Sansome Streets

Saint Patrick's Church - 756 Mission Street, between Third and Fourth Streets

Saint Francis of Assisi Church - Vallejo Street at Columbus Avenue

Holy Cross Parish Hall (Old Saint Patrick's Church) - 1820 Eddy Street, near Scott Street

Audiffred Building - Mission Street and The Embarcadero

South San Francisco Opera House - Newcomb and Mendell Streets, near Third Street

Belli Building (Landerman's Building) - 722 Montgomery Street

Genella Building (Belli Annex) - 728-30 Montgomery Street

Hotaling Stables Building - 32-42 Hotaling Place

Hotaling Building - 451 Jackson Street

Hotaling Annex East - 445 Jackson Street

Medico-Dental Building - 441 Jackson Street

Ghirardelli Building - 415-31 Jackson Street

Ghirardelli Annex Jackson Street - 407 Jackson Street

Colonial Dames Octagon House - 2645 Gough Street, near Union Street

Garden Court of the Palace Hotel - New Montgomery Street at Market Street

Golden Era Building - 732 Montgomery Street

Hotaling Annex West - 463-73 Jackson Street

San Francisco City Hall - Block bounded by Polk and McAllister Streets, Van Ness Avenue and Grove Street

Solari Building East (Larco's Building) - 470 Jackson Street

Solari Building West (Old French Consulate) - 472 Jackson Street

Yeon Building - 432 Jackson Street

Moulinie Building - 458-60 Jackson Street

Bank of Lucas, Turner & Co. - 800-804 Montgomery Street, at Jackson Street

Grogan-Lent-Atherton Building - 400 Jackson Street

Old Holy Virgin Russian Orthodox Cathedral - 858-64 Fulton Street

Old Fire House, Engine 22 - 1348 Tenth Avenue

Ghirardelli Square - Block bounded by North Point, Larkin, Beach and Polk Streets

San Francisco City Hall

Burr House - 1772 Vallejo Street

Abner Phelps House - 329 Divisadero Street between Oak and Page Streets, on interior of the block

Columbus Tower (Sentinel Building) - Columbus Avenue and Kearny Street

Original United States Mint and Subtreasury - 608 Commercial Street, near Montgomery Street

Stadtmuller House - 819 Eddy Street

Feusier Octagon House - 1067 Green Street

Hallidie Building - 130 Sutter Street

Bourn Mansion - 2550 Webster Street

Saint Francis Lutheran Church - Church Street, between Market and Duboce Streets

First Unitarian Church - Block bounded by Franklin Street, Geary Boulevard and Starr King Way

Saint Mark's Evangelical Lutheran Church - O'Farrell Street (vacated portion) between Franklin and Gough Streets

Dennis T. Sullivan Memorial Fire Chief's Home - 870 Bush Street

Cable Car Barn and Power House - Washington and Mason Streets, northwest corner

Donaldina Cameron House - 920 Sacramento Street

Leale House - 2475 Pacific Street

House of the Flag - 1652-56 Taylor Street

Talbot-Dutton House - 1782 Pacific Avenue

Nightingale House - 201 Buchanan Street

DeMartini House - 294 Page Street

Sherman House - 2160 Green Street

Conservatory, Golden Gate Park - West of Kennedy Drive and Stanyan Street

Casebolt House - 2727 Pierce Street

Transamerica Building (old) - 4 Columbus Avenue

Wormser-Coleman House - 1834 California Street

Edward Coleman House - 1701 Franklin Street

Lilienthal-Orville Pratt House - 1820 California Street

Roos House - 3500 Jackson Street

Merryvale Antiques - 3640 Buchanan Street

Haslett Warehouse - 680 Beach

Hunters Point Springs and Albion Brewery - 881 Innes Avenue

Sylvester House - 1556 Revere Ave.

Old Mesh House - 1153 Oak Street

Quinn House - 1562 McKinnon Ave.

Old Flood Mansion (Pacific Union Club) - 1000 California Street

Trinity Episcopal Church - 1668 Bush Street

Atherton House - 1990 California St.

Police Department

In 1847, before San Francisco was chartered, the police force consisted of six men. By 1850 the force was increased to 12 men, hardly sufficient in number to control crime and the many riotous disturbances.

In June, 1851, and again in 1856, a small band of citizens formed themselves into a Committee of Vigilance for the purpose of arresting lawbreakers, trying them, and pronouncing and carrying out sentence. Following the adjournment of the Vigilantes, the regular police force was again made responsible for enforcing the laws and keeping the peace.

After the Consolidation Act was passed in 1856 the responsibility for enforcing law and order rested with a Board of Police Commissioners. This board selected the members of the force, the Chief being chosen by popular vote, until 1878, when the position became appointive.

Marshals
(Title of City Marshal no longer used after 1856)

	Date of Office		Date of Office
Malachi Fallon	May 11, 1850	Brandt Seguine	Sept. 14, 1853
Robert G. Crozier	April 28, 1851	John W. McKenzie	Oct. 2, 1854
David W. Thompson	Jan. 1852	Hampton North	July 1, 1855
Robert G. Crozier	Nov. 2, 1852	James McElroy	July 6, 1856

Police Chiefs

	Date of Office		Date of Office
James F. Curtis	Nov. 4, 1856	George Wittmann	Nov. 21, 1901
Martin J. Burke	Sept. 11, 1858	Jermiah F. Dinan	April 5, 1905
Patrick Crowley	Dec. 3, 1866	William J. Biggy	Sept. 13, 1907
Theodore G. Cockrill	Dec. 1, 1873	Jesse B. Cook	Dec. 25, 1908
Henry H. Ellis	Dec. 6, 1875	John B. Martin	Jan. 28, 1910
John Kirkpatrick	Dec. 3, 1877	John Seymour	Oct. 3, 1910
Patrick Crowley	Dec. 1, 1879	David A. White	June 15, 1911
Isaiah W. Lees	April 7, 1897	Daniel J. O'Brien	Dec. 1, 1920
William P. Sullivan, Jr.	Feb. 13, 1900	William J. Quinn	Jan. 1, 1929

San Francisco's Finest

Charles W. Dullea . . . . . . Feb. 15, 1940
Michael Riordan . . . . Oct. 9, 1947
Michael Mitchell . . . . Jan. 13, 1948
Michael Gaffey . . . . Jan. 2, 1951
George Healy . . . . Nov. 15, 1955

Francis J. Ahern . . . . Feb. 1, 1956
Thomas J. Cahill . . . . Sept. 5, 1958
Alfred J. Nelder . . . . Feb. 4, 1970
Donald M. Scott . . . . Sept. 23, 1971

Badge

A seven-pointed star, known as "The Mystic Star" is an emblem of "The seven gifts of the Holy Spirit." These seven points signify: Virtue, Divinity, Prudence, Fortitude, Honor, Glory, & Praising (God).

Presidential Visits to San Francisco

Rutherford B. Hayes . . . . Sept. 9, 1880
Benjamin Harrison . . . . . April 25, 1891
William McKinley . . . . . . May 12, 1901
Theodore Roosevelt . . . . . May 14, 1903

William Howard Taft . . . Oct. 13, 1911
Woodrow Wilson . . . . Sept. 17, 1919
Warren Harding . . . . July 29, 1923*
Herbert Hoover . . . . Nov. 8, 1932

President Eisenhower visits in 1955.

Franklin D. Roosevelt...July 14, 1938; Sept. 24, 1942

Harry S. Truman......June 25, 1945; June 13, 1948; Oct. 16, 1950; Sept. 3, 1951; Oct. 3, 1952

Dwight D. Eisenhower..Oct. 8, 1952; June 1, 1955; August 21, 1956; Oct. 21, 1958; Oct. 20, 1960

John F. Kennedy .....March 23, 1962

Lyndon B. Johnson.....June 19, 1964; Oct. 11, 1964; June 25, 1965

Richard M. Nixon ......July 23, 1969; August 21, 1969; Sept. 4, 1972; Sept. 27, 1972

*Died in San Francisco at the Palace Hotel, August 2, 1923.

National Conventions Held in San Francisco

	Place	Date Opened
Democratic Convention	Civic Auditorium	June 28, 1920
Republican Convention	Cow Palace	August 20, 1956
Republican Convention	Cow Palace	June 19, 1964

San Francisco Ranchos

Rancho	Granted by	Granted to	Date
Camaritas 300 varas located at the Willows	Juan B. Alvarado	José de Jésus Noe	*Jan. 21, 1840*
Canada de Guadalupe Visitacion y Rodeo Viejo 2 square leagues	Juan B. Alvarado	Jacob P. Leese	*July 31, 1841*
Laguna de la Merced 1½ leagues	José Castro	José Antonio Galindo	*Sept. 27, 1835*
Ojo de Agua de Figueroa 100 varas Lyon & Vallejo Sts.	José Sanchez	Apolinario Miranda	*Nov. 16, 1833*
Paraje del Arroyo ½ league (Presidio)	Pio Pico	Henry D. Fitch	*July 24, 1846*

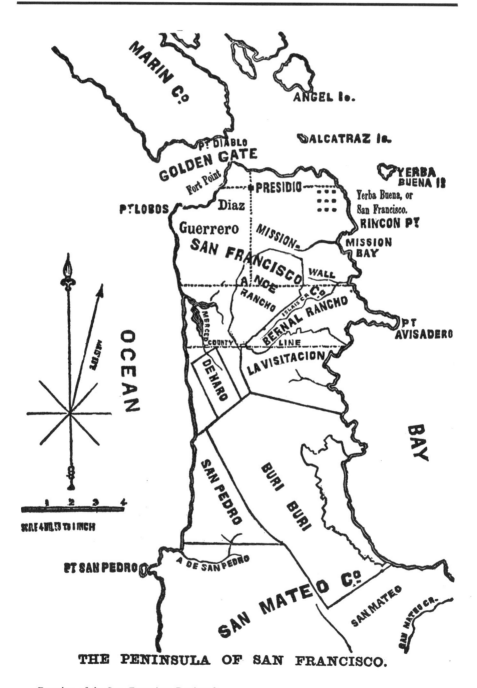

Ranchos of the San Francisco Peninsula

Rancho	Granted by	Granted to	Date
Potrero de San Francisco 2,288 varas	Manuel Micheltorena	Ramon & Francisco de Haro	*April 30, 1844*
Punta de la Loma Alta 200 by 100 varas Telegraph Hill	Gov. Alvarado	Leese & Salvador Vallejo	*1839*
Punta de Lobos 2 square leagues Point Lobos	Pio Pico	Benito Diaz	*June 25, 1846*
Rincon 800 varas	Manuel Micheltorena	Peter Sherreback	*1844*
Rincon de las Salinas y Potrero Nuevo 1 square league	Manuel Jimeno	José Cornelio de Bernal	*Oct. 10, 1839*
San Miguel 1 square league (includes Twin Peaks)	Pio Pico	José de Jésus Noe	*Dec. 23, 1845*
Willows 600 varas 18th & Mission	Pio Pico	José M. Andrade	*1846*

Patron Saint

The Patron Saint of Mission Dolores and the City and County of San Francisco is the best known and loved of the saints: Saint Francis.

He was born John Bernardone in 1182 at Assisi, Italy, the son of a wealthy merchant who early changed his son's name from John to Francisco.

In the fall of 1208 Francis of Assisi founded the order of Friars Minor. Francis died at the age of 45 on October 3, 1226 and was canonized two years later by Pope Gregory IX.

Beniamino Bufano's statue of St. Francis.

Seal of San Francisco

There have been two seals in the history of San Francisco. The first was the seal of the City of San Francisco. The second is the Seal of the City and County of San Francisco.

The Seal of the City of San Francisco was adopted on November 4, 1852 and was quite similar to the Seal of the State of California. It showed the Golden Gate and the hills on each side, and ships sailing around the harbor. At the bottom a Phoenix, the legendary Greek bird arising from burning fire. Around the margin of the seal were the words, "Seal of the City of San Francisco".

The Board of Supervisors on March 1, 1859, adopted a new seal for the City and County. In this the main figures, a miner and a sailor, stand on either side of a shield on which is depicted a steamer entering the Golden Gate. At the bottom is a scroll with the words, "Oro en Paz, en Guerro Fierro". At the top of the shield is the Phoenix. At the bottom also are the symbols of commerce, agriculture, and mining. Around the outside circle are the words "Seal of the City and County of San Francisco".

On March 26, 1900 the Board of Supervisors passed Ordinance #39 which states:

That a corporate seal of the City and County of San Francisco bearing upon its face: A shield supported by a miner on the left and a sailor on the right, with a device of a steamship passing the Golden Gate. At the foot of the supporters emblems of commerce, navigation and mining. Crest,

1st Seal of San Francisco, adopted in 1852.

Phoenix issuing from flames. Motto, "Oro en Paz, en Guerra Fierra (Gold in Peace, in War Iron)". Around the margin the words, "Seal of the City and County of San Francisco."

Sheriffs

The sheriff is the keeper of the county jail, transports prisoners to and from court, and delivers them to the state prison and other institutions. It is also his duty to carry out all lawful orders and serve all legal notices of the court.

John C. Hays 1850-1851
Thomas P. Johnson 1851-1852
William R. Gorham 1853-1854
David Scannell 1855-1856
Charles Doane 1857-1861
John S. Ellis 1862-1864
Henry L. Davis 1864-1867
P.J. White 1868-1871
James Adams 1872-1873
William McKibbin 1874-1875
Matthew Nunan 1876-1879
Thomas Desmond 1880-1881
John Sedgwick 1882

Patrick Connolly 1883-1884
Peter Hopkins 1885-1886
William McMann 1887-1888
Charles S. Laumeister 1889-1892
John J. McDade 1893-1894
Richard I. Whelan 1895-1898
Henry S. Martin 1899
John Lachmann 1900-1904
Peter J. Curtis 1904-1906
Thomas F. O'Neil 1906-1908
Lawrence J. Dolan 1908-1910
Thomas F. Finn 1910-1911
Fred S. Eggers 1912-1915
Thomas F. Finn 1916-1927
William J. Fitzgerald 1928-1935
Daniel C. Murphy 1936-1952
Dan Gallagher 1952-1956
Matthew C. Carberry 1956-1971
Richard D. Hongisto .... Dec. 31, 1971

Ships

U.S.S. San Francisco

The first *U.S.S. San Francisco* was a cruiser built at the Union Iron Works of San Francisco. The ship was commissioned in 1890 and later converted into a mine layer called the *Yosemite*.

The new heavy cruiser *U.S.S. San Francisco* was launched at Mare Island March 9, 1933. She was the first warship to be commissioned during the administration of President Franklin D. Roosevelt. Captain Royal E. Ingersoll was the first commanding officer.

On December 7, 1941, the *San Francisco* was alongside the dock at the Navy Yard, Pearl Harbor, when Japanese planes attacked. The ship was not directly attacked, but the dock was strafed.

Under command of Rear Admiral Daniel J. Callaghan, she was the flagship of his fleet of four other cruisers and eight destroyers. The vessel participated in an engagement off Guadalcanal in the Solomons against a Japanese fleet of two battleships, a cruiser and force of de-

The cruiser U.S.S. San Francisco, *launched in 1933.*

stroyers in an action that was fought at point blank range. The *San Francisco* in leading the attack received 45 hits and 25 fires were started aboard her. Her death toll included Admiral Callaghan; the commanding officer of his flagship, Captain Cassin Young; and 98 crew members.

The *San Francisco's* survivors, under command of Lt. Comdr. Herbert E. Schonland, saved their ship to fight again in the Aleutians, at Wake; in the Gilbert, Marshall, Caroline and Palau Islands; off New Guinea; and in the Marianas. Later she joined forces supporting the amphibious landings in the Philippine Islands, on Iwo Jima and Okinawa and in Korea and China. The *San Francisco* was deactivated at the Philadelphia Navy Yard, January 19, 1946.

The *U.S.S. San Francisco* won the Presidential Unit Citation, the Nation's highest tribute to a ship and all her company.

The Memorial to the *U.S.S. San Francisco* (actual bridge structure, riddled with shells together with the ship's mast upon which is mounted the ship's bell) is emplaced 200 feet above the shore line of the Pacific Ocean on the edge of a natural esplanade on Land's End.

U.S.S. Coral Sea

In a letter written to Mayor John F. Shelley, in July, 1967, Captain William Shawcross, of the *U.S.S. Coral Sea*, asked the City of San Francisco to "adopt" his ship, as his men had always considered San Francisco their home port. Shelley agreed to the adoption and presented the matter to the Board of Supervisors who formalized the agreement with Resolution No. 417-67.

On July 24, 1967 in ceremonies in the City Hall rotunda, Captain Shawcross accepted the 96-piece set of wardroom silverware, which had originally been presented to the old cruiser *San Francisco* in 1890, and then to the new cruiser *San Francisco* in 1934. The ship was also presented two 40 by 6 foot banners inscribed "SAN FRANCISCO'S OWN" to be flown port and starboard on the island of the ship as she enters and leaves port.

The Coral Sea *and* Midway *pass under the Bay Bridge.*

Sister Cities

Assisi, Italy

Assisi, Italy, is a quiet medieval town located on the southern slope of Monte Subosio. It was the place of birth of St. Francis of Assisi, patron saint of San Francisco.

The informal proposal for the establishment of the sister city affiliation was made by the Honorable Joseph L. Alioto and accepted by the Honorable Giorgio Costantino, Mayor of Assisi, who stated "the sister city affiliation will provide a living and actual proof of the love, harmony and brotherhood of the two municipalities, so far away from the other, but idealistically near and united in the name of Saint Francis."

Resolution No. 366-69 was adopted by the Board of Supervisors on May 19, 1969.

Osaka, Japan

Osaka, Japan, is the second largest city of Japan, with a population of more than three million. It is one of the principal international trading, banking and insurance centers of Japan and is known as the "Western Headquarters City" and "Western Capital" of the nation. Like San Francisco it is also noted for its fine hotels and restaurants.

It was the opinion of the Board of Supervisors that a sister city affiliation would be beneficial to the residents of both San Francisco and Osaka-Kobe, and would provide an excellent opportunity for the people of the cities involved to learn about the community life of each other through the exchange of cultural material and token gifts, including photographs, recordings, movies, books, local histories, etc.

Resolution No. 17773 was adopted by the Board of Supervisors on April 29, 1957.

Sydney, Australia

Sydney was the first British settlement in Australia. It was founded in 1788 by British officials in charge of a group of convicts. Today, the city of 2,712,610 persons is a center of industrial and commercial activities. It is endowed with an abundance of natural advantages, such as climate, topography, and has one of the world's finest harbors, capable of accommodating the largest vessels.

Since the citizens of Sydney and the citizens of San Francisco in many instances share a common heritage and in all instances share a common future based on the expansion of cultural and economic relations throughout the great Pacific Basin, the Board of Supervisors approved as official City policy the creation of a sister-city relationship between the cities of San Francisco and Syd- ney on May 16, 1968 (Resolution No. 367-68).

Taipei, Formosa

Taipei, Formosa, seat of government of the Nationalist Republic of China is the largest and most modern city in the country with a population of nearly 1,700,000. The city is located in a broad valley surrounded by high mountains where two rivers come together to form the Tamsui River.

The sister city affiliation between San Francisco and Taipei provides an impregnable tie of friendship, goodwill and commerce so necessary in today's family of nations, and especially important to our Chinese community, the largest outside of the Orient.

In 1969 Taipei's Mayor Henry Yu-Shu Kao, passed a resolution to become a sister city to San Francisco. Their action was approved by the Board of Supervisors in Resolution No. 865-69.

City Song
"I Left My Heart in San Francisco"

The loveliness of Paris
Seems some-how sadly gay.
The glory that was Rome
Is of another day.
I've been terribly alone
And forgotten in Manhattan.
I'm going home
To my city by the bay.

I left my heart in San Francisco
High on a hill, it calls to me.
To be where little cable cars
Climb half-way to the stars!
The morning fog may chill the air
I don't care!
My love waits there
In San Francisco,
Above the blue and windy sea.
When I come home to you, San Francisco,
Your golden sun will shine for me!

On October 6, 1969 Douglass Cross and George Cory were ushered to the Board of Supervisors rostrum to be introduced after their "I Left My Heart in San Francisco" was officially voted the City song.

Douglass Cross told the supervisors and the spectators, "this is a very proud moment for George Cory and me. If our song is a success, it is because it reflects in some small measure, perhaps, the history, the legend, the magic of this beautiful City, that has fascinated the imagination of the world. "I recall my favorite lines about San Francisco (not mine) by the distinguished San Francisco journalist, poet and novelist of the early 1900's—Ambrose Bierce:
'Careful now,
'We're dealing here with a myth.
'This city is a point upon a map of fog;
'Lemuria in a city unknown.
'Like us,
'It doesn't quite exist.' "

363d Infantry (San Francisco's Own)

The 363d Infantry was formed at Camp Lewis, Washington, on September 5, 1917, as a part of the 91st Division, one of the 16 "National Army" Divisions created by General Order No. 101, August 3, 1917. The original enlisted personnel of the Regiment was composed of men inducted into the service from Central and Northern California counties and a majority of these came from San Francisco, which caused the Regiment to be named: "San Francisco's Own."

The Regiment returned to San Francisco April 22, 1919 at which time Mayor James Rolph, Jr., said: "Some of those to whom we bade good-bye in 1917 from the steps of our City Hall lie today beneath the fields of France and Belgium and we will see them no more. Gold-star mothers and wives and sisters there are who will watch your triumphant home-coming with tear-dimmed eyes, weeping for their own boys whom you left sleeping 'over there.' To these we extend our boundless sympathy. To these we do honor, as do you, who know better than any others the noble manner in which the flower of our man-hood laid down their lives. Again boys of the 363d, boys of the Glorious West, we say to you: 'Welcome, a hundred times Welcome Home.' We love you. We admire you. You are our own."

The Regiment was later mustered out at a ceremony at the Palace of Fine Arts.

Geography

San Francisco Boundaries

1834 — Boundaries set down by M. G. Vallejo in 1834.

> "...commencing at the little cove at E. of the Fortaleza, following the line traced by you as far as the shore leaving to the north the Casamata and the Fortaleza; thence following the border of the said shore to the Point of Lobos on its southern side; thence following a straight line as far as the peak of the Devisadero, (Lookout,) continuing to the said line towards the E. as far as the Point of Rincon, embracing the Canutales and the Gentil. Said line shall terminate within the bay of the Mission Dolores, whose estuary shall serve for a natural boundary between the municipal jurisdiction of that Pueblo and the aforesaid Mission de Dolores."

1844 — Boundaries related to Henry L. Ford by Captain Hinckley, Alcalde of San Francisco.

> "...pueblo line commenced at a point of rocks on the coast, beyond the Presidio, and ran over in a direct line, crossing Mission Creek near its mouth, to a point of rocks or boulders, at a place known at that time, as the 'Potrero'."

1849 — Boundaries of San Francisco as related to Julius K. Rose, attorney, by Francisco Guerrero.

> "...the northern line of Buriburi, and the lines of Rancho de la Merced, Mr. Noe's rancho, which, I think, was called 'San Miguel'; Mr. Ridley's rancho, which I think, is called 'Visitacion,' and a rancho belonging to a Spanish woman, called I think, 'The Widow Bernal,' and the rancho known as 'The Potrero.' He described the boundaries as commencing just at the entrance of the bay at the Golden Gate, running from that point, to a hill about half a mile distant from that point; to the hill on which we stood, (Devisadero) and which is a very high, round hill, from that place to the southern extremity of Rincon Point, where it runs into Mission Bay, and from that point by the line of the bay to the Golden Gate, at the place of beginning."

(Documents, Depositions and Brief of Law Points Raised Thereon on Behalf of the United States, in Case Number 28.., Before the U.S. Board of Land Commissioners. San Francisco. 1854)

1850 — In the year 1850 the State Legislature defined the limits of San Francisco as follows:

> "The southern boundary shall be a line two miles distant in a southerly direction from the center of Portsmouth Square, and which line shall be a parallel to the street known as Clay Street.
> The western boundary shall be a line one and a half miles distant in a westerly direction from the center of Portsmouth Square, and which line shall be parallel to the street known as Kearny Street.
> The northern and eastern shall be the same as the County of San Francisco."

1851 — Boundaries of the City under act to reincorporate, passed April 18, 1851.

> "On the south by a line parallel with Clay Street, two and one-half miles distant, in a southerly direction from the centre of Portsmouth Square; on the west by a line parallel with Kearny Street, two miles distant, in a westerly direction from the centre of Portsmouth Square. Its northern and eastern boundaries shall be coincident with those of the county of San Francisco."

1856 — "The boundaries of the City and County of San Francisco shall be as follows: Beginning in the Pacific Ocean, three miles from the shore, and on the line (extended) of the United States Survey, separating townships two and three, south (Mount Diablo meridian) and thence running northerly and parallel with the shore so as to be three miles therefrom opposite Seal Rocks; thence in the same general direction to a point three miles from the shore, and on the northerly side of the entrance to the bay of San Francisco; thence to low-water mark on the northerly side of said entrance, at a point opposite Fort Point; thence following said low-water mark to a point due north-west of Golden Rock; thence due south-east to a point within three miles of the natural high water mark on the eastern shore of the bay of San Francisco; thence in a southerly direction to a point three miles from said eastern shore, and on the line first named (considered as extending across said bay); and thence along said first named line to the place of beginning. The islands in said bay, known as Alcatraces and Yerba Buena, and the island in said ocean, known as the Farallones, shall be attached to and form a part of said City and County." (Section 1 - Consolidation Act)

(Prior to the consolidation of the governments of the City and County of San Francisco, July 1, 1856, the present County of San Mateo, containing an area of 154,981 acres, formed the southerly portion of San Francisco. The County of San Mateo is bounded on the south by Santa Clara and Santa Cruz.)

1971 — "Beginning at the southwest corner, being the northwest corner of San Mateo, in the Pacific Ocean, on the extension of northern line of T. 3 S., of Mount Diablo base; thence northerly along the Pacific Coast, to its point of intersection with the westerly extension of the low-water line on the northern side of the entrance to San Francisco Bay, being the southwest corner of Marin and northwest corner of San Francisco; thence easterly, through Point Bonita and Point Cavallo, to the most southeastern point of Angel Island, all on the line of Marin; thence northerly, along the easterly line of Marin to the northwest point of Golden Rock (also known as Red Rock), being a common corner of Marin, Contra Costa, and San Francisco; thence due southeast four and one-half statute miles to a point established as the corner common to Contra Costa, Alameda, and San Francisco; thence southeasterly, on the western line of Alameda County to a point on the north line of T. 3S., R. 4W., M. D. B. & M.; thence westerly on the township lines and an extension thereof to the place of beginning. The islands known as the Farralones (Farallons) are a part of said city and county."

District & Place Names

Old & New

Anita Rock - Shows above water at low tides, and is situated 1-1/6 miles inside of Fort Point, and bears E. by N. from it.

Anza Vista District - Formerly occupied by Calvary and Laurel Hill cemeteries. 110 acres bounded by Geary St., St. Joseph's Ave., Turk St., and Masonic Ave. Work began on project in February, 1946.

Apparel City - Located in the Potrero District on 34 acres. Bounded by Oakdale Ave., Industrial and Loomis streets. Construction on project began in 1946.

Arch & Seal Rocks - Arch Rock blown up August 15, 1901. Cadwalader Ringgold in his 1852 charts of San Francisco Bay described them as, "two detached and conspicious rocks with bold approach, of some elevation, and sufficiently distinct. A small rock lies off N.W. end of Alcatraces isle, submerged at usual flow of tide."

Ashbury Heights - Ashbury Park Tract bounded on the west by Lincoln Way and Golden Gate Park, on the east by Ashbury St., on the south by Pemberton Place. Developed by the Simons-Fout Company in 1911.

Banana Belt - Area where the United Fruit Company unloaded its boats at Third & Channel.

Barbary Coast - Northerly part of the city comprising both sides of Broadway and Pacific streets, and the cross streets between them, from Stockton St. to the waterfront.

Battle Mountain - Dolores Heights

Bernal Heights - Bounded by Bayshore on the east; Mission St. on the west; Army St. on the north; Alemany Blvd. on the south.

Black Point - Fort Mason area, known first as Point Medanos, later as Point San Jose.

Blossom Rock - Blown up April 23, 1871. Cadwalader Ringgold in his 1852 charts of San Francisco Bay described it as, "a dangerous submerged rock, five feet water on its apex at low tide, lies in line between Alcatraces and Yerba Buena islands, rises up in conical form, with bold and deep water on every side."

Blue Mountain - Name given to Mt. Davidson by George Davidson in the 1850's.

Boca del Puerto de San Francisco - Spanish name for the Golden Gate.

Butchertown - Area purchased in March 1868 from California Legislature by three San Franciscans, "to carry on and maintain the business of slaughtering beef cattle, hogs, sheep and calves." Butchertown was bounded by First Ave., west by Kentucky St. and Railroad Ave., east by I St. and south by Bayshore.

Candlestick Cove - In the Hunter's Point area. Sometime prior to 1910 the shoreline in this area was quite irregular, with mud and shallow water adjacent to it. Before filling operations began to extend the shoreline outward there existed a land form in the shape of a candelabra. This form has now disappeared.

Carville - In the early 1900's a community of families lived in slightly remodeled street cars occuping the sand dunes near what is now 48th Ave. and Kirkham Street.

Castille de San Joaquin - Spanish fort built in 1776 where Fort Point now stands.

Cathedral Hill - 16 square block natural eminence bounded by Van Ness, Post, Eddy and Webster streets.

Centre's Bridge - A tenuous viaduct of the Mission Dolores Plank Road Company in the vicinity of Seventh, Mission and Folsom streets.

China Basin - Named for the "China Clippers" of the Pacific Mail Steamship Line, which frequently tied up in the area in the 1860's.

Chinatown - Bay Street south to California and from Sansome at the edge of downtown west to Van Ness (includes most of Russian and Nob Hill).

Chrysopylae - Name given the Golden Gate by John Frémont in 1848.

Civic Center - Built on basis of a 1911 plan in an area bounded by Market, Golden Gate Ave., Van Ness Ave., and Hayes Street.

Clarke's Point - Broadway and Battery.

Cook's Lake - Located in Golden Gate Park east of the Aviary and south of Main Drive. Once the site of a rock quarry.

Corona Heights - Craggy area above 16th Street and Roosevelt Way.

Cow Hollow - Fillmore to Lyon, Jackson to Greenwich.

Crocker Amazon Tract - Tract developed by the Crocker Realty Company at Geneva & Mission streets, on land formerly part of the Rancho Canada de Guadalupe de la Visitacion y Rodeo Viejo, a Spanish land grant.

The Dell - Located in the western end of Lone Mountain cemetary, an area sheltered by a girdle of sand-dunes.

Diamond Heights - 325 acres bounded by Portola Drive and Clipper Street on the north, O'Shaughnessy Blvd. on the west. Boundary lines generally follow Sussex, Diamond and Bemis streets on the south, and Beacon, Diamond and Douglass on the east.

Dogpatch - Area southeast of Potrero Hill and north of Bayview. Name originally given to area by a gang from Potrero Hill who noticed swarming dogs during a fight.

Ensenada de Los Llorenes (Cove of Weepers - Spanish name for Mission Bay.

Estero Angosto - Spanish name given Islais Creek by Jose de Canizares in 1775.

Eureka Valley - Area below the southern slope of Twin Peaks.

Excelsior - The area received its name from the Excelsior Homestead Association in 1869. The boundaries are Silver Street on the north, McLaren Park on the east, Geneva Ave. on the south, and Alemany Blvd. on the west.

Fern Hill - Early name for Nob Hill.

Fish Alley - Area where most of the fish processing is done. Located on the bayside two blocks off Jefferson east of Hyde Street.

Fisherman's Wharf - The westerly terminus of the Embarcadero, between Hyde Street Pier and Pier 45.

Forest Hills - Area promoted by Newell & Murdock in 1912. Forest Hill is bounded by Laguna Honda and Dewey Blvds.,

Hayes Valley in 1864.

rising to the west of Sutro Forest and Twin Peaks.

Francisco Heights - A tract of 22 acres developed by Coldwell, Cornwall & Banker in 1935. It is bounded by Parker Ave., Turk, Arguello, and Geary Blvd.

Gas House Cove - West side of Black Point (Fort Mason).

Gold Mountain - Name given California by early Cantonese Chinese.

Golden Gate Heights - 115 acres from Kirkham to Quintara streets and from 10th to 17th Aves.

Golden Gateway - A planned urban residential community developed by the Perini Land Development Company. The project is bounded by Battery, Broadway, the Embarcadero and Clay Street.

Great Highway - All that portion of land which lies south of a line drawn due, south through Seal Rock, and west of a line easterly not less than 200 feet from ordinary high-water mark.

Guadalupe Valley - South of Visitacion, lying between a ridge of unnamed hills and the San Bruno mountains.

Gulliver's Hill - Vicinity of Green &

Webster, named after diaryman Capt. Charles Gulliver.

Haight-Ashbury - 17th Street to Fulton and Golden Gate Park to Buena Vista Park & Baker Streets.

Happy Valley - First, Second, Market & Mission.

Harbor View - Name given to waterfront section which stretched from Fort Mason to Fort Point, now called the Marina.

Hayes Valley - 160-acre land grant northwest of Mission and west of Larkin Streets, named for and owned by Colonel Tom Hayes.

Holladay Heights - Between Clay, Washington, Gough and Octavia streets, now known as Lafayette Park.

Holly Park - The limits of Holly Park are the limits of the park itself. The park and the hill are enclosed by an oval street named Holly Park Circle.

Hunter's Point - Hunter's Point and its contiguous territory of Bay View were jointly known as Potrero Viejo in the early 1830's. It is an isolated district in the southeastern section of San Francisco, adjacent to the Hunter's Point Naval Shipyard. The area was possibly named after Robert and Philip Hunter, early developers of this section, but more likely called "Hunter's Point" by the many sportsmen who hunted there.

India Basin - Lies adjacent to Islais Creek on the south extending to Hunter's Point. Received its name from the many ships from India which used to tie up there in the 1870's.

Ingleside Heights - 122 acres between Garfield and Randolph streets and Junipero Serra Blvd. and Faxon Ave.

Islais Creek - An Indian word "islay" meaning wild cherry suggests origin of name. Once part of the Bernal Grant it was known as Du Vrees Creek, later as Islais Channel and Islais Creek. Creek was fed by many sources as it descended from the southern slope of Twin Peaks and emptied into Islais Creek estuary. The 1868 Legislature viewed Islais Creek as a navigable stream from "Franconia Landing, on or near Bay View Turnpike to its outlet into San Francisco Bay, and thence easterly along the southerly line of Tulare Street to the city water front on Massachusetts Street".

Jackson Square - Bounded on the east by Sansome Street; on the south by Washington Street; on the west by Columbus Ave. from Washington to Kearny; and on the north by an irregular line approximately midway between Pacific Ave. and Broadway.

Japantown - Boundaries are Geary on the south; Fillmore on the west; Pine on the north; Octavia on the east.

Kite Hill - Bare area atop hill bounded by Shields, Sargent and Ramsell streets.

Laguna de Nuestra Senora de Los Dolores (Lake Dolores) - 18th & Dolores Streets.

Laguna Dulce - Fresh water pond at Sacramento and Montgomery Streets.

Laguna Pequena (Washerwoman's Lagoon) - Fresh water lake bounded by Franklin, Octavia, Filbert & Lombard streets.

Laguna Salina - Pear-shaped body of salt water at Jackson and Montgomery streets.

Lake Geneva - Lake formed by the widening of Isalis Creek between Niagara & Geneva Avenues.

Larsen's Peak - Area now known as Golden Gate Heights, called by many Larsen's Peak after Carl G. Larsen, who owned the Tivoli Café.

Las Lomitas (The Little Hills) - Name given to the pueblo Yerba Buena by the early Spanish.

Latin Quarter - Extends from the vicinity of Broadway, Columbus Ave., and Kearny St. up the precipitous slopes of Telegraph Hill.

Laurel Hill - 54 acres bounded by California on the north; Geary on the south; Parker on the west; and the east by Presidio Ave.

Little China - (1850's) Upper part of Sacramento Street, the whole length of Dupont Street, and portions of various other streets adjoining these named.

Loma Alta - Name given Telegraph Hill by the early Spaniards.

Ma Dulce (Sweet plant) - Name given by early Spaniards to Strawberry Hill in Golden Gate Park.

Marina - Bounded on the north by Marina Blvd., west by Lyon Street, east by Laguna, south by Lombard. First named the Marina-Vanderbilt Tract after its former primary owner, Mrs. Virginia Vanderbilt.

Merced Heights - Located east to west at Summit and Thrift Streets; Shields Street and Orizaba Ave., and Ramsell Street near Shields.

Mission Creek - From Harrison and 19th Streets southeast to the Bay.

Mission District - The district lying at the eastern base of Twin Peaks and adjacent to Old Mission Dolores.

Mission Valley - An opening into the bay between Rincon Point and Potrero Point and extending back westward and then southward, with a minor fork to the northwest.

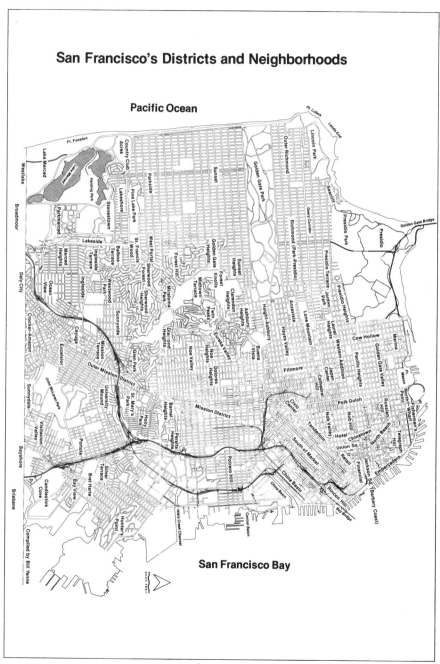

San Francisco's Districts and Neighborhoods

Districts of San Francisco today

Mooneysville - A settlement established by Con Mooney and Denis Kearney on the Ocean Beach below the Cliff House in 1883.

Nanny Goat Hill - 18th to 19th Streets, between Church and Noe Streets. So named by George M. Jaeger who lived in this area with his family and a number of goats.

Nob Hill - Beginning at the northwest corner of Sutter and Kearny Streets, north on Kearny Street to Pacific Ave., west on Pacific Ave. to Larkin Street, south on Larkin Street to Sutter Street, east on Sutter Street to point of beginning.

Noe Valley - Clipper & Douglas to Dolores and over Dolores to 25th Street. Down to Mission, out Mission to San Jose, south on San Jose to Miguel, west on Miguel to Laidley Street, over Laidley to 30th Street to Castro, over Castro to Valley, Valley to Diamond and back to Clipper Street.

North Beach - So named because it follows the northern shore of San Francisco Bay. The district covers approximately 300 blocks extending from the Embarcadero to Octavia Street, and from Broadway to Fisherman's Wharf.

Ojo de Figueroa - A prominent water well located at Lyon Street, midway between Vallejo and Green Streets.

Old Town - An eight block area south of Market Street, with the intersection at Kansas and Division Streets as the focal point.

Pacific Heights - California to Broadway, Fillmore to Arguello.

Parkmerced - 200 acres of apartments developed by Metropolitan Life Insurance Company in 1948. Located east of Lake Merced.

Park Presidio - Golden Gate Park on the south to the Presidio and Golden Gate on the north, and from Arguello Blvd. to Ocean Beach.

Parkside - Noriega on the north, 14th Ave on the east, Great Highway on the west, Sloat Blvd on the south.

Pine Lake Park - Area bounded by Sloat Blvd. from 24th Ave. to 37th Ave. and Vicente on the north, developed by Parkside Realty Company in 1927.

Pleasant Valley - Area east of Happy Valley, First to Third, Folsom to Brannan.

Point Alvisadera - Name given to Hunter's Point by Capt. Beechey in 1833. Name changed to Point Avisadero in 1884.

Point Lobos - Westernmost point of San Francisco. Spanish word for wolf, meaning seal or sea lion.

Point Medanos - Fort Mason area, later called **Point San Jose**.

Polk Gulch - Name given to Polk Street business area, Geary to Broadway, during celebration of Bridge and Fair opening in the 1930's.

The Potreros - Spanish word for "pasture." Under the pueblo system a potrero was classed as land for the common use of the inhabitants of the pueblo. San Francisco had two potreros, one known as *viejo* (old), the other *nuevo* (new).

Precita Valley - Originally a swamp flooded by Islais Creek. The Mexicans built a dam and from this dam the name "Precita" (a little dam).

Presidio - Spanish word meaning garrison or fortified barracks. San Francisco's Presidio was founded in 1776. It fronts the Golden Gate with an area of 1,590 acres.

Presidio Heights - Portion of Pacific Heights which overlooks the Presidio.

Presidio Terrace - Adjacent to Presidio on the north and west, Arguello on the east, Lake on the south. Access to from Arguello at Washington Street. Developed by A.S. Baldwin, president of Baldwin & Howell in 1905.

Produce District (old) - Washington Street, between Front, Drumm & Davis, until relocated at Islais Creek in 1963.

Punta de Concha - Spanish name given to Hunter's Point.

Punta San Quentin - Easterly corner of Mission Bay.

Richmond District (Park Presidio) - District lies just south of the Presidio and north of the Park, extending from Arguello on the east to the ocean on the west. Early maps designated the area as the "Great Sand Waste".

Rincon Hill - The hill bounded by the Bay, Third, Folsom and Fremont Streets, comprised 14 blocks of land, with an area of 86 acres.

Russian Hill - Beginning at the northwest corner of Pacific Ave. and Grant Ave., north on Grant Ave. to Columbus Ave., northwest on Columbus Ave. to Bay Street, west on Bay Street to Van Ness Ave., south on Van Ness Ave. to Pacific Ave., east on Pacific Ave. to point of beginning.

St. Anne's Valley - Where the Emporium stands today was a rift in the sandhills which was called St. Anne's Valley.

St. Francis Wood - 175 acres bounded by Portola Drive, Monterey Blvd and Mount Davidson, purchased in May 1911 and developed by the Mason McDuffie Company.

Scotch Hill - Now called Potrero Hill. In the 1880's known as "Scotch Hill" due to the Scottish boat builders and iron workers who lived above the Union Iron Works.

Sea Cliff - Developed by the Allen Company with streets and terraces completed in April, 1924. Boundaries are those streets north of California from 28th Ave to Lincoln Park and those north of Camino Del Mar from 25th Ave.

Seashell Point - Hunter's Point now, but called Seashell Point by the Spanish explorers in 1775.

Shag Rock (Barrel rock) - Until blown up April 30, 1900, located about ⅜-mile from the mainland southeast of Hunter's Point.

Signal Hill - Name given to Telegraph Hill in the early 1850's after the erection of a semaphore to announce the arrival of ships.

Silver Hummock - Name given to what is now called Lone Mountain by Capt.

Beechey in 1827.

Skid Row - Area bounded approximately by Mission, Harrison, 9th, and the Embarcadero.

Snob Hill - Nob Hill

South Beach - Area southwest of Rincon Point, beach extended to Steamboat Point.

South of Market - Area south of Market from the Bay to the Mission, called earlier "South of the Slot."

South of the Slot - After the cable car tracks were installed on Market Street the district south of Market was called "South of the Slot."

South Park - Area bounded by Second, Third, Bryant and Brannan Streets.

Spring Valley - Small oasis at the foot of Nob Hill, a low place between Powell, Mason, Clay and Broadway.

Steamboat Point - Intersection of Third and Berry Streets.

Stonestown - 67 acre site off 19th Ave, between Eucalyptus Drive and State College. Ground broken Nov. 4, 1948.

Strawberry Island - Area in Harbor View when cut off from mainland by high tide formed an island. Strawberries grew plentifully there.

Sunset - Fron Stanyan on the east, Sloat Blvd on the south, Pacific Ocean on the west, and the Golden Gate Park on the north.

Sunshine Hill - Hill sloping to the north, along the east side of Potrero Ave from 18th to 21st Streets.

Sutro Heights - 21 acres located on the bluffs above the Cliff House, purchased in 1881 by Adolph Sutro.

Sydney Gulch - Around the base of Telegraph Hill to the north, from Filbert and Montgomery Streets to the Bay.

Tar Flat - Named from the tar that ran down Rincon Point from the old gas house, casting oil upon the bay waters. The boundaries were from 11th and Harrison over to Brannan Street and down to the waterfront.

Telegraph Hill - Beginning at the northwest corner of Broadway and Battery

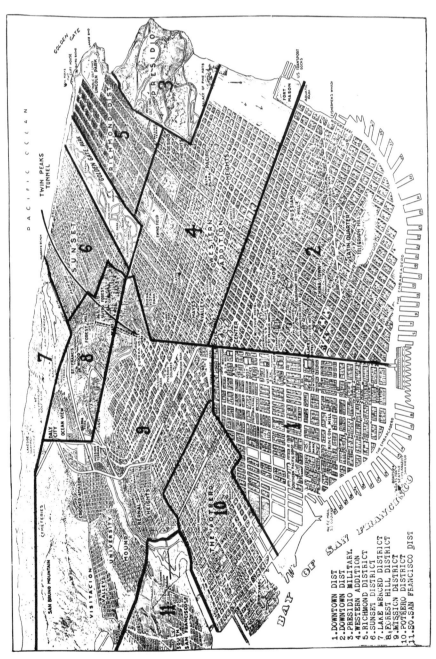

Districts of San Francisco in 1920

Street, north on Battery Street to Filbert Street, west on Filbert Street to Sansome Street, north on Sansome Street to Chestnut Street, west on Chestnut Street to Montgomery Street, north on Montgomery to Francisco Street, west on Francisco Street to Kearny Street, north on Kearny Street to Bay, west on Bay Street to Stockton Street, south on Stockton Street to Francisco Street, west on Francisco Street to Powell Street, south on Powell Street to Columbus Ave, southwest on Columbus Ave to Broadway, east on Broadway to point of beginning.

Tonquin Shoal - Cadwalader Ringgold in his 1852 charts of San Francisco Bay defines the shoal as being "extensive lying off North Bay it extends off and connects with Tonquin Point".

Transvestite Center - Area surrounding Mason & Turk Streets.

Tuckerville - From Buchanan Street to Webster and from Washington Street to Pacific. Area developed by J.W. Tucker, a jeweler.

University Mound - Area north of McLaren Park bounded by Burrows, Wayland, Cambridge and University.

Visitacion Valley - Visitacion Valley is roughly a V-shaped area, opening east-ward to San Francisco Bay. It is walled on both sides by hills lying between Mansell Street and the San Mateo County line.

Washerwoman's Lagoon - See Laguna Pequena.

Western Addition - The area which extends from Divisadero Street to the Ocean Beach. This section includes wholly or partially, several important districts, bearing individual names. Farthest west are Sutro Heights, Point Lobos and Sea Cliff Districts. Eastward sweeps the Richmond District to Arguello Blvd, where directly east and northeast it runs into the original Western Addition, and southeast into the Panhandle and Haight-Ashbury Districts, taking in Buena Vista Park.

Windmill Hill - Name given to Telegraph Hill in the 1840's after the construction of a coffee mill on it.

Yerba Buena Cove - A shallow extending in a crescent between Clark's Point on the north to the Rincon on the south.

Yerba Buena Redevelopment Project - A 25 acre site in the South of Market, between Third & Fourth streets, from Market to Folsom.

Yulupa - Indian word for Golden Gate or "Sunset Strait."

Hills

We frequently hear the term "San Francisco and Her Seven Hills," but the city by the Golden Gate is not really limited to that number. Her topography is such that as many as 43 hills of varying heights have been counted. But the "seven" doubtless suggested by the number of hills that form the city of Rome, has struck popular fancy and visitors to the city often make inquiries concerning them. The so-called seven hills are: **Telegraph Hill** (named for the signal station erected on its summit during the early days that informed the citizenry of the arrival of ships); **Nob Hill** (where the mining and railroad millionaires built their palatial mansions. The name is derived from "nabob", an Indian prince); **Rincon Hill** (close to the southern portion of the Embarcadero or water front, now cut down to act as anchorage for the Bay Bridge. Rincon is Spanish for "corner"); The **Twin Peaks** (forming the background at the western end of Market Street); **Russian Hill** (named in honor of the early Russian colony and burying ground on its slopes); **Lone Mountain** (around which the early cemeteries of San Francisco were laid out); and the highest hill, **Mt. Davidson** (where Easter morning services are held annually).

San Francisco's Forty-Three Hills

Alamo Heights	225 **feet**	Edgehill Heights	600 **feet**
Anza Hill	260	Excelsior Heights	315
Bernal Heights	325	Forest Hill	700
Buena Vista Heights	569	Gold Mine Hill	679
Candlestick Point	500	Holly Hill	274
Castro Hill	407	Hunters Point Ridge	275
Cathedral Hill	206	Irish Hill	250
City College Hill	350	Lafayette Heights	378
College Hill	200	Larsen Peak	725
Corona Heights	510	Laurel Hill	264
Dolores Heights	360	Lincoln Heights	380
		Lone Mountain	448
		McLaren Ridge	515
		Merced Heights	500
		Mt. Davidson	938
		Mt. Olympus	570
		Mt. St. Joseph	250
		Mt. Sutro	918
		Nob Hill	376
		Pacific Heights	370
		Parnassus Heights	400
		Potrero Hill	300
		Presidio Heights	370
		Red Rock Hill	689
		Rincon Hill	120
		Russian Hill	294
		Strawberry Hill	412
		Sutro Heights	200
		Telegraph Hill	284
		Twin Peaks (North)	903 ft. 8 in.
		(South)	910 ft. 5 in.
		University Mound	265
		Washington Heights	260 **feet**

Homes terrace the hills.

Islands

Alcatraz

The 22½ acre Isla de Alcatraces (Spanish word for pelican) was named in August, 1775, by Lt. Juan Manuel de Ayala, Spanish commander of the survey vessel *San Carlos*, the first ship to enter San Francisco Bay.

Alcatraz was granted by Governor Manuel Micheltorena in 1843 to José Yvés Limantour, and later claimed by Julian Workman and John Frémont.

The Alcatraz lighthouse, built in 1854, was the first on San Francisco Bay. The station switched to remote control on November 4, 1963.

In 1859 Fort Alcatraz was established and occupied by troops. The island was held by the Army until January 1, 1934 when it became a Federal penitentiary. The prison closed July 1, 1963 after housing such notorious criminals as Al Capone, Mickey Cohen, George "Machine Gun" Kelly, Joseph "Dutch" Critzer, and Robert Stroud, better known as the "Bird Man of Alcatraz."

On January 10, 1963 Representative John F. Shelley introduced the bill to establish a Federal Commission on the disposition of Alcatraz. However, Bay Area residents were far from unanimous on the question of Alcatraz. There was talk of making it a park, erecting a peace monument, opening a revolving restaurant, a hotel, etc.

In the 1870's troublesome Indians from the Arizona territory and some participants from the Modoc War were held as federal prisoners for disciplinary purposes. Almost 200 years later, on March 8, 1964, five Sioux Indians staked claim to the island. They acted on an 1868 treaty with the Sioux Nation that allowed Indians off the reservation to claim "unoccupied government land." On November 9, 1969 Indian leader

Aerial view of Alcatraz.

Richard Oakes and four others landed on the island but were talked off the next day by Thomas Hannon, regional director of the General Services Administration. However, on November 20, about 80 college-aged Indians again took possession of the island and held it until removed by U.S. marshals on June 11, 1971.

The island is approximately 1½ miles from the mainland and is entirely without resources within itself. The soil is scarcely perceptible, the island being rocky and precipitous on all sides. The purple growth visible at certain times of the year is mesembryanthemum, more popularly known as ice plant.

Alcatraz Island is now a part of the 24,000 acre, $119-million park plan called the Golden Gate National Recreation Area approved by President Nixon in 1972.

Aerial view of Angel Island

Angel Island

Largest island in the Bay, (640.2 acres in area) located seven miles northeast of San Francisco.

Visited and named Nuestra Señora de los Angeles by Lt. Juan Manuel de Ayala in 1775, the island later served early whalers as an anchorage for replenishing supplies of wood and water. In 1839 Governor Alvarado granted Antonio Osio the entire island to breed horses and mules, but the grant was later voided by the U.S. Supreme Court.

President Fillmore reserved the island for military purposes on November 6, 1850, and on September 12, 1863 Camp Reynolds was established. The name of the military reservation was changed to Fort McDowell by War Department Order, on April 4, 1900. The Army remained on the island until September 20, 1946 when the War Department officially declared the island and its installations "surplus." The remains of 131 soldiers and civilians buried on the island were removed to Golden Gate National Cemetery in 1947.

The U.S. Quarantine Station was established on 28.6 acres of land, December 22, 1888. It was followed in 1909 by the Immigrant Station, which later served as a temporary detention area for enemy aliens during World War I. The station closed in 1940.

Today Angel Island is a part of the

new Golden Gate National Park System providing hiking, fishing, and picnicking areas. Transportation to the island is provided from the following points: San Francisco (Fisherman's Wharf), Sausalito, Tiburon, and the Berkeley Yacht Harbor.

The Farallones

The Farallone Islands, 32 miles west of the Golden Gate, are a group of seven islands visible to San Franciscans on a clear day.

The islands were sighted by Cabrillo on November 16, 1542, followed by Sir Francis Drake in 1579. Drake was the first to land on the islands and named them "The Islands of St. James."

Sebastian Vizcaino in 1603 called the islands "Los Frailes" and Juan Francisco Bodega y Quadra in 1775 gave them the name "Los Farallones de los Frayles." (Los Farallones comes from the Spanish word meaning "cliff or small pointed island in the sea.")

The gathering of murre eggs for table consumption brought early Russian settlers to the islands during the years 1812-1841. Later the Americans, too, consumed large quantities of eggs taken from the islands until the government banned all egg gathering in 1897. The Farallones became a Federal Bird Reserve February 27, 1907 by Theodore Roosevelt's Executive Order No. 1043.

The U.S. Light Station established in 1855 is now automated and

The Farallones.

radio-controlled. The station is located atop Beacon Rock, 350 feet above mean sea level and the highest peak.

The island's only humans now are the biologists and volunteers of the Point Reyes Bird Observatory, who founded a Farallone field research station in an abandoned Coast Guard barracks in 1968.

Treasure Island

On February 11, 1936 construction of the 400 acre (5,520 feet long, 3,400 feet wide) Treasure Island was begun as the site of the 1939 Golden Gate International Exposition. The manmade island would lie on shoals adjacent to Yerba Buena's northern shore and the reclamation work would be under command of Lt. Col. Janus A. Dorst, Army Engineers Corps. Dredging was completed August 26, 1937. Later, in 1943, an additional 6.7 acres were added.

The secondary task was the creation of a rock seawall over three miles in length and 13 feet above mean low water level. This seawall contains 287,000 tons of quarried rock.

Funds for the seawall and fill were provided through a $3,043,000 Federal WPA grant. The roadways, causeway, trestles, landscaping, drainage of water systems were provided through an additional WPA grant of $1,306,000.

Water for the island is pumped to a 3-million gallon reservoir on Treasure Island through a 10 inch steel pipeline 10,000 feet in length, supported under the upper deck of the San Francisco, Oakland Bay Bridge.

On February 28, 1941, after the Golden Gate International Exposition, the island was leased from the City and County of San Francisco by the U.S. Government. The U.S. Navy moved in on July 1, 1941 and still maintains the island as headquarters of the Western Sea Frontier.

Yerba Buena

José de Canizares in 1776 gave Yerba Buena the name "Isla del Carmen." Later, Californians referred to it as Wood Island and Bird Island. Today the island is best known as the connecting link between the San Francisco and Oakland Bay Bridge.

The 198-acre island was granted by Juan B. Alvarado to José Castro in 1838 and in 1843 claimed by José Y. Limantour.

The first legislature on February 18, 1850 passed an act establishing the limits of San Francisco County and gave the island the name of Yerba Buena. This name was changed in 1895 by the U.S. Geographic Board to Goat Island. It remained Goat Island until June 3, 1931 when the name Yerba Buena was reinstated by the U.S. Geographic Board.

The military history of the island

begins with the Army, which established a post on December 19, 1866, consisting of one sergeant, 10 privates and a commissioned officer; the Coast Guard, responsible for the lighthouse; and the Navy, which opened a Naval Training Station on April 12, 1898.

The tunnel linking the bridges was built by the Clinton Construction Company of San Francisco with work commencing May 15, 1933.

A 900-foot-long causeway links Yerba Buena Island to Treasure Island.

Present Day Lakes

Golden Gate Park Lakes

North Lake, Middle Lake, South Lake, also known as the Chain of Lakes in the west end of the park, are the only lakes in the park not man made. The following lakes are man made.

Alvord Lake
Elk Glen Lake
Lloyd Lake
Mallard Lake

Metson Lake
Spreckles Lake
Stow Lake

Waterfowl abound at Stow Lake.

Lake Merced
(Sp., Laguna de Nuestra Senora de la Merced)

The Lake of Our Lady of Mercy is situated in the southwest corner of the City and County of San Francisco, crossing the boundary line into San Mateo County. The lakes have a water surface of 336 acres with a total lake shore of about 38,000 feet. They are 30 feet deep and fed by innumerable springs in the bottom and around the shores.

Mountain Lake
(Sp., La Laguna de Las Presidio de San Francisco)

It was here March 27, 1776 that Juan Bautista de Anza camped. In Spanish times it was known as Laguna de Loma Alta, (Lake of the High Hill) referring to the 400 foot elevation of the Presidio.

Pine Lake

Once called Laguna Puerca (Dirty Lake), it is bordered by Crestlake and Wawona Streets.

San Francisco Water

Hetch Hetchy

Hetch Hetchy takes its name from a small flat mountain valley north of Yosemite. The Central Miwok Indians referred to the area as "Hatchatchie", meaning plant or grass, bearing edible seeds, which grew in the valley.

The expense of building the Hetch Hetchy system was met entirely by the City of San Francisco, without State or Federal assistance. It was therefore built as economically as possible, at an approximate cost of $100-million from the initial drawing of the plans by City Engineer C. E. Grunsky and Marsden Manson, to the first flowing of water into the city in 1934.

San Francisco's water flows west by gravity from the Hetch Hetchy Project in Tuolumne County, 149 miles to the terminal reservoir, Crystal Springs. Construction of this water system followed passage of the Raker Act in 1913, granting necessary permission for use of a portion of Yosemite National Park. The Raker Act did not constitute a free gift as there were many conditions and requirements to be met before San Francisco could draw water from the Tuolumne River.

89 men lost their lives during the course of construction and 12 days before the completion of the project chief engineer Michael Maurice O'Shaughnessy died of a heart attack. The O'Shaughnessy Dam in Yosemite is named in his honor.

The mountain water supply system includes three impounding reservoirs: Hetch Hetchy on the Tuolumne River, Lloyd on the Cherry River, and Lake Eleanor on Eleanor Creek. Water stored in lakes Lloyd and Eleanor is utilized to generate power at Dion R. Holm Powerhouse and to meet the downstream irrigation priorities. Hetch Hetchy Reservoir is drawn upon mainly for San Francisco's domestic and suburban water supply, in the course of its journey generating electric power at Robert C. Kirkwood and Moccasin powerhouses. This source supplies over three-quarters of the total consumption in the City's water service area.

CITY RESERVOIRS

	Capacity in Millions of Gallons		Capacity in Millions of Gallons
Balboa	150.0	Potrero	1.0
College Hill	13.5	Stanford Heights	11.0
Francisco	2.5	Sunset	176.0
Lake Merced		Summit	14.3
(*emergency supply only*)	2,500.0	Sutro	31.4
Lombard	2.7	University Mound	140.9
Merced Manor	9.5	Wilde Avenue	0.5

San Francisco Water Chemical Analyses

Sierra-Calaveras Sample

	Parts per Million		Parts per Million
Total Solids	82.0	Carbonates (CO_3)	0.0
Calcium (Ca)	8.0	Bicarbonates (HCO_3)	18.0
Magnesium (Mg)	1.0	Alkalinity (Methyl Orange	
Sodium (Na)	3.0	as $CaCO_3$)	15.0
Iron (Fe)	0.2	Total hardness as $CaCO_3$	24.0
Silica (SiO_2)	0.6		
Sulfates (SO_4)	24.0	Coliform (most probable number)	
Chlorides (Cl)	21.3	per 100 milliters of	
Nitrates (NO_3)	less than 0.1	sample	less than 2.0

San Mateo County Watershed Sample

	Parts per Million		Parts per Million
Total Solids	78.0	Carbonates (CO_3)	less than 0.1
Calcium (Ca)	12.0	Bicarbonates (HCO_3)	37.0
Magnesium (Mg)	1.9	Alkalinity (Methyl Orange	
Sodium (Na)	4.0	as $CaCO_3$)	30.0
Iron (Fe)	less than 0.1	Total hardness as $CaCO_3$	38.0
Silica (SiO_2)	0.4	Coliform (most probable number)	
Sulfates (SO_4)	3.3	per 100 milliters of sample	2.0
Chlorides (Cl)	16.0	(Both samples were taken when ideal weather	
Nitrates (NO_3)	less than 0.1	conditions prevailed.)	

San Francisco's Land Surveys

May, 1835   William Antonio Richardson drew unofficial plan of the pueblo Yerba Buena for Mexican Governor Figueroa.

Oct., 1835   William Antonio Richardson drew first official plan of the pueblo Yerba Buena.

1839   Jean Jacques Vioget surveyed area bounded by Montgomery, Pacific, Sacramento and Dupont Streets.

1847   Jasper O'Farrell surveyed area included between Vallejo, Powell and Sutter Streets. Later surveyed the district bounded by Post, Leavenworth, and Francisco Streets and the waterfront.

1849   William Eddy began his survey with Front Street and extended westward to Larkin and 8th Streets.

1852   Clement Humphreys surveyed the northern portion of San Francisco County.

1868   George F. Allardt surveyed the Salt Marsh and Tide Lands by order of the Tide Lands Commissioners.

1868   James Stratton surveyed Tide and Pueblo Lands. Survey approved by the U.S. Surveyor General on August 13, 1868.

1883   Ferdinand Von Leicht resurveyed the Pueblo Lands, completed January 17, 1884. Brought the southern boundary of the Pueblo about 980 feet further north and excluded from the Pueblo boundaries a strip of land about 980 feet wide by two miles long, bounded by the Pacific Ocean on the West, the San Miguel Ranch on the east, the Patent Line on the north, and Stratton's Four League Line and the Merced Ranch on the south.

1905   Daniel H. Burnham surveyed and laid out a plan for the improvement and adornment of San Francisco.

Parks

Golden Gate Park

Golden Gate Park is San Francisco's largest park, comprising 1013 acres. It is a narrow parallelogram approximately 3 miles long by ½-mile wide, extending from its eastern boundary at Stanyan Street, between Fulton Street on the north and Lincoln Way on the south, to the Great Highway on the west.

The park was an outgrowth of the city's legal fight to establish its title to the four square leagues (17,000 acres) originally granted it under Mexican law, called the Outside Lands, and settled by squatters.

Shortly before 1866 a clamor for a large public park started and the city authorities directed their efforts to obtaining the land. A compromise settlement (Order #800) between the city and squatters and other so-called land owners was approved by

The Conservatory during the Park Centennial

the Mayor and the Board of Supervisors on January 14, 1868 and approved by the Legislature March 27, 1868.

The first Park Commissioners (S.F. Butterworth, D.W. Connely and Charles F. MacDermott) appointed William Hammond Hall to survey and make maps of the park area on August 8, 1870. He was later elected the first Superintendent of Golden Gate Park on August 14, 1871. He was succeeded by the following superintendents: William Bond Prichard (1876-1881). F. P. Hennessey (1881-1882), John J. McEwen (1882-1886), John McLaren (July 29, 1890 to his death January 12, 1943), Julius Girod (1943-1957), Bartle S. Rolph (1958-1964), Frank Foehr, (1964-1970), Emmett O'Donnell (1971-1974), Jack Spring (Nov. 1974-).

First meeting of commission: May 3, 1870

First money received by Commission from sale of bonds: August 1, 1870

First permanent employee: Patrick J. Owens, "Keeper of the Grounds," hired November 17, 1870.

First contract for work on Panhandle awarded to : B. Kenny on May 12, 1871.

First restaurant: "Casino", built in 1881 by Jake & Rheinhart Daemon.

First Park Lodge: A frame Victorian structure built in 1874. Second lodge built in 1895.

First Life Saving Station: established in Park in 1879. Station discontinued in 1950.

First transportation to Park: "Geary, Park, & Ocean Railroad" 1881 - (Steam Dummy)

First buffalo purchased: February 26, 1891.

First windmill built: "The Dutch Mill" built in 1902. It was designed by Alpheus Bull, and had a capacity to pump 30,000 gallons per hour.

Oldest building in Park: Conservatory. Erected 1879. Designated as California Historical Landmark #841 on November 19, 1970.

Oldest monument: Garfield, erected 1884.

Music Stands: First, built 1881; second, built 1886; third, built 1900, still in use.

Japanese Tea Garden: Built in 1894 by G. T. Marsh for the Midwinter Fair.

De Young Museum: established in 1895 from Midwinter Fair. New building opened Jan. 2, 1921.

Brundage Collection of Oriental Art, opened May 9, 1960.

California Academy of Sciences:

North American Hall, dedicated Sept. 22, 1916

Steinhart Aquarium, opened Sept. 29, 1923

Simson African Hall, dedicated Dec. 14, 1934

Morrison Planetarium, opened Nov. 6, 1952

Cowell Hall, opened May 16, 1969

Moon Bridge in the Japanese Tea Garden.

Other San Francisco Parks

Location   Location

Alamo Square . . . . Hayes & Steiner Sts.
Alta Plaza . . . . Scott & Washington Sts.
Aptos . . . . Aptos & Ocean Ave.
Argonne . 18th Ave. bet. Geary & Anza
Balboa . . . . Ocean & Circular Aves.
Bayview . . . . . . Third & Armstrong Sts.
Bernal Heights . . . . . Moultrie Street &
                               Jarboe Ave.
Cabrillo . . . . 38th Ave. near Cabrillo
Cayuga . . . . Cayuga & Naglee Ave.
Chalmers, Alice . Brunswick & Whittier
Chinese Playground . . . . . Sacramento &
                               Waverly Street
Cow Hollow . . . . Baker bet. Filbert
                               & Greenwich
Crocker-Amazon . . . . . . Geneva Ave. &
                               Moscow Street
Douglass . . . . . . 26th St. & Douglass St.
Duboce . . . . . . Duboce Ave. & Scott St.
DuPont Tennis Courts . . 30th Ave. bet.
                               Clement & California
Eureka Valley . . . . Collingwood St. near
                               18th Street
Excelsior . . . . Russia & Madrid Sts.
Folsom . . . . 21st St. & Folsom St.
Fulton . . . . . . 27th Ave. & Fulton Sts.
Funston . . . . Chestnut & Buchanan Sts.
Garfield . . . . 26th & Harrison Sts.
Gilman . . . . . Gilman Ave. & Griffith St.
Glen Park . . . . Chenery & Elk Sts.
Grattan . . . . Stanyan & Alma Sts.
Hamilton Center . Geary & Steiner Sts.
Hayes Valley . . Hayes & Buchanan Sts.
Herz, Francis J. . . . . Visitacion & Hahn
Hunters Point Milton Meyer
       . . . . 195 Kiska Road
Jackson . . . . 17th St. & Carolina St.
Junipero Serra . . . 300 Stonecrest Drive
Kahn, Julius . . . . Spruce at Pacific
Kimball, Raymond S. . . . . Geary &
                               Steiner Streets
Lafayette . . . Washington & Laguna Sts.

Larsen Park . . . 19th Ave. & Vicente St.
Laurel Hill . . . . . . Euclid & Collins Sts.
Lee, Joseph . . . . Oakdale Ave. &
                               Mendell St.
McCoppin . . . . 24th Ave. & Taraval St.
Merced Heights . Byxbee & Shields Sts.
Midtown Terrace . . . . Clarendon Dr. &
                               Olympia Way
Miraloma . . . . . . Omar & Sequoia Ways
Mission Dolores . 19th Street & Dolores
Mountain Lake . . 12th Ave. & Lake St.
Murphy, J. P. . . . . . . 1960 - 9th Avenue
Noe Valley Courts . . . . . . 24th Street &
                               Douglass Street
North Beach . . . Lombard & Mason Sts.
Ocean View . . . . Capitol Ave. &
                               Montana Street
Parkside Square . . . . 26th Ave. &
                               Vicente Street
Peixotto, Sidney . . . . 15th St. bet.
                               Beaver & Roosevelt Way
Portola . . . . Felton & Holyoke Sts.
Potrero Hill . . . 22nd St. & Arkansas St.
Presidio Heights . . . . . . Clay Street near
                               Walnut Street
Richmond . . . . 18th Ave. bet. Lake
                               & California
Rochambeau . . . . . . 24th Ave. bet Lake
                               & California
Rolph, James Jr. . . . . . . Potrero Ave. &
                               Army Street
Rossi, Angelo J. . . . . . Arguello Blvd. &
                               Edward Street
St. Mary's . . . . Murray St. & Justin Dr.
Silver Terrace . . . . Thornton Ave. &
                               Bayshore Blvd.
South Sunset . . . . 40th Ave. bet.
                               Wawona & Vicente
Stern Grove . . . 19th Ave. & Sloat Blvd.
Sunnyside . . . Forrester & Melrose Sts.
Sunset Recreation Center . 28th Ave. &
                               Lawton Street

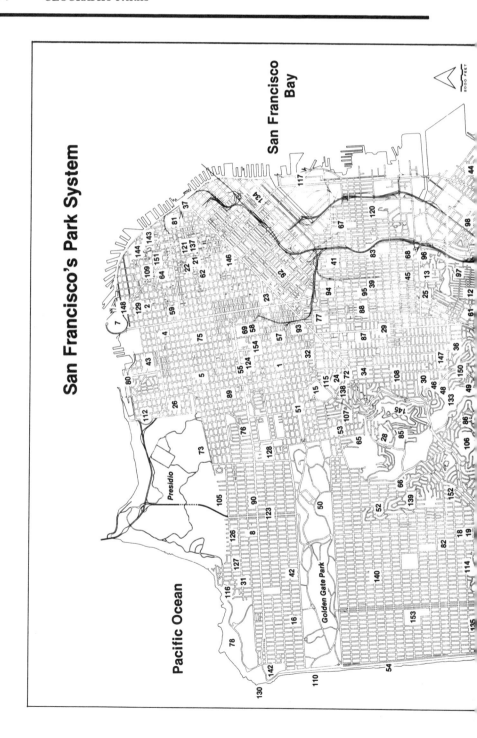

San Francisco's Park System

Pacific Ocean

San Francisco Bay

Presidio

Golden Gate Park

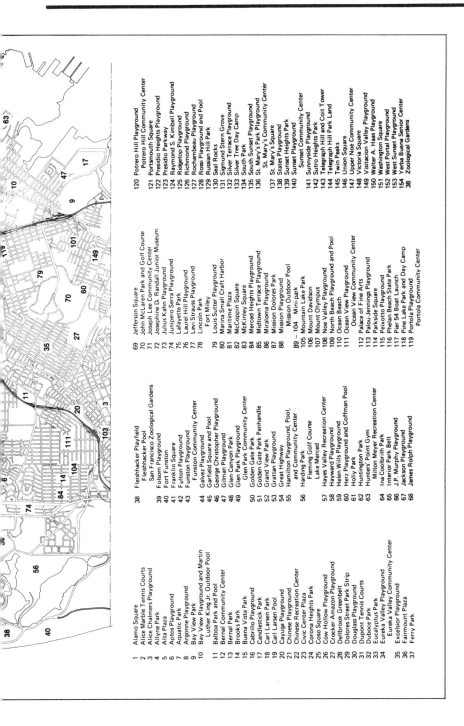

1 Alamo Square
2 Alice Marble Tennis Courts
3 Alice Chalmers Playground
4 Allyne Park
5 Alta Plaza
6 Aptos Playground
7 Aquatic Park
8 Argonne Playground
9 Bay View Park
10 Bay View Playground and Martin Luther King Jr. Outdoor Pool
11 Balboa Park and Pool
12 Bernal Community Center
13 Bernal Park
14 Brooks Park
15 Buena Vista Park
16 Cabrillo Playground
17 Candlestick Park
18 Carl Larsen Park
19 Carl Larsen Pool
20 Cayuga Playground
21 Chinese Playground
22 Chinese Recreation Center
23 Civic Center Plaza
24 Corona Heights Park
25 Coso Square
26 Cow Hollow Playground
27 Crocker Amazon Playground
28 Dellbrook Greenbelt
29 Dolores Street Park Strip
30 Douglass Playground
31 Dupont Tennis Courts
32 Duboce Park
33 Eucalyptus Park
34 Eureka Valley Playground
   Eureka Valley Community Center
35 Excelsior Playground
36 Fairmount Plaza
37 Ferry Park

38 Fleishhacker Playfield
   Fleishhacker Pool
   San Francisco Zoological Gardens
39 Folsom Playground
40 Fort Funston
41 Franklin Square
42 Fulton Playground
43 Funston Playground
   Funston Community Center
44 Galvez Playground
45 Garfield Square and Pool
46 George Christopher Playground
47 Gilman Playground
48 Glen Canyon Park
49 Glen Park Playground
   Glen Park Community Center
50 Golden Gate Park
51 Golden Gate Park Panhandle
52 Grand View Park
53 Grattan Playground
54 Great Highway
55 Hamilton Playground, Pool, and Community Center
56 Harding Park
   Fleming Golf Course
   Lake Merced
57 Hayes Valley Recreation Center
58 Hayward Playground
59 Helen Wills Playground
60 Herz Playground and Coffman Pool
61 Holly Park
62 Hunters' Point Gym
63 Hunters' Point Park
   Milton Meyer Recreation Center
64 Ina Coolbrith Park
65 Interior Park Belt
66 J.P. Murphy Playground
67 Jackson Playground
68 James Rolph Playground

69 Jefferson Square
70 John McLaren Park and Golf Course
71 Joseph Lee Community Center
72 Josephine D. Randall Junior Museum
73 Julius Kahn Playground
74 Junipero Serra Playground
75 Lafayette Park
76 Laurel Hill Playground
77 Levi Strauss Playground
78 Lincoln Park
   Fort Miley
79 Louis Sutter Playground
80 Marina Small Craft Harbor
81 Maritime Plaza
82 McCoppin Square
83 McKinley Square
84 Merced Heights Playground
85 Midtown Terrace Playground
86 Miraloma Playground
87 Mission Dolores Park
88 Mission Playground
   Mission Outdoor Pool
89 – 104 Mini-park
105 Mountain Lake Park
106 Mount Davidson
107 Mount Olympus
108 Noe Valley Playground
109 North Beach Playground and Pool
110 Ocean Beach
111 Ocean View Playground
   Ocean View Community Center
112 Palace of Fine Arts
113 Palou-Jennings Playground
114 Parkside Square
115 Peixotto Playground
116 Phelan Beach State Park
117 Pier 54 Boat Launch
118 Pine Lake Park and Day Camp
119 Portola Playground
   Portola Community Center

120 Potrero Hill Playground
   Potrero Hill Community Center
121 Portsmouth Square
122 Presidio Heights Playground
123 Presidio Parkway
124 Raymond S. Kimbell Playground
125 Ridgetop Playground
126 Richmond Playground
127 Rochambeau Playground
128 Rossi Playground and Pool
129 Russian Hill Park
130 Seal Rocks
131 Sigmund Stern Grove
132 Silver Terrace Playground
133 Silver Tree Day Camp
134 South Park
135 South Sunset Playground
136 St. Mary's Park Playground
   St. Mary's Community Center
137 St. Mary's Square
138 States Playground
139 Sunset Heights Park
140 Sunset Playground
   Sunset Community Center
141 Sunnyside Playground
142 Sutro Heights Park
143 Telegraph Hill and Coit Tower
144 Telegraph Hill Park Land
145 Twin Peaks
146 Union Square
147 Upper Noe Community Center
148 Victoria Square
149 Visitacion Valley Playground
150 Walter A. Haas Playground
151 Washington Square
152 West Portal Playground
153 West Sunset Playground
154 Yerba Buena Senior Center
38 Zoological Gardens

Sunset Heights . . . . .12th Ave. &
                          Pacheco Street
Sutter, Louis . . .University & Wayland
Upper Noe . . . . . . .Day & Sanchez Sts.
Visitacion Valley . . . . .Cora St. &
                          Leland Avenue
Wawona Bowling Greens . .19th Ave. &
                          Wawona Street
West Portal. . . .Ulloa St. & Lenox Way

West Sunset . . . . . .39th Ave. & Ortega
Wills, Helen . .Broadway & Larkin Sts.
Yerba Buena Center
         . . . . .1111 Buchanan Street
Silver Tree Day Camp
         . . . . .Glen Canyon
Pine Lake Day Camp
         . . .West end of Sigmund Stern Grove

City Planning

Early city planning was rudimentary, stemming from the rectilinear block plan laid out by the early surveyors.

Capt. Jean Jacques Vioget, a Swiss sailor and surveyor, made the first survey and plan of Yerba Buena in 1839. His survey was bounded by Pacific, Montgomery, Sacramento and Dupont Streets.

Later surveys, each more extended than its predecessor, were made officially by Jasper O'Farrell in 1847 and William Eddy in 1849.

In 1904 Chicago architect Daniel Burnham, working with the Association for the Improvement and Adornment of San Francisco, laid out a plan for the city's improvement and beautification. This plan was completed and published just before the earthquake and fire of 1906, but San Franciscans in their haste to rebuild ignored the plan. Later some of the Burnham proposals were initiated, specifically the Great Highway development, the Yacht Harbor, Aquatic Park, the Civic Center location, John McLaren Park and the Telegraph Hill Park.

After the 1906 catastrophe San Francisco began developing new areas further to the west. Mayor Edward R. Taylor was fearful that the city might be broken up into boroughs and said "I don't believe San Francisco will ever consent to have her body carved up into boroughs. I don't believe that San Francisco or San Franciscans will ever consent to put aside all of her great traditions, all of her great glories, all of her great deeds, all of her sorrows, all of her triumphs, and be known no more—as she would be known no more. Would San Francisco be San Francisco if you have a Western Addition Borough, if you have a Mission Borough, if you have a Telegraph Hill Borough? San Francisco would not be San Francisco anymore. Of course it would not be. You would have greater San Francisco, but that greater San Francisco would be made up of innumerable boroughs, and not one of those boroughs would be San Francisco. I for one should never consent to any such project."

On December 28, 1917 Mayor James Rolph appointed the members of the first City Planning Commission. However, it wasn't until 1929 that the City Planning Commission became a separate agency of local government, charged with the responsibility under the Charter to make, adopt, and maintain a Master Plan for the physical development of the city.

The 1948 Progress Report issued by the City Planning Commission stated: "San Franciscans, in the process of developing a Master Plan, have been comparing the city that exists with the city that could be—a city with a smooth-functioning circulation system, healthful housing, neighborhoods with adequate parks, playgrounds, schools, social halls, branch libraries, and public health offices, efficiently organized business and industrial areas, and outstanding cultural and recreation facilities. They have discovered ex-cellent features of the city of today that can be integrated into the city of tomorrow. But they have learned that much must be replaced, and the task, viewed in its entirety, poses problems that might be discouraging to the fainthearted."

A matured metropolitan city like San Francisco that has used all the available land within its boundaries for housing, business, industry, parks and open areas, must develop planning areas for study purposes to determine its ultimate capacity for growth without losing the established and recognized characteristics.

Boundaries of these planning areas are definite and seldom change as depicted on the area map.

Streets

Oldest—Grant Avenue. Formerly Calle De La Fundacion and later DuPont Street. Known as DuPont Gai to the Chinese community.

Steepest—Filbert Street from Hyde to Leavenworth: 31½° grade. Parnassus Ave. to Arguello Blvd.: 31.½ ° grade.

Longest—Mission Street: 7.29 miles long.

Widest—Van Ness Ave.: 125 feet.

Crookedest—Lombard Street, 8 turns in one block from Hyde to Leavenworth. Vermont Street, full 5 turns and two half turns, from McKinley to 22nd Street.

First Numbered—No. 1 Montgomery was the first house number known to have been used in San Francisco, following Jasper O'Farrell's survey in 1845.

First Paved—Kearny between Clay and Washington was the first street paved in 1854.

First street signs—Ordinance No. 468 is-sued on Nov. 17, 1853 provided for the making and affixing of street signs at various intersections.

Names—Final approval of all names (except highways) comes from the Board of Supervisors. In practice, developers supply the names for the subdivisions with which they are concerned. When the city opens new streets, names are sup-plied by the Board of Public Works.

Widths - The streets of San Francisco are not of uniform width. Eldredge in his history, *The Beginnings of San Francisco*, states: "In the Vioget survey of 1839 the streets were, as has been stated, very narrow. Vioget ran no east line for Montgomery street and consequently that street, being completed later, was the widest in the village and was made sixty-two and a half feet wide. Kearny street was made forty-five feet, five inch-

"The crookedest street in the world."

es wide, and Dupont Street, forty-four feet, this irregularity being probably due to want of knowledge in regard to the lines and when buildings were erected the street lines were made, in a degree, to conform. Kearny street was afterwards widened to seventy-five feet between Market street and Broadway, and Du-Pont to seventy-four feet from Market street to Bush. Vioget laid out five streets running east and west, viz: Pacific, Jackson, Washington, Clay, and Sacramento. These streets were forty-

nine feet, one and a half inches wide. The Vioget survey was extended some time before the American occupation to include Stockton and Powell streets on the west, Broadway and Vallejo on the north, and California, Pine, and Bush on the south. Stockton and Powell were made sixty-six feet nine inches wide, Broadway, eighty-two and a half feet, California, eighty-five feet, and the others sixty-eight feet, nine inches, which became the regulation width for the Main streets of the Fifty vara and the Western addition surveys; the exceptions being, in addition to California street and Broadway, Van Ness avenue one hundred and twenty-five feet, and Divisadero street, eighty-two and a half feet wide. The five westerly streets of the Vioget survey extend with their narrow width to Larkin street, the limit of the Fifty vara survey, and from Larkin street they were widened to sixty-eight feet, nine inches, by taking from the lots on either side. Market street is one hundred and twenty feet wide, and the main streets of the Hundred vara survey are eighty-two and a half feet wide. In the Mission the main streets are eighty-two and a half feet, except Dolores, which is one hundred and twenty; Tenth, Eleventh, Twelfth, Thirteenth, and Sixteenth streets, which are eighty feet wide and the streets from Fourteenth to Twenty-sixth inclusive (excepting Sixteenth street) which are sixty-four feet wide."

Origin of Street Names

Street	Named for
Acevedo Avenue	Luis Joachin Alvarez de Acevedo
Alemany Boulevard	Archbishop Joseph S. Alemany
Alvarado	Juan B. Alvarado
Annie	Annie Russ
Anza	Capt. Juan Bautista Anza
Arballo Drive	Señora Feliciana Arballo
Arellano Ave.	Manuel Ramirez Arellano
Arguello	José Dario Arguello
Armstrong	Gen. Samuel Strong Armstrong
Arthur	Chester A. Arthur
Ashbury	Munroe Ashbury

Baker	Col. E. D. Baker	Clay	Henry Clay
Balboa	Vasco Nunez de Balboa	Clayton	Charles Clayton
Bancroft	George Bancroft	Cleary	Alfred J. Cleary
Barnard	Major J. C. Barnard	Clement	Roswell P. Clement (?)
Bartlett	Lt. Washington A. Bartlett	Cleveland	Charles T. Cleveland
Bartol	Abraham Bartol	Cole	R. Beverly Cole

Battery
Named for early city fortification, originally called Fort Montgomery.

Beale	Lt. Edward E. Beale, U.S.N.
Bernal	Juan Francisco Bernal
Berry	Richard W. Berry
Bluxome	Isaac Bluxome, Jr.
Brannan	Samuel Brannan
Brenham	Charles J. Brenham
Bret Harte	Bret Harte

Broadway
Named after a street in New York City

Broderick	David Colbert Broderick

Brotherhood Way
A highway jointly owned by the Roman Catholic Archbishop of San Francisco, Congregation Judea, The Seventh Church of Christ of San Francisco, the Richmond Masonic Temple and the Greek Orthodox Church.

Bryant	Edwin Bryant

Bucareli
Lt. Gen. Baylio Fray Don Antonio Maria Bucareli y Ursua

Buchanan	John C. Buchanan
Burke	General John Burke
Burnett	Peter H. Burnett
Bush	Dr. J. P. Bush
Cabrillo	Juan Rodriguez Cabrillo
California	State of California
Cambon	Fray Pedro Cambon
Cameron	Donaldina Cameron
Carroll	Charles Carroll
Cardenas	Señora Juana Cardenas
Castelo	Gertrudis Castelo
Castro	Joaquin Isidro de Castro
Chesley	George W. Chesley
Chumasero	Maria Angela Chumasero
Clark	William S. Clark

Coleman	William T. Coleman
Colton	C. O. Colton
Columbus	Christopher Columbus
Colusa	Indian tribe
Crespi	Fray Juan Crespi
Custer	Gen. George A. Custer
Davidson	Professor George Davidson
Davis	William Heath Davis
De Boom	Cornelius De Boom
De Haro	Francisco De Haro
Diaz	Fray Juan Diaz

Divisadero
Received its name on account of its position, the sumit of a high hill. The name comes from the Spanish verb *divisar*—to descry at a distance.

Dolores	Named for the Mission
Donahue	Peter Donahue
Donner	George & Jacob Donner
Dow	William H. Dow
Doyle Drive	Frank Pierce Doyle
Drumm	Lt. Richard C. Drumm
Duboce	Col. Victor D. Duboce

DuPont (now Grant Ave.)
Capt. Samuel F. DuPont

Earl	John O. Earl
Ecker	George O. Ecker
Eddy	William M. Eddy
Egbert	Col. Egbert
Ellis	Alfred J. Ellis

Embarcadero
Spanish name for place of embarkation

Essex	U.S. Warship *Essex*
Evans	Adm. Robley D. Evans
Fair	James G. Fair
Fairfax	Thomas Fairfax
Fallon	Thomas Fallon
Fanning	Charles Fanning

Federal
Probably named for the U.S. Bonded

Warehouse established in its vicinity.

Fell	William Fell
Fillmore	President M. Fillmore
Fitch	George K. Fitch
Fitzgerald	Edward Fitzgerald
Flood	James C. Flood
Folsom	Capt. Joseph L. Folsom
Font	Fray Pedro Font
Franklin	

May have been named for pioneer merchant Selim Franklin or Benjamin Franklin.

Frémont	Lt. Col. John C. Frémont
Freelon	Judge T. W. Freelon
Fuente	Pedro Perez de Fuente
Funston	Gen. Frederick Funston
Galindo	José Galindo
Galvez	José de Galvez
Garces	Fray Francisco Garces
Geary	John W. Geary
Gerke Alley	Henry Gerke
Gilbert	Lt. Edward Gilbert
Gilman	Daniel C. Gilman
Golden Gate Ave.	Golden Gate Park
Gonzalez	Joseph Manuel Gonzalez
Gordon	George C. Gordon
Gough	Charles H. Gough
Grant	Gen. U. S. Grant
Green	Talbot H. Green
Greenwich	

Named after a New York Street

Griffith	Millen Griffith
Grijalva	Sgt. Juan Pablo Grijalva
Guerrero	Francisco Guerrero
Haight	Henry Haight
Halleck	

Capt. Henry W. Halleck, U.S.A.

Hare	Elias C. Hare
Harlan	George C. Harlan
Harney	Charles L. Harney
Harrison	Edward H. Harrison
Hawes	Horace Hawes
Hayes	Col. Thomas Hayes
Hearst	Sen. George Hearst
Hermann	Sigismund Hermann
Heron	James Heron

Higuera	Ygnasio Anastasio Higuera
Hinckley	William Sturgis Hinckley
Holland	Nathaniel Holland
Hollister	Sgt. Stanley Hollister
Hotaling	Anson P. Hotaling
Howard	William Davis Howard
Hudson	Henry Hudson
Hunt	Henry Brown Hunt
Huntington	Collis P. Huntington
Hyde	George Hyde
Ingalls	Gen. Rufus Ingalls
Ingerson	Dr. H. H. Ingerson
Innes	George Innes
Irving	Washington Irving
Jackson	Andrew Jackson
Jennings	Thomas Jennings
Jerrold	Douglas W. Jerrold
Jessie	Jessie Russ
Jones	Dr. Elbert P. Jones
Josepha	Señora Petronila Josepha
Judah	Theodore D. Judah
Junipero Serra	Fray Junipero Serra
Kearny	Stephen Watts Kearny
Keith	William Keith
Key	Francis Scott Key
King	Thomas Starr King
Kirkham	Gen. Ralph W. Kirkham
Kirkwood	Samuel J. Kirkwood
Kramer Place	Jacob Kramer
Laguna	

Named for pond in area known as Washerwoman's Lagoon

Lane	Dr. L. C. Lane
Lapham	Roger Lapham
La Playa	Spanish word for beach
Larkin	Thomas O. Larkin
La Salle	

Robert Cavalier, Sieur de la Salle

Lawton	Gen. Henry W. Lawton
Leavenworth	

Thaddeus M. Leavenworth

Le Conte	Prof. Joseph Le Conte
Lee	Lt. Curtis Lee
Leese	Jacob Primer Leese
Leidesdorff	William A. Leidesdorff
Lick	James Lick

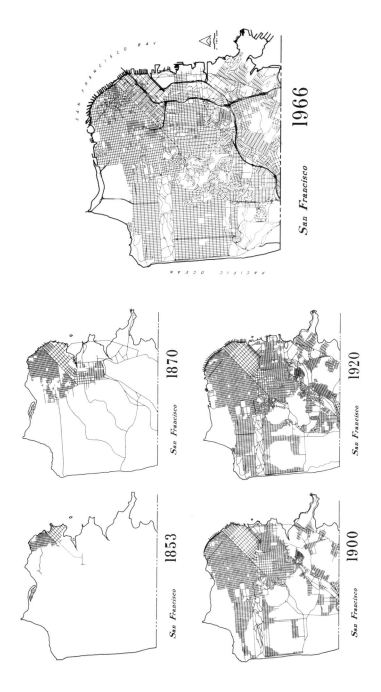

THE GROWTH OF SAN FRANCISCO
Showing streets along which property was developed

1966
San Francisco

1870
San Francisco

1920
San Francisco

1853
San Francisco

1900
San Francisco

Lincoln	Abraham Lincoln
Lombard	
	Named after a New York street
Lyon	Nathaniel Lyon
McAllister	Hall McAllister
Main	Charles Main
Market	
	Probably named after Market Street, Philadelphia
McKinnon	Father William McKinnon
McLaren	John McLaren
Mason	Col. Richard B. Mason
Meade	Gen. George C. Meade
Mendell	George H. Mendell
Mission	
	First st. from city to Mission Dolores
Montgomery	John B. Montgomery
Moraga	Lt. José Joaquin Moraga
Morris	George R. Morris
Moss	J. Mora Moss
Muir	John Muir
Natoma	
	Indian tribe inhabiting banks of Sacramento & Feather Rivers
Nelson	General William Nelson
Newcomb	Simon Newcomb
Newhall	Henry M. Newhall
Noe	José de Jésus Noe
Noriega	José de la Guerra y Noriega
Octavia	Octavia Gough
O'Farrell	Jasper O'Farrell
Opera Alley	Adjoins Opera House
Ora Way	Mrs. Elmer (Ora) Robinson
Ortega	José Francisco de Ortega
O'Shaughnessy	
	Michael M. O'Shaughnessy
Otis	James Otis
Pacheco	Juan Salvio Pacheco
Page	Robert C. Page
Palou	Fray Francisco Palou
Peralta	Gabriel Peralta
Perry	Dr. Alexander Perry
Peter Yorke Way	Father Peter Yorke
Phelan	James Phelan
Phelps	Timothy Phelps

Pico	Pio Pico
Pierce	President Franklin Pierce
Pine	Isaac B. Pine
Pinto	Pablo Pinto
Pioche	Francis Pioche
Polk	President James K. Polk
Portola	Gaspar de Portola
Post	Gabriel Post
Potrero	Spanish word for pastureland
Powell	Dr. William J. Powell
Quesada	Gonzalo Ximinez de Quesada
Quint	Leander Quint
Quintara	Spanish family
Ralston	William C. Ralston
Rausch	Joseph N. Rausch
Revere	Paul Revere
Richardson	William A. Richardson
Ringgold	Lt. Cadwalader Ringgold
Rivas	Señora Gertrudis Rivas
Rivera	
	Capt. Fernando Rivera y Moncada
Robinson	Elmer Robinson
Rossi	Angelo J. Rossi
Russ	Russ family
Sacramento	
	Named after the city of Sacramento
Sampson	Adm. William T. Sampson
Sanchez	José Antonio Sanchez
Sandoval	Christoval Sandoval
Santiago	Spanish battle cry
Sansome	
	Named after a Philadelphia street
Scott	Gen. Winfield Scott
Serrano	Doña Ana Regina Serrano
Shafter	Gen. William R. Shafter
Sharon	William Sharon
Shelley	John F. Shelley
Shrader	A. J. Shrader
Sloat	Commodore John D. Sloat
Spear	Nathan Spear
Stanford	Leland Stanford
Stanley	Lee Stanley
Stanyan	C. A. Stanyan
Steiner	L. Steiner
Steuart	William M. Steuart

Stevenson
    Col. Jonathan Drake Stevenson
Stockton
    Commodore Robert F. Stockton
Sutro Heights   Adolph Sutro
Sutter   John A. Sutter
Tapia   Felipe Santiago Tapia
Taraval
    Named for an Indian guide on the Anza expedition.
Taylor   President Zachary Taylor
Thomas   Gen. George H. Thomas
Tiffany   Robert J. Tiffany
Toland   Dr. H. H. Toland
Tovar   Don Pedro de Tovar
Townsend   Dr. John Townsend
Treat   George Treat
Turk   Frank Turk
Ulloa   Francisco de Ulloa
Underwood   Gen. Franklin Underwood
Upton   Mathew C. Upton
Valencia   José Manuel Valencia

Vallejo
    Gen. Mariano Guadalupe Vallejo
Van Dyke   Walter Van Dyke
Van Ness   James Van Ness
Varela   Casimiro Varela
Vicente   Spanish name
Vidal   Don Mariano Vidal
Wallace   William T. Wallace
Waller   R. H. Waller
Washington
    President George Washington
Wawona   Indian name
Webster   Daniel Webster
Welsh   Charles Welsh
Whipple
    Major Gen. Emile W. Whipple
Yorba   Antonio Yorba

Many streets are named for obvious reasons, such as presidents, trees, states, and counties, and certain locations (such as Bay, North Point).

Street Name Changes - Prior to 1909, San Francisco had three sets of numbered streets and two sets of streets designated by letters of the alphabet. Two sets of the numbered streets were called "avenues" and one had the suffix "south"; one set of lettered streets had the same treat-ment. To remedy this condition the mayor appointed a commission to recommend such changes as might be considered necessary. The Board of Supervisors in December, 1909, adopted Ordinances Nos. 988, 989, and 1029 which changed the names of the following streets:

A

A St. to Anza St.
A St. South to Alvord St.
Ada Alley to Amity Alley
Adele Alley to Ade Alley
Aileen Ave. to Aileen St.
Albert Alley to Alert Alley
Albion Ave. to Albion St.
Alder Alley to Ames St.
Aldine Street to Golden Gate Avenue
Alemany St. to Abbey St.
Allen St. (that portion thereof from Union St. to angle north of Union St.) to Eastman St.
Alma Ave. to Alma St.
Alta Alley to Acme Alley
Amazon St. to Amazon Ave.
Andover Ave. to Andover St.
Ankeny Pl. to Anson Pl.
Anna Ln. to Glasgow St.
Arlington Ave. to Ashton Ave.
Army St. North to Andrew St.
Ash Ave. to Ash St.
Ashbury St. (that portion thereof extending from junction of Clayton St. to Corbett Ave.) to Clayton St.
Austin Ave. to Austin St.

B

B St. to Balboa St.
B St. South to Boalt St.
Bacon Pl. to Quincy St.
Bagley Pl. to Savings Union Pl.
Baker Ave. to Barton St.
Barry St. to Campbell Ave.

Bartlett Alley to Beckett St.

Bay View Place to Black Place

Belcher Court to Boynton Court

Bellevue Ave. to Burnham St.

Belmont Ave. (that portion thereof extending from junction of Willard St. to Woodland Ave.) to Willard St.

Benton St. (from Octavia St. to Laguna St., between Francisco and Bay Sts.), to Bennett St.

Berkshire St. to Bosworth St.

Berry Pl. to Harlan Pl.

Beta St. to Rutland St.

Blanche Alley to Blanche St.

Bessie Ave. to Bessie St.

Birch Ave. to Birch St.

Bird Ave. to Bird St.

Bond Alley to Brant Alley

Bourbin Pl. to Bourbin St.

Bourbon St. to Bristol St.

Bowie Ave to Kissling St.

Brannan Pl. to Butte Pl.

Broadway St. to Broadway

Browns Alley to Breen Pl.

Bruce Pl. to Brush Pl.

Bryant Ct. (off Bryant St., between Sterling St. and Rincon Pl.), to Bradley Ct.

Bryant Terrace to Brice Terrace

Buena Vista St. to Bonview St.

Burnside St. to Bishop St.

Burnett Pl. to Treasury Pl.

Butler Ave. to Butler St.

Byington Ave. to Byington St.

C

C St. to Cabrillo St.

C St. South to Coleman St.

Caledonia Alley to Caledonia St.

California Ave. to Coleridge St.

California St. South to Cornwall St.

Cannon or Condon St. (between York St. and Holladay Ave.) to Hampshire St.

Caroline Pl. to Carmine Pl.

Carson Ave. to Carson St.

Cotta St. to Lamartine St.

Cedar St. to Ceylon St.

Cedar Ave. to Cedar St.

Central Ct. to Conway Ct.

Central Pl. to St. Anne St.

Charles Pl. to Charlestown Pl.

Church Alley to Cameron Alley

Church Ave. to Churchill St.

Church Ln. to Chula Ln.

Clara Ave. to Ord St.

Clara Ln. to Claude Ln.

Clarence Ct. to Canning Ct.

Clary St. to Clara St.

Clay Ave. to Collier St.

Cliff Ave. to Point Lobos Ave.

Clinton Ave. south of Glen Ave. to Chilton Ave.

Clinton Ave. between Surrey St. and Glen Ave. to Lippard Ave.

Clover Alley to Clover St.

College St. to Colby St.

Colton Ct. to Chase Ct.

Colton Pl. to Colusa Pl.

Concord Ave. to Concord St.

Corbet Pl. to Corbin Pl.

Cottage Pl. to Colin Pl.

Cumberland Pl. to Cunningham Pl.

Cypress Alley to Cypress St.

D

D St. South to Donahue St.

Dearborn Pl. to Dearborn St.

Delaware Ave. to Delano Ave.

De Long Ave. to Delmar St.

Devisadero St. to Divisadero St.

Diamond Alley to Dixie Alley

Division St. (that portion thereof from Florida St. to Eighteenth St.) to Treat Ave., its continuation.

Dore Alley to Doric Alley

E

E St. South to Earl St.

Eagle St. (that portion thereof extending from Douglass St. to point 206 feet westerly) to Nineteenth St.

Eagle St. (that portion thereof extending from easterly junction of Short and Eagle Sts. northeasterly) to Yukon St.

East St. North and East St. South to The Embarcadero

East Ave. to Highland Ave.

East Arbor St. to Orchard St.

East Lake Ave. to Winnipeg Ave.

East Park St. to Park St.

Eddy St. West to Edward St.

Edgar Pl. to Edgardo Pl.

Eleventh Ave. South to Kirkwood Ave.

Eighteenth Ave. South to Revere Ave.

Eighth Ave. South to Hudson Ave.

Eighteenth St. (that portion thereof extending from point east of Lower Terrace to Clayton St.), to Deming St.

Eighteenth St. (that portion thereof extending from point east of Stanyan St. to Stanyan St.), to Estee St.

Ellery St. to Rincon St.

Elliot Park to Endicott Park

Elliot Ln. to Elton Ln.

Elm Ave. to Elm St.

Elizabeth Pl. to Eliza Pl.

Esmond St. to Concord St.

Eugenie St. to Emerson St.

Eureka Alley to Drummond Alley

Ewing Pl. to Hemlock St.

F

F St. South to Fitch St.

Falcon Pl. to Fallon Pl.

Farren Ave. to Farren St.

Farrollones St. to Farallones St.

Fay St. to Sawyer St.

Fern Ave. to Fern St.

Fifth Ave. South to Evans Ave.

Fifteenth Ave. South to Oakdale Ave.

Filbert Pl. to Genoa Pl.

Fillmore Pl. to Calumet Pl.

First Ave. to Arguello Bl.

First Ave. South to Arthur Ave.

Fitch Alley to Fenton Alley

Flint Alley to Cowell Pl.

Florence Ave. to Florentine St.

Folsom Pl. to Richardson Pl.

Folsom Ave. to Rodgers St.

Forty-first Ave. South to Quebec Ave.

Forty-second Ave. South to Richter Ave.

Forty-third Ave. South to Sampson Ave.

Forty-fourth Ave. South to Tovar Ave.

Forty-fifth Ave. South to Ugarte Ave.

Forty-ninth Ave. to La Playa

Fourth Ave. South to Davidson Ave.

Fourteenth Ave. South to Newcomb Ave.

Fortieth Ave. South to Pulaski Ave.

Franconia Ave. to Franconia St.

Fremont Alley to Frisbie Alley

Fremont Court to Freeman Court

Front Ave. to Contra Costa Ave.

Fulton Ave. to Brompton Ave.

G

G St. South to Griffith St.

Garden Ave. to Garden St.

Garfield Ave. to Lucky St.

Gavin Pl. to Grover Pl.

Geneva St. to Lucerne St.

Germania Ave. to Germania St.

Glen Ave. (from Diamond and Chenery Sts. to Elk St.) to Chenery St.

Gold Alley to Golding Alley

Good Children St. to Child St.

Grand St. to Grace St.

Grant St. to Buell St.

Grant Pl. to Grote Pl.

Green Pl. to Windsor Pl.

Groveland Ave. to Groveland St.

H

H St. to Lincoln Way

H St. South to Hawes St.

Hamilton Ave. to Hamerton Ave.

Hamlin St. (from Mansell St. to Arieta Ave.) to Cambridge St.

Hanna St. to Hanover St.

Hardy St. to Harlow St.

Harkness Ave. to Harkness St.

Harrison Ave. to Hallam St.

Harry Pl. to Harris Pl.

Heath St. to Holladay Ave.

Hermann St. (that portion thereof extending from West Mission St. to Market St.) to McCoppin St.

Hickory Ave. to Hickory St.

Hodge Avenue (from Greenwich Street to Lombard Street., between Steiner and Pierce Sts.), to Holden St.

Hoff Ave. to Hoff St.

Hoffman St. to Homans St.

Holly Park Ave. to Holly Park Circle

Holly St. to Leese St.

Horace Alley to Horace St.

Howard Ct. to Holland Ct.

I

I St. to Irving St.

I St. South to Ingalls St.

India Ave. to Peru Ave.

Ivy Ave. to Ivy St.

J

J St. to Judah St.

J St. South to Jennings St.

Jackson Alley to James Alley

Jackson Ct. to Jason Ct.

Jefferson Ave. to Jarboe Ave.

Jones Alley to Jessop Pl.

K

K St. to Kirkham St.
K St. South to Keith St.

L

L St. to Lawton St.
L St. South to Lane St.
Lafayette Pl. to Varennes St.
Laura Pl. to Petrarch Pl.
Laurel Ave. to Larch St.
Laurel Pl. to Lansing St.
Laussat Ave. to Laussat St.
Lee St. to Hilton St.
Lewis Pl. to Cosmo Pl.
Lexington Ave. to Lexington St.
Lick Alley to Elim Alley
Lilac Alley to Lilac St.
Lily Ave. to Lily St.
Linadil Ave. to Niagara Ave.
Lincoln Ave. to Burnett Ave.
Lincoln Pl. to Hastings Pl.
Lincoln St. to Macondray St.
Linden Ave. to Linden St.
Locust Ave. to Redwood St.
Lombard Alley to Tuscany Alley
Lyon Terrace to Leona Terrace

M

M St. to Moraga St.
M St. South to Mendell St.
Madison Ave. to Merlin St.
Magnolia Ave. to Magnolia St.
Maple Ct. to Rosemont Pl.
Margaret Pl. to Margrave Pl.
Mariposa Terrace to Berwick Pl.
Market St. (that portion thereof extending from point 796 feet east of Thirty-ninth Ave., now forming a portion of Sloat Blvd.) to Sloat Blvd.
Marshall St. to Maynard St.
Mary Ln. to Mark Ln.
Medwey Alley to Severn St.
Merced Ave. (Hillcrest Tract) to San Mateo Ave.
Mersey Alley to Mersey St.
Michigan Pl. to Chatterton Pl.
Midway St. (South from Stillings Ave.) to Nordhoff St.
Miles Pl. to Miller Pl.
Milliken St. to San Bruno Ave.
Milton Ave. to Marston Ave.
Mint Ave. to Mint St.
Montgomery Ave. to Columbus Ave.
Montgomery Ct. to Verdi Pl.
Morris Ave. to Morris St.
Morse Pl. to Cyrus Pl.
Moss Alley to Mono St.
Moulton Ave. to Moulton St.
Moulton Pl. to Montague Pl.
Myrtle Ave. to Myrtle St.

N

N St. to Noriega St.
N St. South to Newhall St.
Nebraska Ave. to Nebraska St.
New Anthony St. to Anthony St.
Nevada Ave. to Nevada St.
New Grove Ave. to Newburg St.
Ninth Ave. South to Innes Ave.
Nineteenth Ave. South to Shafter Ave.
Nome Ave. to Danvers St.
Norma St. to Altamont St.
North Ave. to Bocana St.
Norton Pl. to Darrell Pl.

O

O St. to Ortega St.
Oak Grove Ave. to Oak Grove St.
Ocean Terrace to Sunset Terrace
Ohio Pl. to Osgood Pl.
Old Hickory St. to Ogden Ave.
Olive Ave. to Olive St.
Olive Ct. to Charlton Ct.
Orient Alley to Orient St.

P

P St. to Pacheco St.
P St. South to Phelps St.
Pacific Alley to Pelton Pl.
Palmer St. (that portion thereof between Harper and Randall Sts.) to Randall St.
Palmer St. (that portion thereof extending from Randall St. to Chenery St.) to Whitney St.
Park Ct. to Prior Ct.
Park Ln. North to Taber Pl.
Park Ln. South to Varney Pl.
Park Way to Payson St.
Parker Alley to Parkhurst Alley
Parkside Ave. to Parsons St.
Paul St. to Saul St.
Pearl Alley to Morgan Alley
Perry Ave. to Reynolds St.
Ploche Alley to Pagoda Place
Pixley Ave. to Pixley St.
Point Lobos Ave. to Geary St.
Poplar Alley to Poplar St.
Porter Ave. to Ellington Ave.
Powell Ave. to Powers Ave.

Powhattan St. to Powhattan Ave.

Presidio St. to Miley St.

Prospect Pl. to Joice St.

Q

Q St. to Quintara St.

Q St. South to Quint St.

Quince Alley to Quane St.

R

R St. to Rivera St.

R St. South to Rankin St.

Railway Ave. to Railway St.

Randall Pl. to Southard Pl.

Reed Pl. to Reno Pl.

Riley St. to Pleasant St.

Rincon Ct. to Elkhart St.

Rincon Pl. to Rincon St.

Rivoli Ave. to Rivoli St.

Rose Ave. to Rose St.

Rose Alley to Aldrich Alley

Rose Lyon Ave. to Primrose St.

Rutledge Ave. to Rutledge St.

S

S St. to Santiago St.

S St. South to Selby St.

Salina Pl. to Sabin Pl.

San Carlos Avenue (from Sycamore Avenue to Twenty-first Street) to San Carlos Street

San Carlos Ave. (Hillcrest Tract) to Santa Cruz Ave.

Scott Ave. to Scotia Ave.

Scott Pl. to Wayne Pl.

Second Avenue South to Burke St.

Serpentine Pl. (that portion thereof extending southwesterly from the easterly end of Lower Terrace to Saturn Street) to Lower Terrace

Serpentine Pl. (that portion thereof extending westerly from Saturn St. to Lower Terrace) to Saturn St.

Serpentine Rd. to Locksley Ave.

Seventh Ave. South to Galvez Ave.

Seventeenth Ave. South to Quesada Ave.

Seymour Ave. to Seymour St.

Sherman Ave. to Lawrence Ave.

Short St. (that portion thereof extending south from junction of Eagle and Short Sts. to Short Alley) to Yukon St.

Short Alley to Yukon St.

Silver Alley to Argent Alley

Silver St. to Stillman St.

Sixth Ave. South to Fairfax Ave.

Sixteenth St. (from point east of Juno St. to Ashbury St.) to Clifford St.

Sixteenth Ave. South to Palou Ave.

South Ave. to Murray St.

South St. to Daggett St.

South Broderick St. to Buena Vista Terrace

Spreckels Ave. to Staples Ave.

St. Charles Pl. to Nottingham Pl.

St. Mary's Pl. to St. Anne St.

Stable Alley to Sparrow St.

Stanton St. (that portion thereof extending west and northwest from Douglass St.) to Corwin St.

Stanley Ct. to Stetson Ct.

Stanley Pl. to Sterling St.

Stanyan Ave. to Kenyon Ave.

Stockton Pl. to Campton Pl.

Stout's Alley to Ross Alley

Surman St. to Severance St.

Sutter Pl. to Belknap Pl.

Sycamore Ave. to Sycamore St.

T

T St. to Taraval St.

T St. South to Toland St.

Tacoma Ave. to Tacoma St.

Taylor Terrace to Aladdin Terrace

Tehama Alley to Sloan Alley

Tehama Pl. to Tenny Pl.

Telegraph Pl. (that portion thereof from Greenwich St. to angle north of Greenwich St.) to Child St.

Tenth Ave. South to Jerrold Ave.

Third Ave. South to Custer Ave.

Thirteenth Ave. South to McKinnon Ave.

Thirtieth Ave. South to Fitzgerald Ave.

Thirty-first Ave. South to Gilman Ave.

Thirty-second Avenue South to Hollister Ave.

Thirty-third Ave. South to Ingerson Ave.

Thirty-fourth Avenue South to Jamestown Ave.

Thirty-fifth Ave. South to Key Ave.

Thirty-sixth Ave. South to Le Conte Ave.

Thirty-seventh Avenue South to Meade Ave.

Thirty-eighth Ave. South to Nelson Ave.

Thirty-ninth Ave. South to Olney Ave.

Thornton St. to Beverly St.

Tiffany Pl. to Everett Pl.

Tilden St. (from Castro St. to Fifteenth St.) to Beaver St.

Tilden Street (from Fifteenth St. to Park Hill Ave.) to Fifteenth St.

Treat Avenue (between Thirteenth Street and Fourteenth Street) to Trainor St.

Tremont Ave. to Downey St.

Trent Alley to Mersey St.

Tustin Ave. (that portion thereof from end of Congo St. to first angle north of Stillings Ave.) to Congo St.

Twelfth Ave. South to La Salle Ave.

Twentieth St. (from Burnett Avenue to point west of Stanyan St.) to Palo Alto Ave.

Twentieth Ave. South to Thomas Ave.

Twenty-first Ave. South to Underwood Ave.

Twenty-second Avenue South to Van Dyke Ave.

Twenty-third Ave. South to Wallace Ave.

Twenty-fourth Avenue South to Yosemite Ave.

Twenty-fifth Ave. South to Armstrong Ave.

Twenty-sixth Ave. South to Bancroft Ave.

Twenty-seventh Avenue South to Carroll Ave.

Twenty-eighth Avenue South to Donner Ave.

Twenty-ninth Ave. South to Egbert Ave.

U

U St. to Ulloa St.

U St. South to Upton St.

Unadilla Ave. to Niagara Ave.

Union Ave. to Tompkins Ave.

Union Pl. to Jasper Pl.

Union Square Avenue to Manila St.

Uranus St. to Lower Terrace

V

V St. to Vicente St.

Vallejo Alley to Tracy Pl.

Vernon Pl. to Warner Pl.

View Ave. to Grand View Ave.

View Road (from intersection of Grand View Ave. and Acme Street north to Stanton St.) to Blair St.

Vincent St. to Garibaldi St.

Virginia St. to Oklahoma St.

Virginia Ct. to Vinton Ct.

Virginia Pl. to Cordelia St.

Vulcan Ln. to Emery Ln.

W

W St. to Wawona St.

Wall Pl. to Coolidge Pl.

Walnut Ave. to Hemlock St.

Washington Avenue to Washburn St.

Washington Pl. to Wentworth St.

Webb St. to Spring St.

Webster Pl. to Bromley Pl.

West Ave. to Appleton Ave.

West Clay St. to Drake St.

West Diamond Street to Berkeley St.

West El Dorado St. to Barstow St.

West End Alley to Eastman St.

West Lake Ave. to Otsego Ave.

West Mission St. to Otis St.

West Park St. to Park St.

White Pl. to Victor St.

Wieland Ave. to Judson Ave.

Wilde Ave. to Wilde St.

Wildey Ave. to Wilmot St.

Willow Ave. to Willow St.

William St. to Shannon St.

Winfield Avenue to Winfield St.

Winslow St. to Franconia St.

Worden Ave. to Whipple Ave.

Woodwards Avenue to Woodwards St.

Wyoming Ave. to Winnipeg Ave.

X

X St. to Yorba St.

Y

Yerba Buena St. to Cushman St.

Z

Zoe Pl. to Zeno Pl.

Natural History

Flora & Fauna

The information contained herein on the flora and fauna of San Francisco was obtained from and compiled by the following staff members of the California Academy of Sciences; Dr. Robert T. Orr, Dr. Elizabeth McClintock, Dr. Laurence C. Binford, Mr. Thomas Davies and Mr. Kenneth Lucas.

The 49 square miles occupied by the City of San Francisco are almost completely urbanized and industrialized. The hills, sand dunes, and marshes once so conspicuous have all but disappeared and along with these features the native plants have also gone. Of the hills, Mt. Sutro and Mt. Davidson are covered now with a man-made forest and residences; only on Twin Peaks in a few places are still to be found remnants of natural areas with grassland and rocky outcroppings and some native plants. Almost nothing of the sand dunes remains except along the ocean as in the Fort Funston area and of the marshes probably nothing at all remains.

San Francisco even before its urbanization was a region with few trees. California buckeye (*Aesculus californica*) and California laurel (*Umbellularia californica*) here once in reduced numbers are long since gone. Only the California live oak (*Quercus agrifolia*), the arroyo and yellow willows (*Salix lasiolepis* and *Salix lasiandra*) and probably the California wax-myrtle (*Myrica californica*) can still be seen in a few places. The planted trees making up the man-made woodland of Mt. Sutro, Mt. Davidson, the Presidio and Golden Gate Park are mostly two conifers, Monterey pine (*Pinus radiata*), Monterey cypress (*Cupressus macrocarpa*) and the blue gum from Australia (*Eucalyptus globulus*). Introduced at the end of the last century these (particularly the blue gum) are becoming naturalized and dense enough to resemble a woodland.

As urbanization progressed and the native plants disappeared, another group of plants appeared on bits and pieces of disturbed and vacant ground. These spontaneously appearing plants are called weeds. These newcomers to our scene were brought by man either directly or indirectly. Some were brought intentionally, being either edible or ornamental, while others were carried unintentionally and serve no useful purpose to man—at times they may even become a nuisance.

Another group of plants which we often call ornamentals has appeared along with urbanization. These are always carried about intentionally and are always planted. They are made available by the nursery industry to gardeners, home owners and landscape architects. These are the plants seen most frequently in San Francisco, in gardens, along the streets and in the parks. Like weeds, they are mostly not native to San Francisco or even to California but have been brought here for their esthetic value from other parts of the world where climates are similar to ours. They beautify the city and make it an attractive, pleasant and enjoyable place to live.

The plants listed here belong to the first two categories, those native to San Francisco and the non-native naturalized weeds. No ornamentals are listed; however, a few of the weeds were once ornamentals which have "escaped" from cultivation and are now naturalized. A few localities are listed, such as Twin Peaks and the Presidio, where still may be seen some of the native plants which once covered the northern San Francisco Peninsula.

(Reference: *A Flora of San Francisco, California* by John Thomas Howell, Peter Raven and Peter Rubtzoff.)

Since this was published in 1958, certain areas which had been undisturbed are now urbanized and their plants have disappeared.

Elizabeth McClintock
California Academy of Sciences

SELECTED PLANTS OF SAN FRANCISCO

(N-natives; W-weeds)

Polypodiaceae. Fern Family

Athyrium filix-femina. Western Lady-Fern. (N) Wet or marshy areas in gullies and canyons. Lobos Creek, Lake Merced.

Pityrogramma triangularis. Goldback Fern. (N) Rocky and brushy slopes. Presidio, Lake Merced, Bayview Hills.

Polypodium californicum. California Polypody. (N) Rocky slopes of hills. Above Bakers Beach, Lands End, Lake Merced, Twin Peaks, Russian Hill.

Polypodium scouleri. Leather Fern. (N) Crevices and surfaces of exposed rocks. Twin Peaks, Bayview Park, McLaren Park.

Polystichum munitum. Western Sword Fern. (N) Widespread on brushy or rocky slopes and canyon bottoms. Point Lobos, Golden Gate Park, Lake Merced, Twin Peaks, Bayview Hills.

Pteridium aquilinum. Bracken Fern. (N) Widespread on dune hills, grassland and brushy slopes. Presidio, Golden Gate Park, Sunset Heights, Lake Merced, Bayview Hills.

Woodwardia fimbriata. Western Chain Fern. (N) In moist places. West end of Lake Merced.

Equisetaceae. Horsetail Family

Equisetum telmateia. Giant Horsetail. (N) On the edge of marshes and along streams and seepages on coastal bluffs and hills. Laguna Honda, Lake Merced, Bayview Hills.

Pinaceae. Pine Family

Pinus radiata. Monterey Pine. (W) Commonly cultivated in parks and gardens. Presidio, Golden Gate Park, Laguna Honda, McLaren Park.

Cupressaceae. Cypress Family

Cupressus macrocarpa. Monterey Cypress. (W) A commonly cultivated tree. Presidio, Golden Gate Park, Laguna Honda, Pine Lake, Lake Merced, Bayview Hills.

Typhaceae. Cat-Tail Family

Typha domingensis. Cat-tail (N) Wet and marshy places. Bayview Hills.

Typha latifolia. Soft-flag. (N) Ponds and marshes. Bayview Hills.

Gramineae. Grass Family

Agropyron repens. Quackgrass. (W) Often a weed in gardens. Sutro Heights, Golden Gate Park.

Agrostis semiverticillata. (W) Common in moist waste places. Fort Point, Golden Gate Park, Laguna Honda, Lake Merced, San Miguel Hills, McLaren Park.

Aira caryophyllea. Silvery Hair-grass. (W) Grassy or brushy slopes. Presidio, Point Lobos, Golden Gate Park, Lake Merced, Mt. Davidson, Twin Peaks, San Miguel Hills, McLaren Park, Bayview Hills.

Ammophila arenaria. Beachgrass. (W) Common on dunes along the coast. Presidio, Lake Merced.

Avena fatua. Wild Oat. (W) On grassy hillsides. Golden Gate Park, Lake Merced, Twin Peaks, Bayview Hills.

Briza maxima. Rattlesnake Grass. (W) In waste places. Golden Gate Park.

Briza minor. Little Quaking Grass. (W) On grassy slopes. Golden Gate Park. Lake Merced, Bayview Hills.

Bromus marginatus. (N) Shallow soil on sunny slopes. Presidio, Bernal Heights, Bayview Hills.

Bromus mollis. Soft Chess. (W) Abundant in grassland. Presidio, Lake Merced, Twin Peaks, Bayview Hills.

Cynodon dactylon. Bermuda Grass. (W) Common in waste places and about the margins of lawns and sidewalks. Seacliff district, Lake Merced, Golden Gate Park.

Dactylis glomerata. Orchard Grass. (W) Common in lawns. Presidio, Golden Gate Park, Lake Merced.

Danthonia californica. (N) Grassy or brushy hillsides. Presidio, San Miguel Hills, McLaren Park, north slope of Bayview Hills.

Elymus glaucus. Blue Wild-Rye. (N) In grassland and on brushy slopes. Presidio, Lands End, Golden Gate Park, Pine Lake, Lake Merced, Laguna Honda, Mt. Davidson, San Miguel Hills, McLaren Park.

Festuca dertonensis. (W) Grassy and brushy slopes. Presidio, Golden Gate Park, Twin Peaks, San Miguel Hills, Bayview Hills.

Festuca megalura. (N) On grassy slopes, flats, and dunes. Near Bakers Beach, Presidio, Golden Gate Park, Lake Merced, Twin Peaks, Mt. Davidson, San Miguel Hills, McLaren Park, Bayview Hills.

Holcus lanatus. Velvet Grass. (W) Moist places and about the margins of lawns. Presidio, Golden Gate Park, Lake Merced, Mt. Davidson, San Miguel Hills.

Hordeum brachyantherum. Meadow Barley. (N) On grassy or brushy slopes and flats. Presidio, Point

Lobos, Laguna Honda, Mt. Davidson, San Miguel Hills, McLaren Park, Bayview Hills.

Hordeum leporinum. Farmer's Foxtail. (W) Widespread and often abundant on grassy slopes and flats. Presidio, Golden Gate Park, Lake Merced, Mt. Davidson, San Miguel Hills, Bayview Hills.

Lagurus ovatus. Hare's-Tail Grass. (W) Occasional dense colonies on sandy slopes. Point Lobos, Golden Gate Park.

Lolium multiflorum. Italian Ryegrass. (W) On grassy slopes. Presidio, Lands End, Golden Gate Park, Lake Merced, Laguna Honda, Mt. Davidson, San Miguel Hills, Bayview Hills.

Lolium perenne. Perennial Ryegrass. (W) In lawns and commonly naturalized in waste places and in moist ground. Golden Gate Park, Lake Merced, San Miguel Hills, Bayview Hills.

Melica californica. (N) Fairly common in rocky grassland. Corona Heights, Twin Peaks, Mt. Davidson, San Miguel Hills, Bernal Heights, Bayview Hills.

Phalaris canariensis. Canarygrass. (W) Widespread in waste ground. Golden Gate Park, Lake Merced, near Russian Hill, Bayview Hills.

Poa annua. Annual Bluegrass. (W) Abundant about gardens, especially where the soil is moist. Presidio, Golden Gate Park, Lake Merced, Mt. Davidson, Twin Peak, San Miguel Hills, Bayview Hills.

Poa pratensis. Kentucky Bluegrass. (N) Common in lawns, also on brushy canyon slopes. Presidio, Golden Gate Park, Lake Merced.

Poa unilateralis. (N) On rocky open slopes. Presidio, Lake Merced, Corona Heights, Mt. Davidson, Twin Peaks, San Miguel Hills, Bernal Heights, McLaren Park, Bayview Hills.

Polypogon monspeliensis. Rabbitfoot Grass. (W) Common in wet areas or in areas which have been moist. Presidio, Point Lobos, Golden Gate Park, Lake Merced, Laguna Honda, Mt. Davidson, San Miguel Hills, Bayview Hills.

Stipa pulchra. (N) Common in rocky grassland. Presidio, Golden Gate Park, Lake Merced, Corona Heights, Laguna Honda, Mt. Davidson, Twin Peaks, San Miguel Hills, Bernal Heights, Bayview Hills.

Cyperaceae. Sedge Family

Carex barbarae. (N) Open grassy or brushy slopes that are wet in the spring. Lake Merced, Mt. Davidson, San Miguel Hills, Bayview Hills.

Carex brevicaulis. (N) Forming turfy patches on open exposed slopes, frequently in shallow soil. Presidio, Lone Mountain, Lake Merced, Twin Peaks, McLaren Park, Bayview Hills.

Carex densa. (N) Moist soil of flats and hillside seepages. Presidio, San Miguel Hills, McLaren Park, Bayview Hills.

Carex harfordii. (N) Wet places on open or brushy hills. Mountain Lake, Lone Mountain, Golden Gate Park, Sutro Forest, Laguna Honda, Bayview Hills.

Carex subbracteata. (N) In moist grassland, brush or woods. Presidio, Lone Mountain, Golden Gate Park, Sutro Forest, Lake Merced, between Mt. Sutro and Twin Peaks, Mt. Davidson, San Miguel Hills, Bayview Hills.

Cyperus eragrostis. (W) Common in wet places in wild and cultivated areas. Presidio, Golden Gate Park, Lake Merced, San Miguel Hills, McLaren Park, Bayview Hills.

Cyperus esculentus. Nut-Grass. (W) Often seen as a garden weed. (Golden Gate Park, Lake Merced.

Scirpus californicus. California Tule. (N) In shallow water of lakes and ponds or in wet ground in marshes. Mountain Lake, Golden Gate Park, Pine Lake, Lake Merced.

Scirpus cernuus. (N) Wet soil of marshes, strands and seepages. Fort Point, Lands End, Golden Gate Park, Pine Lake, Lake Merced, San Miguel Hills, marsh north of McLaren Park, Bayview Hills.

Scirpus microcarpus. (N) Common in wet and marshy places. Mountain Lake, Lobos Creek, Golden Gate Park, Lake Merced, San Miguel Hills.

Araceae. Calla Family

Zantedeschia aethiopica. Common Calla.(W) In wet or marshy ground. Lobos Creek, Sutro Heights above Point Lobos, Chain of Lakes and Stow Lake, Golden Gate Park.

Juncaceae. Rush Family

Juncus bufonius. Toad Rush. (N) Common and widespread in moist or wet soil, both in wild and disturbed places. Mountain Lake, Point Lobos, Golden Gate Park, Lake Merced, San Miguel Hills, Bayview Hills.

Juncus effusus. Bog Rush. (N) In wet ground of marshes and about seepages. Presidio, Point Lobos, Golden Gate Park, Laguna Honda, Twin Peaks, San Miguel Hills, Bayview Hills.

Juncus leseurii. Salt Rush. (N) On wet slopes and flats, frequently in sandy soil, sometimes bordering salt marshes. Presidio, Point Lobos, Lake Merced, Golden Gate Park, Twin Peaks, Mt. Davidson, San Miguel Hills, Bayview Hills.

Juncus occidentalis. Western Rush. (N) Open slopes and flats that are moist in the spring. Presidio, Mt. Davidson, San Miguel Hills, McLaren Park, Bayview Hills.

Juncus patens. (N) Sandy soil that is wet in the spring. Presidio, Pacific Heights, Twin Peaks, Golden Gate Park, Laguna Honda, San Miguel Hills, Bayview Hills.

Juncus phaeocephalus. (N) Wet soil of sandy flats or marshy places. Presidio, Lake Merced, San Miguel Hills, Bayview Hills.

Luzula multiflora. Wood Rush. (N) Grassland and borders of brush in shallow soil. Lands End, Presidio, east of Lake Merced, Twin Peaks, San Miguel Hills, Bayview Hills.

Liliaceae. Lily Family

Allium dichlamydeum. Coastal Onion. (N) Open rocky slopes, in shallow soil. Presidio, often on serpentine, McLaren Park, Bayview Hills.

Brodiaea laxa. Grass-Nut. (N) Open grassy places in sandy or rocky soil. Presidio, McLaren Park, Bayview Hills.

Brodiaea pulchella. Blue Dicks. (N) Common in grassy or brushy places. Presidio, Twin Peaks, Mt. Davidson, Lake Merced, Corona Heights, McLaren Park, Bayview Hills.

Brodiaea terrestris. (N) Open grassy slopes in shallow sandy or rocky soil. San Francisco is the type locality. McLaren Park, Bayview Hills.

Calochortus luteus. Yellow Mariposa. (N) Rocky soil of open flats and slopes. Serpentine hills near Hunters Point.

Chlorogalum pomeridianum. Soap Plant. (N) Rocky or shallow soil of open slopes. Presidio, Lake Merced, Twin Peaks, Bayview Hills.

Fritillaria lanceolata. Mission Bells. (N) In brushy or grassy places. Presidio, Twin Peaks and the gully east of Lake Merced.

Iridaceae. Iris Family

Iris douglasiana. Douglas Iris. (N) Open grassland and brushy slopes. Presidio, the gully east of Lake Merced, Twin Peaks, near McLaren Park.

Iris longipetala. Field Iris. (N) Open grassy slopes. Presidio, Laguna Honda, McLaren Park, Bayview Hills.

Sisyrinchium bellum. Blue-Eyed-Grass. (N) Widespread in open grassland and on brushy slopes. Presidio, Golden Gate Park, gully east of Lake Merced, Bayview Hills.

Orchidaceae. Orchid Family

Habenaria greenei. Rein-orchis. (N) In grassland or on brushy slopes. Presidio, Point Lobos, Laguna Honda, Pine Lake, Mt. Davidson.

Salicaceae. Willow Family

Salix lasiandra. Yellow Willow. (N) Along the edge of creeks and lakes. Mountain Lake, Lake Merced, Bayview Hills.

Salix lasiolepis. Arroyo Willow. (N) In marshes, and along streams, or on slopes that are wet in the spring and dry in the summer. Golden Gate Park, Lake Merced, McLaren Park, Bayview Hills.

Corylaceae. Hazel Family

Corylus californica. California Hazel. (N) On brushy slopes. On the gully east of Lake Merced, Strawberry Hill in Golden Gate Park.

Fagaceae. Oak Family

Quercus agrifolia. Coast Live Oak. (N) Shrubs or low trees on brushy slopes, canyon sides and dune hills. Golden Gate Park, Lake Merced, McLaren Park, Bayview Hills.

Myricaceae. Bayberry Family

Myrica californica. California Wax-Myrtle. (N) In wet and marshy places in gullies and on dunes. Moist gullies east of Lake Merced.

Urticaceae. Nettle Family

Urtica holosericea. Nettle. (N) Brushy places in wet or dry soil. Presidio, above Bakers Beach, Mountain Lake, Golden Gate Park, Lake Merced.

Aristolochiaceae. Birthwort Family

Asarum caudatum. (N) Naturalized in moist shaded places in Golden Gate Park.

Polygonaceae. Buckwheat Family

Eriogonum latifolium. (N) In sandy soil or on rocky slopes. Presidio, Twin Peaks, Bayview Hills.

Polygonum aviculare. Dooryard Knotweed. (W) Along sidewalks and in gardens. One of the commonest plants in San Francisco. Presidio, Golden Gate Park, Laguna Honda, Lake Merced, Hunters Point, Bayview Hills.

Rumex acetosella. Sheep Sorrel. (W) Widespread in wild grassland and in gardens. Presidio, Golden Gate Park, Lake Merced, San Miguel Hills, Nob Hill, Bayview Hills.

Rumex crispus. Curly Dock. (W) Common in low weedy places and about marshes. Mountain Lake, Golden Gate Park, Lake Merced, Bayview Hills.

Chenopodiaceae. Goosefoot Family

Chenopodium album. Pigweed. (W) Rather common in weedy places. Presidio, Golden Gate Park.

Chenopodium ambrosioides. Mexican Tea. (W) In low ground or in weedy places. Presidio, Golden Gate Park, Lake Merced.

Chenopodium multifidum. Cutleaf Goosefoot. (W) A common weed. Presidio, Point Lobos, Golden Gate Park, Lake Merced, Twin Peaks, Russian Hill, Bayview Hills.

Chenopodium murale. Nettle-Leaf Goosefoot. (W) Widespread in waste and cultivated ground, also occasional in undisturbed areas. Presidio, Golden Gate Park, San Miguel Hills, Nob Hill, Embarcadero, Bayview Hills.

Amaranthaceae. Amaranth Family

Amaranthus powellii. (W) A weed of cultivated or waste ground. Golden Gate Park, near San Francisco State College, southeastern San Francisco.

Nyctaginaceae.
Four-O'Clock Family

Abronia latifolia. Yellow Sand-Verbena. (N) Dune Hills and sandy flats. Bakers Beach, Pine Lake, coastal dunes south of Fort Funston.

Aizoaceae. Carpetweed Family

Mesembryanthemum chilense. Sea-Fig. (N) Sandy slopes and flats near the ocean. Above Bakers Beach, Point Lobos.

Mesembryanthemum edule. Hottentot-Fig. (W) Extensively planted to prevent erosion. Presidio, Golden Gate Park, Twin Peaks, Bayview Hills.

Tetragonia tetragonioides. New Zealand Spinach. (W) A weed in sandy places. Presidio, Lands End, Golden Gate Park, Lake Merced, Bayview Hills.

Portulacaceae. Purslane Family

Calandrinia ciliata. Red Maids. (N) Open places in sandy or rocky soil. East of Lake Merced, Bayview Hills.

Montia perfoliata. Miner's Lettuce. (N) Common in grassland or brush. Presidio, Golden Gate Park, Lake Merced, Bayview Hills.

Portulaca oleracea. Common Purslane. (W) A common weed. Golden Gate Park, Embarcadero, near Mission Rock Terminal.

Caryophyllaceae. Pink Family

Silene gallica. Windmill Pink. (W) Common and widespread in wild areas. Presidio, Golden Gate Park, Sunset Heights, Lake Merced, Twin Peaks, Bayview Hills.

Silene verecunda. (N) Forming colonies on sandy or rocky slopes. Above Bakers Beach, Lake Merced.

Spergularia macrotheca. (N) Common on ocean bluffs, also in salt marshes and occasionally on open grassy hillsides. Presidio, Point Lobos, Lake Merced, Hunters Point.

Spergularia rubra. Sand-Spurrey. (W) In hard ground of roads or paths. Golden Gate Park, Twin Peaks, San Miguel Hills, Bayview Hills.

Stellaria media. Chickweed. (W) Common and widespread in gardens and on moist brushy or grassy slopes. Presidio, Golden Gate Park, Lake Merced, Mt. Davidson, San Miguel Hills, Pacific Heights, Russian Hill, Bayview Hills.

Ranunculaceae. Buttercup Family

Ranunculus californicus. California Buttercup. (N) Ocean bluffs, grassy hills, dunes and wooded slopes. Presidio, Golden Gate Park, Lake Merced, Laguna Honda, Twin Peaks, McLaren Park, Hunters Point, Bayview Hills.

Ranunculus repens. Creeping Buttercup. (W) Common in lawns. Golden Gate Park, Pacific Heights, Fort Mason.

Berberidaceae. Barberry Family

Berberis pinnata. Coast Barberry. (N) Rocky slopes and summits of hills. Lake Merced, Twin Peaks, Mt. Davidson, San Miguel Hills, McLaren Park, Bayview Hills.

Papaveraceae. Poppy Family

Eschscholzia californica. California Poppy. (N) Coastal bluffs, grassy hills and rocky ridges. Presidio, Lands End, Golden Gate Park, Lake Merced, Corona Heights, McLaren Park, Bayview Hills.

Platystemon californicus. Cream Cups. (N) Sandy soil of open or brushy hills and dunes. Lake Merced, Twin Peaks.

Cruciferae. Mustard Family

Arabis blepharophylla. Coast Rock-Cress. (N) Ocean bluffs and rocky outcrops in the hills. Above Bakers Beach, Twin Peaks, McLaren Park, Bayview Hills.

Arabis glabra. Tower Mustard. (N) Grassy and brushy slopes. Above Bakers Beach, Lands End, Laguna Honda, Twin Peaks, Bayview Hills.

Barbarea verna. Winter-Cress. (W) Coastal slopes, grassland, and cultivated ground. Lands End, Golden Gate Park, Mt. Davidson, Lake Merced, Laguna Honda, San Miguel Hills, McLaren Park, Bayview Hills.

Brassica campestris. Field Mustard. (W) Common on grassy hills. Presidio, Golden Gate Park, Nob Hill, Bayview Hills.

Cakile maritima. (W) On beaches and dunes. Presidio, Lands End, Stow Lake, Golden Gate Park, beach west of Lake Merced.

Cardamine oligosperma. Bitter-Cress. (N) Moist wild and cultivated places. Presidio, Golden Gate Park, gully east of Lake Merced.

Dentaria integrifolia. Toothwort. (N) Open or brushy slopes. Lands End, Laguna Honda, Twin Peaks, McLaren Park, Bayview Hills.

Erysimum franciscanum. Franciscan Wallflower. (N) Grassy or brushy slopes, dune hills and ocean bluffs in the western part of the city. Above Bakers Beach, Point Lobos, Laguna Honda, Lake Merced.

Lepidium nitidum. Shining Pepper-Grass. (N) Rather common on rocky slopes and in grassland in the central and eastern part of the city. Corona Heights, McLaren Park.

Lobularia maritima. Sweet Alyssum. (N) Commonly naturalized on coastal slopes and dunes. Lands End, Twin Peaks, Bayview Hills.

Raphanus sativus. Radish. (N) On the edge of wild areas. Presidio, Golden Gate Park, Lake Merced, Bayview Hills.

Crassulaceae. Stone Crop Family

Echeveria farinosa. Bluff Lettuce. (N) Coastal bluffs and rocky outcrops in the hills. Lands End, Golden Gate Park, Twin Peaks, McLaren Park, Bayview Hills.

Saxifragaceae. Saxifrage Family

Lithophragma affine. Woodland Star. (N) Moist shaded slopes in brush or grassland. East of Lake Merced, Bayview Hills.

Ribes sanguineum. Flowering Currant. (N) Moist slopes. Between Bakers Beach and Fort Point, Lands End, Golden Gate Park.

Rosaceae. Rose Family

Fragaria californica. California Strawberry. (N) Grassy and brushy slopes. Twin Peaks, Bayview Hills.

Fragaria chiloensis. Beach Strawberry. (N) Coastal slopes and dunes or in grassland in shallow rocky soil. Lands End, above Bakers Beach, Golden Gate Park, Lake Merced, Fort Funston, Twin Peaks, San Miguel Hills.

Holodiscus discolor. Ocean Spray. (N) Brushy slopes. Gully east of Lake Merced, Twin Peaks, McLaren Park, Bayview Hills.

Osmaronia cerasiformis. Oso Berry. (N) Moist brushy slopes, along the coast and inland. Laguna Honda, gully east of Lake Merced, McLaren Park, Bayview Hills.

Photinia arbutifolia. Christmas Berry. (N) On brushy hills. Golden Gate Park, Laguna Honda, Lake Merced.

Potentilla egedii. Cinquefoil. (N) In marshy places. Golden Gate Park, Pine Lake, Lake Merced, Twin Peaks.

Potentilla glandulosa. Sticky cinquefoil. (N) Grassy and brushy slopes that are dry in the summer. Presidio, Laguna Honda, gully east of Lake Merced, Twin Peaks, Corona Heights, Bayview Hills.

Prunus demissa. Western Choke-Cherry. (N) On brushy or rocky slopes. San Miguel Hills, Bayview Hills.

Prunus ilicifolia. Holly-Leaved Cherry. (N) Ro·ky summit ridge of Bayview Hills.

Rosa californica. California Wild Rose. (N) In brushy places. Presidio, gully east of Lake Merced, north base of Bayview Hills.

Rubus ursinus. California Blackberry. (N) On coastal bluffs, in brushy thickets, among oaks and willows, and on open rocky ridges. Above Bakers Beach, Lobos Creek, Golden Gate Park, Lake Merced, Laguna Honda, Twin Peaks, San Miguel Hills, McLaren Park, Bayview Hills.

Leguminosae. Pea Family

Albizzia lophantha. Stink Bean. (W) Near Bakers Beach, Lake Merced, Bayview Hills.

Astragalus nuttallii. (N) Brushy places, usually in sandy soil. Lake Merced.

Cytisus monspessulanus. French Broom. (W) Weedy in neglected gardens as well as in natural areas. Lands End, Golden Gate Park, Lake Merced, Twin Peaks, Bayview Hills.

Cytisus scoparius. Scotch Broom. (W) Becoming a bad weed. Presidio, Golden Gate Park, Laguna Honda, Corona Heights.

Lathyrus vestitus. Pacific Pea. (N) On grassy and brushy slopes. Near Bakers Beach, Laguna Honda, Twin Peaks, Lake Merced, McLaren Park, Bayview Hills.

Lotus corniculatus. Bird's Foot Trefoil. (W) Occasional in waste ground and lawns. Golden Gate Park, Lake Merced, Bayview Hills.

Lotus scoparius. Deerweed. (N) Sandy flats and brushy hills. Presidio, Golden Gate Park, Lake Merced, Bayview Hills.

Lotus subpinnatus. (N) Open and brushy slopes in sandy or rocky soil. Presidio, Twin Peaks, Hunters Point, McLaren Park, Bayview Hills.

Lupinus albifrons. Silver Bush Lupine. (N) Open rocky ridges. Twin Peaks, Bayview Hills.

Lupinus arboreus. Yellow Beach Lupine. (N) Common and widespread in sandy soil, frequently growing in disturbed places. Presidio, Lone Mountain, Golden Gate Park, Lake Merced, Bayview Hills.

Lupinus bicolor (N) Widespread in sandy or rocky soil, our commonest annual lupine. Above Bakers Beach, Point Lobos, Lone Mountain, Lake Merced, Twin Peaks, McLaren Park, Bayview Hills.

Lupinus chamissonis. Blue Beach Lupine. (N) Sandy soil of dune hills and flats. Above Bakers Beach, Golden Gate Park, Lake Merced.

Lupinus nanus. Sky Lupine. (N) Hillsides in sandy soil. Lake Merced, Presidio, Twin Peaks, McLaren Park, Bayview Hills.

Trifolium amplectens. Sack Clover. (N) Grassy slopes, generally in clay soils. Presidio, Golden Gate Park, Corona Heights, Bayview Hills.

Ulex europaeus. Gorse. (W) Escaping from cultivation and becoming rampantly weedy. Pine Lake, southeastern San Francisco.

Vicia americana. (N) Open grassland or brushy slopes. Presidio, Laguna Honda, Twin Peaks, gully east of Lake Merced, Bayview Hills.

Geraniaceae. Geranium Family

Erodium botrys. Broad-Leaf Filaree. (W)

Grasslands. Golden Gate Park, Lake Merced, Bayview Hills.

Erodium cicutarium. Red-Stem Filaree. (W) Common on grassy hills. Twin Peaks, San Miguel Hills, Bayview Hills.

Erodium moschatum. White-Stem Filaree. (W) Open hillsides and cultivated areas, particularly lawns. Golden Gate Park, Bayview Hills.

Geranium dissectum. Cut-Leaved Geranium. (N) Widespread and rather common in natural areas or cultivated ground. Lobos Creek, Point Lobos, Lone Mountain, Golden Gate Park, Mt. Davidson, Twin Peaks, Fort Mason, Bayview Hills.

Oxalidaceae. Oxalis Family

Oxalis pes-caprae. Bermuda Buttercup. (W) An attractive but difficult weed in cultivated ground. Point Lobos, Lone Mountain, Presidio, Golden Gate Park, Pine Lake, Lake Merced, Mt. Davidson, San Miguel Hills, Telegraph Hill.

Tropaeolaceae. Tropaeolum Family

Tropaeolum majus. Garden Nasturtium. (W) Widely cultivated and becoming established in moist places. Lobos Creek, Golden Gate Park, Telegraph Hill.

Euphorbiaceae. Spurge Family

Euphorbia peplus. Petty Spurge. (W) A widespread weed of gardens and shaded wild areas. Golden Gate Park, Mt. Davidson, San Miguel Hills, Russian Hill.

Anacardiaceae. Sumac Family

Rhus diversiloba. Poison Oak. (N) Common on brushy slopes, rocky ridges and sandy flats. Presidio, Lands End, McLaren Park, Bayview Hills.

Rhamnaceae. Buckthorn Family

Ceanothus thyrsiflorus. Blue Blossom. (N) Forming mats and thickets on coastal bluffs and on brushy slopes. Near Bakers Beach, between Lands End and Golden Gate Bridge, Lake Merced.

Rhamnus californica. Coffee Berry. (N) Hills and bluffs, forming thickets or mats. Presidio, east of Lake Merced, Laguna Honda, Bayview Hills.

Malvaceae. Mallow Family

Lavatera arborea. Tree Mallow. (W) In natural areas, a fugitive from cultivation. Presidio, Golden Gate Park, Lands End, Fort Funston.

Sidalcea malvaeflora. Wild Hollyhock. (N) Open grassy slopes. Lake Merced, Presidio, Laguna Honda, Twin Peaks, McLaren Park, Bayview Hills.

Violaceae. Violet Family

Viola adunca. Blue Violet. (N) Forming colonies on open grassy hills. Bakers Beach, Twin Peaks.

Viola pedunculata. Yellow Violet. (N) Open grassy hills. East of Lake Merced, McLaren Park, Bayview Hills.

Lythraceae. Loose-Strife Family

Lythrum hyssopifolia. (W) Moist or wet places, or in dry places that are wet in the spring. Mountain Lake, Lake Merced, San Miguel Hills, Bayview Hills.

Myrtaceae. Myrtle Family

Eucalyptus globulus. Blue Gum. (W) Often weedy in the vicinity of planted trees. Presidio, Golden Gate Park, Sigmund Stern Grove, Lake Merced, Bayview Hills.

Onagraceae. Evening Primrose Family

Clarkia rubicunda. (N) On grassy or brushy slopes and coastal bluffs. Lands End, Lake Merced, Twin Peaks, Bayview Hills.

Epilobium watsonii. San Francisco Willow-Herb (N) Very common in wet places, often weedy in gardens. Presidio, Lands End, Golden Gate Park, Lake Merced, Laguna Honda, Twin Peaks, Bayview Hills.

Epilobium paniculatum. Willow-Herb. (N) On flats and slopes both in sandy and clay soils. Presidio, Lake Merced, Point Lobos.

Oenothera cheiranthifolia. Beach Primrose. (N) Sandy slopes and flats. Above Bakers Beach, Lands End, Golden Gate Park, Lake Merced.

Oenothera ovata. Sun-Cups. (N) On grassy slopes and flats. Presidio, Golden Gate Park, Lake Merced, Twin Peaks, Bayview Hills.

Araliaceae. Aralia Family

Hedera helix. English Ivy. (W) Widely cultivated in San Francisco. Presidio, Golden Gate Park.

Umbelliferae. Parsley Family

Angelica hendersonii. (N) On brushy hills. Point Lobos, Lake Merced, Bayview Hills.

Conium maculatum. Poison Hemlock. (W) A common weed of fertile soil, and along streams. Golden Gate Park, Lake Merced, Twin Peaks, Bayview Hills.

Foeniculum vulgare. Sweet Fennel. (W) Common in vacant lots. Point Lobos, Laguna Honda, Corona Heights, Mt. Davidson, Russian Hill, Bayview Hills.

Heracleum maximum. Cow-Parsnip. (N) Moist slopes, along streams and on coastal bluffs. Lobos Creek, above Bakers Beach, Lands End, Laguna Honda.

Lomatium caruifolium. Alkali Parsnip. (N) Open rocky grassland, on serpentine. Presidio, Corona Heights, Laguna Honda, Twin Peaks, McLaren Park, Bayview Hills.

Lomatium dasycarpum. Lace Parsnip. (N) Open rocky grassland. Presidio, Mt. Davidson, Bayview Hills.

Oenanthe sarmentosa. (N) Common in wet places. Mountain Lake, Lobos Creek, Lands End, Golden Gate Park, Lake Merced, Mt. Davidson, San Miguel Hills, swamp north of McLaren Park.

Perideridia kelloggii. (N) Open grassy hillsides. Coastal bluffs between Lobos Creek and Fort Point, Laguna Honda, Mt. Davidson, Twin Peaks, San Miguel Hills, Bayview Hills.

Sanicula arctopoides. Footsteps-of-Spring (N) In open rocky grassland. Above Bakers Beach, Presidio, dunes south of Golden Gate Park, Lake Merced, Laguna Honda, Corona Heights, Mt. Davidson, Twin Peaks, Bayview Hills.

Sanicula bipinnatifida. Purple Sanicle. (N) Open rocky grassland. Presidio, Lake Merced, Corona Heights, Laguna Honda, Twin Peaks, Mt. Davidson, McLaren Park, Bayview Hills.

Sanicula crassicaulis. Pacific Sanicle. (N) Open or shaded places, often under brush. Golden Gate Park, Lake Merced, Laguna Honda, Twin Peaks, Mt. Davidson, Bayview Hills.

Ericaceae. Heather Family

Arctostaphylos franciscana. Franciscan manzanita. (N) Forming colonies on open rocky slopes on serpentine, known only from San Francisco. North of Bakers Beach, Mt. Davidson.

Gaultheria shallon. Salal. (N) Around rocks or in brush of rock-strewn hilltops. Mt. Davidson, San Miguel Hills.

Vaccinium ovatum. Huckleberry. (N) Moist brushy slopes. Mt. Davidson.

Primulaceae. Primrose Family

Anagallis arvensis. Scarlet Pimpernel.

(W) In gardens and natural areas. Presidio, Point Lobos, Lone Mountain, Golden Gate Park, Lake Merced, Laguna Honda, Mt. Davidson, San Miguel Hills, Russian Hill, McLaren Park, Bayview Hills.

Dodecatheon clevelandii. Shooting Stars. (N) Open grassy hilltops. Point Lobos, Bernal Heights, McLaren Park.

Dodecatheon hendersonii. Shooting Stars. (N) Shaded brushy slopes. Summit of Mt. Davidson.

Plumbaginaceae. Thrift Family

Armeria maritima. Sea-Pink. (N) Coastal bluffs, dunes and hills. Point Lobos, Lake Merced.

Apocynaceae. Dogbane Family

Vinca major. Periwinkle. (W) Commonly cultivated and becoming an aggressive weed in shaded places. Above Bakers Beach, Golden Gate Park, Laguna Honda, Mt. Davidson, McLaren Park.

Convolvulaceae. Morning-Glory Family

Convolvulus arvensis. Orchard Morning-Glory. (W) A weed often seen in gardens. Point Lobos, Golden Gate Park, Lake Merced, San Miguel Hills, Russian Hill, Bayview Hills.

Convolvulus occidentalis. (N) Moist brushy slopes and coastal bluffs, sometimes on open rocky slopes. Presidio, Point Lobos to Fort Point, Lands End, Lake Merced, Laguna Honda, Twin Peaks, San Miguel Hills, Mt. Davidson.

Polemoniaceae. Phlox Family

Gilia capitata. (N) On dunes and sandy flats. Presidio, near Bakers Beach, Lake Merced.

Linanthus androsaceus. (N) Forming colonies in grassland in sandy soil. Lake Merced.

Navarretia squarrosa. Skunkweed. (N) Sandy moist depressions. Lobos Creek to Fort Point, Presidio, Golden Gate Park, Laguna Honda, San Miguel Hills.

Hydrophyllaceae. Waterleaf Family

Nemophila menziesii. Baby-Blue-Eyes. (N) Moist open grassland. Presidio, Point Lobos, Lake Merced, Twin Peaks, Mt. Davidson, San Miguel Hills, Bayview Hills.

Nemophila pedunculata. (N) Open grassland or underbrush. Lake Merced, Point Lobos, McLaren Park.

Phacelia californica. (N) In rocky or sandy soil on open or brushy slopes. Lake Merced, Laguna Honda, San Miguel Hills, Corona Heights, Mt. Davidson, McLaren Park, Bayview Hills.

Phacelia distans. Wild Heliotrope. (N) Rocky or brushy slopes. Point Lobos, Golden Gate Park, Lake Merced, Laguna Honda, Mt. Davidson, Bayview Hills.

Phacelia malvaefolia. Stinging Phacelia. (N) Shaded brushy slopes. Lobos Creek, Point Lobos, Golden Gate Park, Lake Merced, Mt. Davidson, San Miguel Hills, Bayview Hills.

Boraginaceae. Borage Family

Allocarya chorisiana. (N) Common in moist places. Near Lobos Creek, Golden Gate Park, Twin Peaks.

Amsinckia intermedia. Common Fiddle-Neck. (N) On grassy slopes. Golden Gate Park, Lake Merced, San Miguel Hills, McLaren Park.

Amsinckia latifolia. Coast Fiddle-Neck. (N) On dunes and on sandy and grassy flats. Above Bakers Beach, Mountain Lake, Point Lobos, Golden Gate Park, Pine Lake, Lake Merced.

Myosotis sylvatica. Forget-Me-Not. (W) Shaded places near cultivation. Presidio, Golden Gate Park, Mt. Davidson, San Miguel Hills, Russian Hill.

Labiatae. Mint Family

Monardella villosa. Coyote-Mint. (N) On brushy or open rocky slopes. Twin Peaks, San Miguel Hills, Bayview Hills.

Satureja douglasii. Yerba Buena. (N) Brushy slopes. Near mouth of Lobos Creek, Laguna Honda, Twin Peaks, Pine Lake, Lake Merced.

Stachys chamissonis. Coast Hedge Nettle. (N) Marshy places. Golden Gate Park.

Stachys rigida. Hedge Nettle. (N) Open grassy slopes and brushy hillsides. Lands End, Golden Gate Park, Lake Merced, Laguna Honda, Corona Heights, Mt. Davidson, Twin Peaks, San Miguel Hills, McLaren Park, Bayview Hills.

Solanaceae. Nightshade Family

Nicotiana glauca. Tree Tobacco. (W) Established in moist places. Golden Gate Park.

Solanum umbelliferum. Blue Witch. (N) Brushy slopes. Bakers Beach, Lobos Creek.

Scrophulariaceae. Figwort Family

Castilleja latifolia. Seaside Paint-Brush. (N) Slopes in coastal brush and grassland. Above Bakers Beach, Lobos Creek to Fort Point, Point Lobos, Lake Merced.

Collinsia multicolor. Franciscan Blue-Eyed Mary. (N) Forming colonies in openings in woodland and brush. Bayview Hills.

Mimulus aurantiacus. Sticky Monkey-Flower. (N) Brushy slopes. Fort Point, above Bakers Beach, Golden Gate Park, Lake Merced, Laguna Honda, Mt. Davidson, Twin Peaks, San Miguel Hills, Bayview Hills.

Orthocarpus densiflorus. Owl's Clover. (N) In shallow soil on open slopes. Presidio, Golden Gate Park, Corona Heights, Mt. Davidson, Twin Peaks, San Miguel Hills, McLaren Park.

Orthocarpus erianthus. Popcorn Beauty. (N) In low fields, on sandy flats, and on bluffs. Presidio, Lake Merced, McLaren Park.

Orthocarpus floribundus. (N) Colonies on coastal bluffs. Above Fort Point, near Bakers Beach, the Presidio.

Orthocarpus pusillus. (N) On grassy flats and slopes, often in shallow soil. Presidio, near Bakers Beach, Lone Mountain, Golden Gate Park, Lake Merced, Corona Heights, Twin Peaks, Mt. Davidson, San Miguel Hills, Bayview Hills.

Scrophularia californica. California Bee-Plant. (N) Brushy slopes and in wooded areas. Lobos Creek, above Bakers Beach, Lands End, Lone Mountain, Golden Gate Park, Pine Lake, Lake Merced, Laguna Honda, Mt. Davidson, Twin Peaks, San Miguel Hills, Bayview Hills.

Veronica americana. American Brooklime. (N) Marshy places. Lobos Creek, Mountain Lake, Sigmund Stern Grove, Lake Merced, Laguna Honda, Mt. Davidson, San Miguel Hills.

Plantaginaceae. Plantain Family

Plantago erecta. (N) On open grassy slopes and dune flats, often in shallow soil. Near Fort Point, above Bakers Beach, Presidio, Golden Gate Park, Pine Lake, Corona Heights, Laguna Honda, Mt. Davidson, Twin Peaks, San Miguel Hills, Bernal Heights, McLaren Park, Bayview Hills.

Plantago lanceolata. Ribwort. (W) Cultivated ground and in wild areas. Above Bakers Beach, Presidio, Lands End, Golden Gate Park, Lake Merced, Laguna Honda, Mt. Davidson, Twin Peaks, San Miguel Hills, Bayview Hills.

Plantago major. Common Plantain. (W) Common in wild areas. Mountain Lake, Golden Gate Park, Laguna Honda, Pine Lake, Lake Merced,

Mt. Davidson, San Miguel Hills, McLaren Park.

Caprifoliaceae. Honeysuckle Family

Lonicera involucrata. Twinberry. (N) Wet soil near streams and marshes. Between Bakers Beach and Fort Point, Lobos Creek, Mountain Lake, Golden Gate Park, Lake Merced, Laguna Honda.

Sambucus callicarpa. Red Elderberry. (N) Moist brushy slopes. Golden Gate Park, Laguna Honda, Mt. Davidson, Twin Peaks.

Sambucus coerulea. Blue Elderberry. (N) On brushy slopes, near streams, and about the margins of swamps. Golden Gate Park, San Miguel Hills, swamp north of McLaren Park.

Symphoricarpos rivularis. Snowberry. (N) Partially shaded brushy slopes. Golden Gate Park, Sunset Heights, Lake Merced, Laguna Honda.

Valerianaceae. Valerian Family

Centranthus ruber. Jupiter's Beard. (W) On rocky slopes, and about gardens. Presidio, Golden Gate Park, Lake Merced, Telegraph Hill, McLaren Park, San Miguel Hills, Russian Hill.

Cucurbitaceae. Gourd Family

Marah fabaceus. Manroot. (N) On dunes and on grassy or brushy slopes. Lands End, Fort Point, near Lobos Creek, above Bakers Beach, Golden Gate Park, Laguna Honda, Twin Peaks, Mt. Davidson, San Miguel Hills, Bayview Hills.

Compositae. Sunflower Family

Achillea borealis. Yarrow. (N) Widespread in sandy soil in natural areas. Lands End, Presidio, Golden Gate Park, Pine Lake, Lake Merced, Laguna Honda, Twin Peaks, Mt. Davidson, San Miguel Hills, Bayview Hills.

Agoseris apargioides. Coast Dandelion. (N) Dunes, grassy hills and rocky slopes. Presidio, Point Lobos, Lake Merced, Twin Peaks, San Miguel Hills, Mt. Davidson, Bayview Hills.

Agoseris grandiflora. California Dandelion. (N) Open or brushy slopes. Mt. Davidson, San Miguel Hills, Bayview Hills.

Anaphalis margaritacea. Pearly Everlasting. (N) Open or brushy slopes. Presidio, Point Lobos, Golden Gate Park, Lake Merced, Laguna Honda, Twin Peaks, San Miguel Hills, McLaren Park, Bayview Hills.

Artemisia californica. California Sagebrush (N) Brushy and open hillsides. Point Lobos, Laguna Honda, Twin Peaks, San Miguel Hills, McLaren Park, Bayview Hills.

Artemisia pycnocephala. (N) Dunes and sandy flats. Lobos Creek, Bakers Beach, Lake Merced.

Aster chilensis. (N) Rocky slopes in natural areas, occasionally cultivated ground. Lands End, Golden Gate Park, Lake Merced, Laguna Honda, Twin Peaks, San Miguel Hills, Bayview Hills.

Aster subspicatus. (N) Brushy slopes. Sutro Heights above Point Lobos, Laguna Honda, Pine Lake, San Miguel Hills.

Baccharis douglasii. (N) Moist soil or in places that are wet in the spring. Sigmund Stern Grove, San Miguel Hills.

Baccharis pilularis. Fuzzy-Wuzzy. (N) Open hillsides. Presidio, Point Lobos, Lake Merced, Twin Peaks, Potrero Hill.

Baccharis pilularis var. *consanguinea.* Coyote-Brush. (N) Brushy hillsides, invading grassland, and disturbed ground. Golden Gate Park, Laguna Honda, Corona Heights, Twin Peaks, San Miguel Hills, Bayview Hills.

Baeria chrysostoma. Gold Fields. (N) Open grassy slopes. Presidio, McLaren Park, Bayview Hills.

Bellis perennis. English Daisy. (W)

Moist grassy places, common in lawns. Presidio, Golden Gate Park, Pine Lake, San Miguel Hills, Pacific Heights, Russian Hill, Fort Mason.

Chrysanthemum coronarium. Crown Chrysanthemum. (W) Common in cultivated areas. Pine Lake, Lake Merced, San Miguel Hills, McLaren Park.

Cirsium occidentale. Western Thistle. (N) On sandy slopes. Above Bakers Beach, Golden Gate Park, Lake Merced, Twin Peaks, Mt. Davidson, San Miguel Hills.

Cirsium quercetorum. Brownie Thistle. (N) Open slopes in grassland. Presidio, Twin Peaks, Mt. Davidson, San Miguel Hills, McLaren Park, Bayview Hills.

Cotula coronopifolia. Brass Buttons. (W) Wet or marshy flats or slopes. Presidio, Golden Gate Park, Pine Lake Lake Merced, Laguna Honda, San Miguel Hills, Bayview Hills.

Erigeron glaucus. Seaside Daisy. (N) Coastal bluffs, and rocky hills. Presidio, Point Lobos, west of Lake Merced, Mt. Davidson, San Miguel Hills.

Eriophyllum confertiflorum. Yellow Yarrow. (N) Brushy and open rocky slopes. Corona Heights, San Miguel Hills.

Eriophyllum staechadifolium. Lizard Tail. (N) Bluffs and brushy hills on or near the coast. Fort Point, Point Lobos, Golden Gate Park, Lake Merced, Twin Peaks, Mt. Davidson, Laguna Honda.

Franseria chamissonis. Beach Bar. (N) Sandy flats, occasionally near the shore. Presidio, Golden Gate Park, Lake Merced.

Grindelia maritima. (N) Coastal bluffs, and open or brushy slopes. Presidio, Point Lobos, Lake Merced, Laguna Honda, Twin Peaks.

Haplopappus ericoides. (N) Common low shrub of dunes and sandy hills. Presidio, Golden Gate Park, Lake Merced, Laguna Honda.

Helenium puberulum. Sneezeweed. (N) Wet ground of marshes, and hillside seepages. Fort Point, Laguna Honda, Lake Merced, San Miguel Hills.

Hypochoeris glabra. Smooth Cat's-Ear. (W) On grassy or brushy slopes. Presidio, Golden Gate Park, Lake Merced, Twin Peaks, Mt. Davidson, Bernal Heights, McLaren Park, Bayview Hills.

Hypochoeris radicata. Hairy Cat's-Ear. (W) Grassy places in cultivated ground. Presidio, Lake Merced, San Miguel Hills, McLaren Park, Bayview Hills.

Layia platyglossa. Tidy-Tips. (N) Common in grassy places in sandy soil. Presidio, Point Lobos, Lake Merced, Twin Peaks, San Miguel Hills.

Madia gracilis. Slender Tarweed. (N) Grassy or brushy slopes. Lake Merced, San Miguel Hills, Bayview Hills.

Madia sativa. Common Tarweed. (N) Grassy or brushy places. Presidio, Point Lobos, Golden Gate Park, Lake Merced, Laguna Honda, Twin Peaks, San Miguel Hills.

Matricaria matricarioides. Pineapple Weed. (W) In natural and cultivated areas. Mountain Lake, Presidio, Golden Gate Park, Lake Merced, Mt. Davidson, San Miguel Hills, Bayview Hills.

Senecio aronicoides. Butterweed. (N) Grassy or brushy slopes, generally in partial shade. Above Bakers Beach, Presidio, Lake Merced, Twin Peaks, Mt. Davidson, Bayview Hills.

Senecio mikanioides. German Ivy. (W) Forming dense tangles on shrubs and trees in moist places. Presidio, Point Lobos, Golden Gate Park, Lake

Merced, Twin Peaks, Mt. Davidson, San Miguel Hills.

Senecio vulgaris. Common Groundsel. (W) A common weed, Presidio, Golden Gate Park, Lake Merced, Mt. Davidson, San Miguel Hills, Bayview Hills.

Solidago spathulata. Dune Goldenrod. (N) Open slopes and flats in rocky, or sandy soil. Lone Mountain, Pine Lake, Lake Merced, Mt. Davidson, San Miguel Hills.

Sonchus oleraceus. Sow-Thistle. (W) One of the most common weeds in San Francisco. Presidio, Lands End, Golden Gate Park, Sigmund Stern

Grove, Lake Merced, Mt. Davidson, San Miguel Hills.

Taraxacum officinale. Dandelion. (W) Common and widespread in wild or cultivated places. Presidio, Golden Gate Park, Twin Peaks, San Miguel Hills.

Wyethia angustifolia. Mule Ears. (N) Grassy or open brushy hills. Presidio, Twin Peaks, Mt. Davidson, Corona Heights, San Miguel Hills, McLaren Park, Bayview Hills.

Xanthium spinosum. Spiny Clotbur. (W) A weed of cultivated areas. Golden Gate Park, Lake Merced, San Miguel Hills, Bayview Hills.

Reptiles and Amphibians of San Francisco

Taricha torosa. California Newt. Ponds, lakes and reservoirs. Golden Gate Park, Presidio, Land's End.

Aneides lugubris. Arboreal Salamander. Under moist logs, boards and rocks. Land's End, Presidio, Golden Gate Park, Sutro Forest, Bayview Park, Mt. Davidson.

Batrachoseps attenuatus. California Slender Salamander. Under moist logs, boards and rocks. Land's End, Presidio, Golden Gate Park, Sutro Forest, Mt. Davidson, Bayview Park.

Ensatina eschscholtzi. Ensatina. Moist bark, logs and deep leaf litter. Golden Gate Park.

Bufo boreas. Western Toad. Grasslands and woodlands. Presidio, Golden Gate Park.

Hyla regilla. Pacific Treefrog. Ponds, and under moist logs. Presidio, Golden Gate Park, Fleishhaker Zoo, Lake Merced.

Rana aurora. Red-legged Frog. Wooded lakes and ponds. Lakes of Golden Gate Park, Presidio, Lake Merced, Land's End.

Rana catesbeiana. Bullfrog. Reservoirs and ponds. Sigmund Stern Grove.

Clemmys marmorata. Western Pond Turtle. Ponds, lakes and reservoirs. Stow Lake, Elk Glen Lake.

Gerrhonotus coeruleus. Northern Alligator Lizard. Under rocks, boards and logs. Sutro Forest, Lake Merced, Golden Gate Park, Land's End.

Eumeces skiltonianus. Western Skink. Under rocks, logs and leaf litter. Presidio, Bayview Park.

Sceloporus occidentalis. Western Fence Lizard. Woodlands and grasslands. Golden Gate Park, Presidio, Lake Merced, Land's End.

Charina bottae. Rubber Boa. Moist woodlands. Lake Merced, Presidio.

Coluber constrictor. Racer. Grasslands and broken woodlands. Golden Gate Park, Lake Merced.

Pituophis catenifer. Gopher Snake. Grasslands and woodlands. McLaren Park.

Lampropeltis getulus. Common King-snake. Grasslands, open forest and woodlands. Presidio.

Thamnophis elegans. Western Garter Snake. Meadows. Golden Gate Park, Land's End, Lake Merced, Mt. Davidson, Presidio, Fort Point, Sutro Forest.

Butterflies of San Francisco

Coenonympha california. California Ringlet. Feeds on grasses. Mt. Davidson, Forest Hills.

Cercyonis sthenele. Sthenele Satyr. Once common on sand dunes in Sunset District. Man's destruction of the dunes pushed this butterfly to extinction.

Danaus plexippus. Monarch. Feeds on milkweeds. Golden Gate Park.

Euphydryas chalcedona. Common Checkerspot. Feeds on plants of the figwort family. Golden Gate Park.

Euphydryas editha bayensis. Editha Bay-Region Checkerspot. Feeds on plants growing on serpentine hills. Twin Peaks.

Phyciodes campestris. Field Crescent. Larva feed on wild asters. Golden Gate Park.

Phyciodes mylitta. Mylitta Crescent. Feeds on various thistles. Forest Hills.

Polygonia satyrus. Satyr Anglewing. Feeds on nettles. Fairly common in vacant lots of the city.

Nymphalis californica. California Tortoiseshell. Feeds on wild lilac, buck brush and other species of *Ceanothus*. Golden Gate Park.

Nymphalis antiopa. Mourning Cloak. Feeds on cottonwoods and willows. Mt. Davidson, West Portal District, Golden Gate Park.

Vanessa atalanta. Red Admiral. Feeds on nettles. West Portal District, Golden Gate Park.

Vanessa cardui. Painted Lady. Feeds on thistles and nettles. Golden Gate Park.

Vanessa virginiensis. American Painted Lady. Feeds on members of the *Compositae*. Golden Gate Park.

Vanessa carye. West Coast Lady. Feeds principally on mallow. Golden Gate Park.

Junonia coenia. Buckeye. Feeds on several plants, including snapdragon, plantain and Gerardia. Forest Hills, Golden Gate Park.

Limenitis lorquini. Lorquin's Admiral. Feeds on cherry, willow, cottonwood and poplar. Golden Gate Park.

Limenitis bredowii californica. California Sister. Larva feeds on Coast Live Oak. Golden Gate Park.

Strymon melinus pudica. Common Hairstreak. Vacant lots and open grasslands. Feeds on numerous native plants.

Incisalia iroides. Western Brown Elfin. Feeds on various species of *Ceanothus*. Golden Gate Park.

Incisalia eryphon. Western Banded Elfin. Feeds on various species of pine. Presidio.

Callophrys dumetorum. Bramble Hairstreak. Feeds on buckwheat and lotus. Seen along sand dunes near Forest Hills.

Callophrys viridis. Green Hairstreak. A butterfly with a limited habitat. Lives along the rocky hills of San Francisco.

Plebejus icarioides missionensis. Mission Blue. Feeds on various species of lupines. Twin Peaks.

Plebejus icarioides pheres. Pheres Blue. Once fed commonly on lupines growing on sand dunes of the Sunset District. Now dunes and Pheres Blue are gone.

Plebejus acmon. Acmon Blue. Feeds on many species of legumes. Golden Gate Park.

Glaucopsyche lygdamus behrii. Behr's Silver Blue. Feeds on various leguminous plants. Grasslands and open woodlands.

Glaucopsyche xerces. Xerces Blue. Now extinct, this butterfly once occurred in sand dunes throughout the city.

Colias eurytheme. Common Sulphur. Feeds on various leguminous plants. Vacant lots.

Pieris rapae. Cabbage Butterfly. Feeds on various vegetables. Golden Gate Park.

Battus philenor hirsuta. Hairy Pipe-vine Swallowtail. Lives near its favorite food plant, Dutchman's Pipe (*Aristolochia*).

Papilio zelicaon. Anise Swallowtail. Feeds on anise and parsley plants. Mt. Davidson.

Papilio rutulus. Western Tiger Swallowtail. Feeds on willow, poplar and hops. Mt. Davidson, Golden Gate Park.

Pyrgus communis. Common Checkered Skipper. Feeds on members of the mallow family. Golden Gate Park.

Erynnis propertius. Propertius Duskywing. Feeds on the Coast Live Oak. Grassland and broken forests.

Hylephila phyleus. Fiery Skipper. Various species of grasses are preferred by this butterfly. Vacant lots and marshes.

Atalopedes campestris. Field Skipper. Feeds on various grasses. Golden Gate Park.

Paratrytone melane. Umber Skipper. Feeds on grasses. Golden Gate Park.

Mammals of San Francisco

Didelphis marsupialis. Opossum. Golden Gate Park.

Scapanus latimanus. Broad-footed Mole. Golden Gate Park.

Neurotrichus gibbsi. Shrew-mole. Moist, broken forests.

Sorex trowbridgei. Trowbridge Shrew. Grass-covered hills.

Sorex vagrans. Vagrant Shrew. Humid grasslands.

Myotis lucifugus. Little Brown Bat. Golden Gate Park.

Lasiurus cinereus. Hoary Bat. Golden Gate Park.

Lasiurus borealis. Red Bat. Deciduous forests.

Tadarida mexicana. Mexican Free-tailed Bat. Often roosts in buildings.

Procyon lotor. Raccoon. Golden Gate Park, Sutro Forest, the Presidio.

Mustela frenata. Long-tailed Weasel. Golden Gate Park.

Mephitis mephitis. Striped Skunk. Golden Gate Park, the Presidio.

Steller sea lions on the Farallones

Taxidea taxus. Badger. Golden Gate Park.

Urocyon cinereoargenteus. Gray Fox. Golden Gate Park, Presidio, Land's End.

Zalophus californianus. California Sea Lion. Seal Rocks.

Eumetopias jubata. Steller Sea Lion. Seal Rocks.

Citellus beecheyi. California Ground Squirrel. Land's End, Twin Peaks.

Sciurus carolinesis. Eastern Gray Squirrel. Golden Gate Park.

Sciurus niger. Fox Squirrel. Golden Gate Park.

Thomomys bottae. Botta Pocket Gopher. Golden Gate Park.

Reithrodontomys megalotis. Western Harvest Mouse. Open grassland.

Peromyscus maniculatus. Deer Mouse. Golden Gate Park.

Microtus californicus. California Vole. Golden Gate Park.

Rattus norvegicus. Norway Rat. Golden Gate Park.

Rattus rattus. Black Rat. Golden Gate Park.

Mus musculus. House Mouse. Golden Gate Park.

Sylvilagus bachmani. Brush Rabbit. Golden Gate Park, the Presidio.

Birds of San Francisco

The following list includes all species of birds ever noted within the city limits of San Francisco. Some species have been noted only once or just a few times.

The localities are presented as a general aid to visitors and are not intended to be complete. A species should be sought whenever suitable habitat is present. The habitats listed are those in which a species is most likely to be found within the city.

Gabiidae, Loons

Gavia immer. Common Loon. Lakes and Bay. Stow Lake (Golden Gate Park), Lake Merced.

Gavia arctica. Arctic Loon. Bay and ocean. Ocean Beach.

Gavia stellata. Red-throated Loon. Lakes and Bay. Golden Gate Park, Lake Merced.

Podicipedidae, Grebes

Podiceps grisegena. Red-necked Grebe. Lakes, Bay and ocean. Presidio of San Francisco, Stow Lake (Golden Gate Park), Lake Merced.

Podiceps auritus. Horned Grebe. Lakes, Bay and ocean. Golden Gate Park, Lake Merced.

Podiceps caspicus. Eared Grebe. Lakes, Bay and ocean. Golden Gate Park, Lake Merced.

Aechmophorus occidentalis. Western Grebe. Lakes, Bay and ocean. Ocean Beach, Golden Gate Park, Lake Merced.

Podilymbus podiceps. Pied-billed Grebe. Lakes and marshes. Golden Gate Park, Lake Merced.

Procellariidae, Fulmar and Shearwaters

Puffinus creatopus. Pink-footed Shearwater. Ocean. Ocean Beach.

Puffinus griseus. Sooty Shearwater. Bay mouth and ocean. Ocean Beach, mouth of San Francisco Bay.

Hydrobatidae, Storm Petrels

Oceanodroma homochroa. Ashy Petrel. Nests on offshore islands; feeds over the open ocean. Ocean Beach (rare).

Pelecanidae, Pelicans

Pelecanus erythrorhynchos. White Pelican. Lakes and Bay. San Francisco Bay.

Pelecanus occidentalis. Brown Pelican. Bay, ocean and occasionally lakes. Ocean Beach, Golden Gate Park.

Phalacrocoracidae, Cormorants

Phalacrocorax auritus. Double-crested Cormorant. Lakes and Bay. Cliff House, Lake Merced.

Phalacrocorax penicillatus. Brandt's Cormorant. Bay and ocean. Ocean Beach; nests on Seal Rocks off the Cliff House.

Phalacrocorax pelagicus. Pelagic Cormorant. Bay and ocean. Ocean Beach.

Ardeidae, Herons and Bitterns

Ardea herodias. Great Blue Heron. Marshes, ponds and lakes. Lake Merced.

Butorides virescens. Green Heron. Marshes, streams, ponds and lakes. Golden Gate Park, Lake Merced.

Nycticorax nycticorax. Black-crowned Night Heron. Marshes, ponds and lakes. Golden Gate Park, Lake Merced.

Ixobrychus exilis. Least Bittern. Marshes. Golden Gate Park.

Botaurus lentiginosus. American Bittern. Marshes. Golden Gate Park, Lake Merced.

Anatidae,
Swans, Ducks and Geese

Olor columbianus. Whistling Swan. Lakes and Bay. Lake Merced.

Branta canadensis. Canada Goose. Marshes, lakes and Bay. Golden Gate Park.

Branta nigricans. Black Brant. Ocean and Bay. Golden Gate Park.

Anser albifrons. White-fronted Goose. Marshes, lakes and Bay. Golden Gate Park.

Chen hyperborea. Snow Goose. Marshes, lakes and Bay. Golden Gate Park.

Anas platyrhynchos. Mallard. Marshes, ponds and lakes. Golden Gate Park, Lake Merced.

Anas strepera. Gadwall. Marshes, ponds and lakes. Golden Gate Park.

Anas acuta. Pintail. Marshes, ponds and lakes. Golden Gate Park.

Anas carolinensis. Green-winged Teal. Marshes, ponds and lakes. Golden Gate Park.

Anas cyanoptera. Cinnamon Teal. Marshes, ponds and lakes. Golden Gate Park, Lake Merced.

Mareca penelope. European Widgeon. Marshes, ponds and lakes, Golden Gate Park.

Mareca americana. American Widgeon. Marshes, ponds and lakes. Stow Lake (Golden Gate Park).

Spatula clypeata. Shoveler. Marshes, ponds and lakes. Golden Gate Park.

Aix sponsa. Wood Duck. Wooded ponds and lakes. Golden Gate Park.

Aythya americana. Redhead. Lakes and Bay. Golden Gate Park.

Aythya collaris. Ring-necked Duck. Marshes, ponds and lakes. Golden Gate Park, Lake Merced.

Aythya valisineria. Canvasback. Lakes and Bay. Golden Gate Park, Lake Merced.

Aythya marila. Greater Scaup. Lakes and Bay. Golden Gate Park.

Aythya affinis. Lesser Scaup. Marshes, lakes and Bay. Stow Lake (Golden Gate Park), Lake Merced.

Aythya fuligula. Tufted Duck. Lakes. Golden Gate Park (one record).

Bucephala clangula. Common Goldeneye. Lakes and Bay. Golden Gate Park.

Bucephala albeola. Bufflehead. Ponds, lakes and Bay. Golden Gate Park, Lake Merced.

Melanitta deglandi. White-winged Scoter. Lakes, Bay and ocean. Ocean Beach, Golden Gate Park, Lake Merced.

Melanitta perspicillata. Surf Scoter. Bay and ocean. Ocean Beach, Golden Gate Park.

Oidemia nigra. Common Scoter. Bay and ocean. Ocean Beach.

Oxyura jamaicensis. Ruddy Duck. Marshes, ponds, lakes and Bay. Golden Gate Park, Lake Merced.

Lophodytes cucullatus. Hooded Merganser. Wooded ponds and lakes. Golden Gate Park.

Mergus serrator. Red-breasted Merganser. Lakes and Bay. Lake Merced.

Cathartidae,
Condors and Vultures

Cathartes aura. Turkey Vulture. Soars over fields and wooded hills. Often flies over Golden Gate Park.

Accipitridae,
Kites, Hawks and Eagles

Elanus leucurus. White-tailed Kite. Marshes and meadows. Lake Merced.

Accipiter striatus. Sharp-shinned Hawk. Woodlands. Sutro Forest, Golden Gate Park.

Accipiter cooperii. Cooper's Hawk. Woodlands. Twin Peaks, Golden Gate Park.

Buteo jamaicensis. Red-tailed Hawk. Meadows and open woodlands. Sutro Forest, Twin Peaks, Golden Gate Park.

Buteo lineatus. Red-shouldered Hawk. Woodlands. Golden Gate Park.

Buteo platypterus. Broad-winged Hawk. Woodlands. Moraga Hill (rare).

Aquila chrysaetos. Golden Eagle. Flying overhead. Twin Peaks.

Circus cyaneus. Marsh Hawk. Marshes and fields. Golden Gate Park, Lake Merced.

Panionidae, **Ospreys**

Pandion haliaetus. Osprey. Lakes and the coastline. Sutro Forest, Lake Merced.

Falconidae, **Falcons and Caracaras**

Falco sparverius. Sparrow Hawk. Open areas. Golden Gate Park.

Phasianidae, **Quail and Pheasants**

Lophortyx californicus. California Quail. Scrub and open woodlands. Golden Gate Park.

Alectoris graeca. Chukar. Grass and brush covered hills. Golden Gate Park (rare).

Rallidae, **Rails**

Rallus limicola. Virginia Rail. Marshes. Golden Gate Park, Lake Merced.

Porzana carolina. Sora. Marshes. Lake Merced.

Gallinula chloropus. Common Gallinule. Marshes. Golden Gate Park, Lake Merced.

Fulica americana. American Coot. Marshes, ponds, lakes and golf courses. Golden Gate Park, Lake Merced.

Charadriidae, **Plovers**

Charadrius semipalmatus. Semipalmated Plover. Sandy beaches and mud flats. Presidio of San Francisco.

Charadrius alexandrinus. Snowy Plover. Sandy beaches and mud flats. Presidio of San Francisco.

Charadrius vociferus. Killdeer. Shorelines, fields and tops of buildings. Golden Gate Park.

Squatarola squatarola. Black-bellied Plover. Sandy beaches and mud flats. Ocean Beach, Cliff House.

Scolopacidae, **Snipe and Sandpipers**

Aphriza virgata. Surfbird. Rocky shorelines of ocean and Bay. Ocean Beach, Cliff House.

Arenaria melanocephala. Black Turnstone. Rocky shorelines of ocean and Bay. Ocean Beach.

Capella gallinago. Common Snipe. Marshes and lake margins. Lake Merced

Numenius phaeopus. Whimbrel. Sandy beaches, mud flats and rocky shorelines. Presidio of San Francisco.

Actitis macularia. Spotted Sandpiper. Lake margins. Lake Merced.

Heteroscelus incanus. Wandering Tattler. Rocky shoreline. Ocean Beach.

Catoptrophorus semipalmatus. Willet. Sandy beaches, mud flats and rocky shorelines. Presidio of San Francisco, Ocean Beach, Lake Merced.

Erolia ptilocnemis. Rock Sandpiper. Rocky shorelines along ocean. Cliff House (rare).

Erolia minutilla. Least Sandpiper. Mud flats and lake margins. Ocean Beach.

Ereunetes mauri. Western Sandpiper. Mud flats. Ocean Beach.

Limosa fedoa. Marbled Godwit. Mud flats. Ocean Beach.

Crocethia alba. Sanderling. Sandy beaches, mud flats and rocky shorelines. Ocean Beach.

Phalaropodidae, **Phalaropes**

Lobipes lobatus. Northern Phalarope. Lakes, Bay and ocean. Golden Gate Park, Lake Merced.

Laridae, **Gulls and Terns**

Larus hyperboreus. Glaucous Gull. Lakes and coastal waterfront. Ocean Beach, Golden Gate Park (rare).

Larus glaucescens. Glaucous-winged Gull. Lakes and coastal waterfront. Ocean Beach, Golden Gate Park.

Larus occidentalis. Western Gull. Lakes and coastal waterfront. Ocean Beach, Golden Gate Park, Lake Merced.

Larus argentatus. Herring Gull. Lakes and coastal waterfront. Ocean Beach, Golden Gate Park.

Larus californicus. California Gull. Lakes and coastal waterfront. Ocean Beach, Golden Gate Park, Lake Merced.

Larus delawarensis. Ring-billed Gull. Lakes and coastal waterfront. Ocean Beach, Golden Gate Park, Lake Merced.

Larus canus. Mew Gull. Lakes and coastal waterfront. Ocean Beach, Golden Gate Park, Lake Merced.

Larus philadelphia. Bonaparte's Gull. Lakes and coastal waterfront. Golden Gate Park, Lake Merced.

Larus heermanni. Heermann's Gull Lakes and coastal waterfront. Ocean Beach, Golden Gate Park.

Xema sabini. Sabine's Gull. Ocean and sandy beach. Ocean Beach.

Sterna hirundo. Common Tern. Lakes, Bay and ocean. Presidio of San Francisco.

Thalasseus elegans. Elegant Tern. Bay and ocean. Fort Point.

Hydroprogne caspia. Caspian Tern. Lakes and Bay. Golden Gate Park, Lake Merced.

Alcidae, **Auks and Murres**

Uria aalge. Common Murre. Ocean and Bay mouth. Ocean Beach.

Cepphus columba. Pigeon Guillemot. Ocean and Bay mouth. Cliff House.

Brachyramphus marmoratum. Marbled Murrelet. Ocean. Ocean Beach (rare).

Columbidae, **Pigeons and Doves**

Columba fasciata. Band-tailed Pigeon. Woodlands. Golden Gate Park.

Columba livia. Rock Dove (Domestic Pigeon). Settled areas. Ubiquitous.

Zenaidura macroura. Mourning Dove. Vacant lots, gardens and open woodlands. Golden Gate Park.

Cuculidae, **Cuckoos and Roadrunners**

Geococcyx californianus. Roadrunner. Open areas. Lake Merced (one record).

Tytonidae, **Barn Owls**

Tyto alba. Barn Owl. Residential areas, open woodlands and fields. Golden Gate Park.

Strigidae, **Owls**

Otus asio. Screech Owl. Woodlands. Golden Gate Park.

Bubo virginianus. Great Horned Owl. Woodlands. Sutro Forest, Sigmund Stern Grove.

Speotyto cunicularia. Burrowing Owl. Open hills. Golden Gate Park, Lake Merced.

Asio otus. Long-eared Owl. Woodlands. Ingleside District.

Asio flammeus. Short-eared Owl. Marshes and fields. Sunset District.

Aegolius acadicus. Saw-whet Owl. Woodlands. Golden Gate Park.

Apodidae, Swifts

Cypseloides niger. Black Swift. Flying overhead, especially along coast. Golden Gate Park.

Chaetura vauxi. Vaux's Swift. Flying overhead. Golden Gate Park.

Aeronautes saxatalis. White-throated Swift. Flying overhead, especially along coast. Golden Gate Park, Candlestick Park.

Trochilidae, Hummingbirds

Calypte anna. Anna's Hummingbird. Scrub, woodlands and gardens. Golden Gate Park.

Selasphorus rufus. Rufous Hummingbird. Scrub, woodlands and gardens. Golden Gate Park.

Selasphorus sasin. Allen's Hummingbird. Scrub, woodlands and gardens. Golden Gate Park.

Alcedinidae, Kingfishers

Megaceryle alcyon. Belted Kingfisher. Streams, ponds and lakes. Golden Gate Park, Lake Merced.

Picidae, Woodpeckers

Colaptes auratus. Yellow-shafted Flicker. Woodlands. Golden Gate Park.

Colaptes cafer. Red-shafted Flicker. Woodlands and gardens. Golden Gate Park.

Melanerpes formicivorus. Acorn Woodpecker. Woodlands, especially oaks. Golden Gate Park.

Asyndesmus lewis. Lewis' Woodpecker. Woodlands. Golden Gate Park.

Sphyrapicus varius. Yellow-bellied Sapsucker. Woodlands. Golden Gate Park.

Dendrocopos pubescens. Downy Woodpecker. Woodlands. Golden Gate Park.

Tyrannidae, Tyrant Flycatchers

Myiarchus cinerascens. Ash-throated Flycatcher. Open woodlands. Golden Gate Park.

Sayornis phoebe. Eastern Phoebe. Margins of fresh water. Golden Gate Park.

Sayornis nigricans. Black Phoebe. Open areas, usually near water. Golden Gate Park, Lake Merced.

Sayornis saya. Say's Phoebe. Grassy areas. Twin Peaks.

Empidonax traillii. Traill's Flycatcher. Scrub and open woodland, often near water. Golden Gate Park.

Empidonax difficilis. Western Flycatcher. Woodlands. Golden Gate Park.

Contopus sordidulus. Western Wood Pewee. Woodlands. Golden Gate Park.

Nuttallornis borealis. Olive-sided Flycatcher. Woodlands. Sutro Forest, Twin Peaks, Golden Gate Park.

Alaudidae, Larks

Eremophila alpestris. Horned Lark. Fields and sand dunes. Presidio of San Francisco, Twin Peaks.

Hirundinidae, Swallows

Tachycineta thalassina. Violet-green Swallow. Open areas. Golden Gate Park, Lake Merced.

Riparia riparia. Bank Swallow. Open areas. Ocean Beach, Lake Merced.

Stelgidopteryx ruficollis. Rough-winged Swallow. Open areas. Ocean Beach, Lake Merced.

Hirundo rustica. Barn Swallow. Open areas. Golden Gate Park, Lake Merced.

Petrochelidon pyrrhonota. Cliff Swallow. Open areas. Lake Merced.

Progne subis. Purple Martin. Open areas. Lake Merced.

Corvidae,
Jays, Magpies and Crows

Cyanocitta stelleri. Steller's Jay. Coniferous forests. Golden Gate Park.

Aphelocoma coerulescens. Scrub Jay. Woodlands. Golden Gate Park.

Corvus corax. Common Raven. Coastal cliffs. Golden Gate Park, Lake Merced.

Corvus brachyrhynchos. Common Crow. Woodlands and open areas. Presidio of San Francisco, Golden Gate Park.

Nucifraga columbiana. Clark's Nutcracker. Woodlands. Presidio of San Francisco, Twin Peaks (rare).

Paridae, **Chickadees and Bushtits**

Parus rufescens. Chestnut-backed Chickadee. Coniferous forests. Golden Gate Park.

Psaltriparus minimus. Common Bushtit. Woodlands and scrub. Golden Gate Park.

Sittidae, **Nuthatches**

Sitta carolinensis. White-breasted Nuthatch. Oak woodland. Golden Gate Park.

Sitta canadensis. Red-breasted Nuthatch. Woodlands. Twin Peaks, Golden Gate Park.

Sitta pygmaea. Pygmy Nuthatch. Pine woodlands. Golden Gate Park.

Certhiidae, **Creepers**

Certhia familiaris. Brown Creeper. Forests. Golden Gate Park.

Chamaeidae, **Wrentit**

Chamaea fasciata. Wrentit. Scrub. Golden Gate Park.

Troglodytidae, **Wrens**

Troglodytes aedon. House Wren. Scrub and woodland undergrowth. Golden Gate Park.

Troglodytes troglodytes. Winter Wren. Woodland undergrowth. Twin Peaks, Golden Gate Park.

Thryomanes bewickii. Bewick's Wren. Scrub and woodland undergrowth. Golden Gate Park.

Telmatodytes palustris. Long-billed Marsh Wren. Marshes. Lake Merced.

Mimidae,
Mockingbirds and Thrashers

Mimus polyglottos. Mockingbird. Residential areas. Presidio of San Francisco.

Turdidae, **Thrushes**

Turdus migratorius. Robin. Meadows, gardens and woodlands. Golden Gate Park.

Ixoreus naevius. Varied Thrush. Forest undergrowth. Golden Gate Park.

Hylocichla guttata. Hermit Thrush. Woodland undergrowth. Golden Gate Park.

Hylocichla ustulata. Swainson's Thrush. Woodland undergrowth. Golden Gate Park.

Sialia mexicana. Western Bluebird. Meadows and other open areas. Golden Gate Park.

Myadestes townsendi. Townsend's Solitaire. Woodlands. Golden Gate Park (rare).

Sylviidae,
Old World Warblers and Kinglets

Regulus satrapa. Golden-crowned Kinglet. Woodland, especially coniferous forests. Golden Gate Park, Lake Merced.

Regulus calendula. Ruby-crowned Kinglet. Woodlands. Golden Gate Park, Lake Merced.

Motacillidae, **Pipits**

Anthus spinoletta. Water Pipit. Fields and margins of fresh water. Golden Gate Park.

Bombycillidae, **Waxwings**

Bombycilla cedrorum. Cedar Waxwing. Woodlands, residential areas. Golden Gate Park.

Laniidae, **Shrikes**

Lanius ludovicianus. Loggerhead Shrike. Fields. Twin Peaks.

Sturnidae, **Starlings**

Sturnus vulgaris. Starling. Open fields and city parks. Golden Gate Park.

Vireonidae, **Vireos**

Vireo huttoni. Hutton's Vireo. Woodlands. Golden Gate Park, Lake Merced.

Vireo solitarius. Solitary Vireo. Woodlands. Golden Gate Park.

Vireo gilvus. Warbling Vireo. Woodlands. Twin Peaks, Golden Gate Park.

Parulidae, **Wood Warblers**

Protonotaria citrea. Prothonotary Warbler. Margins of wooded lakes. Lincoln Park (one record).

Vermivora pinus. Blue-winged Warbler. Woodlands. San Francisco (one record).

Vermivora peregrina. Tennessee Warbler. Woodlands. Lake Merced (rare).

Vermivora celata. Orange-crowned Warbler. Scrub and woodlands. Twin Peaks, Golden Gate Park.

Dendroica petechia. Yellow Warbler. Woodlands. Golden Gate Park.

Dendroica caerulescens. Black-throated Blue Warbler. Woodlands. Lake Merced (rare).

Dendroica coronata. Myrtle Warbler. Woodlands. Lake Merced.

Dendroica auduboni. Audubon's Warbler. Woodlands. Golden Gate Park, Lake Merced.

Dendroica nigrescens. Black-throated Gray Warbler. Woodlands. Golden Gate Park.

Dendroica townsendi. Townsend's Warbler. Woodlands, especially coniferous forests. Golden Gate Park.

Dendroica occidentalis. Hermit Warbler. Woodlands, especially coniferous forests. Twin Peaks.

Seiurus noveboracensis. Northern Waterthrush. Margins of wooded lakes and streams. Golden Gate Park (rare).

Oporornis tolmiei. MacGillivray's Warbler. Scrub and woodland undergrowth. Lincoln Park.

Geothlypis trichas. Yellowthroat. Marshes and lake edge. Golden Gate Park.

Icteria virens. Yellow-breasted Chat. Scrub and open woodland undergrowth. Lake Merced.

Wilsonia pusilla. Wilson's Warbler. Woodlands. Golden Gate Park.

Ploceidae, **Weaverbirds**

Passer domesticus. House Sparrow. Ubiquitous. Gardens, parks and vacant lots.

Icteridae, **Orioles, Meadowlarks & Blackbirds**

Sturnella neglecta. Western Meadowlark. Grassy areas. Golden Gate Park, Lake Merced.

Xanthocephalus xanthocephalus. Yellow-headed Blackbird. Marshes. Golden Gate Park.

Agelaius phoeniceus. Red-winged Blackbird. Marshes, lake margins and parks. Golden Gate Park.

Agelaius tricolor. Tricolored Blackbird. Marshes and fields. Presidio of San Francisco.

Icterus cucullatus. Hooded Oriole. Woodlands and residential areas. San Francisco gardens.

Icterus bullockii. Bullock's Oriole. Woodlands and residential areas. Golden Gate Park.

Euphagus cyanocephalus. Brewer's Blackbird. Open areas. Golden Gate Park, Lake Merced.

Molothrus ater. Brown-headed Cowbird. Woodlands and open areas. Lake Merced.

Thraupidae, Tanagers

Piranga luboviciana. Western Tanager. Woodlands. Twin Peaks, Golden Gate Park.

Fringillidae, Sparrows, Buntings and Finches

Pheucticus ludovicianus. Rose-breasted Grosbeak. Woodlands. Golden Gate Park.

Pheucticus melanocephalus. Black-headed Grosbeak. Woodlands. Golden Gate Park.

Passerina amoena. Lazuli Bunting. Scrub. Golden Gate Park.

Carpodacus purpureus. Purple Finch. Woodlands. Sutro Forest, Golden Gate Park.

Carpodacus mexicanus. House Finch. Woodlands, residential areas, and open areas. Ubiquitous.

Spinus pinus. Pine Siskin. Woodlands. Golden Gate Park.

Spinus tristis. American Goldfinch. Fields and scrub. Lake Merced.

Spinus psaltria. Lesser Goldfinch. Fields and scrub. Glen Park.

Spinus lawrencei. Lawrence's Goldfinch. Fields and scrub. Golden Gate Park.

Loxia Curvirostra. Red Crossbill. Coniferous woodlands. Golden Gate Park.

Piplo erythrophthalmus. Rufous-sided Towhee. Scrub and woodland undergrowth. Golden Gate Park.

Pipilo fuscus. Brown Towhee. Scrub and gardens. Twin Peaks.

Passerculus sandwichensis. Savannah Sparrow. Marshes and fields. Presidio of San Francisco, Twin Peaks, Lake Merced.

Junco oreganus. Oregon Junco. Woodlands. Twin Peaks, Golden Gate Park.

Spizella passerina. Chipping Sparrow. Open woodlands. Twin Peaks.

Zonotrichia leucophrys. White-crowned Sparrow. Scrub and gardens. Golden Gate Park.

Zonotrichia albicollis. White-throated Sparrow. Woodland undergrowth. Golden Gate Park.

Zonotrichia atricapilla. Golden-crowned Sparrow. Scrub and gardens. Golden Gate Park.

Passerella iliaca. Fox Sparrow. Scrub and woodland undergrowth. Golden Gate Park, Lake Merced.

Melospiza melodia. Song Sparrow. Marshes and scrub. Golden Gate Park.

Geology

San Francisco is based on a foundation of sandstone (graywacke type), shale, and volcanic rock with minor amounts of ferruginous. Called by geologists the Franciscan Formation, the rock is first seen on entering the Bay from the Pacific at Point Lobos.

Within San Francisco, colored chert and other Franciscan rocks are visible in Golden Gate Park, Twin Peaks, and along the Alemany Freeway.

San Francisco County Minerals

Apophyllite	Datolite	Pectolite
Aragonite	Diallage	Prehnite
Barite	Diopside (lilac)	Psilomelane
Brucite	Enstatite	Pryolusite
Calcite	Gyrolite	Quartz
Chalcedony	Hydromagnesite	Sphene
Chromite	Jasper (var. Kinvadite)	Wollastonite
Cinnabar	Magnesite	Xonotlite
Curtisite	Mercury	

Some of these minerals were found many years ago, in mines now long abandoned; others are of rare or single occurrence, still others are so unusual for the area in which they are reported to occur that they need verification.

Earthquakes

"The Results and Lessons of the Earthquake"
October 21, 1868. 7:53 A.M.

"The State was visited yesterday by an earthquake, and the shock in San Francisco was the most severe felt here since the foundation of the Mission, ninety-two years ago, with perhaps one exception, in 1808, when several adobe walls were thrown down, but of that shock we know so little that it is impossible to make any satisfactory comparison with it.

"Amidst the multitude of slight movements of the earth's surface observed here since 1848, the only one which did any damage before that of yesterday occurred on the 8th of October, 1865, when several cornices and parts of green brick walls were thrown down. In that shock the motion was mainly perpendicular, and perhaps it was for that reason that the amount of glass broken was far greater in 1865 than in the horizontal movement of 1868. On the other hand, more cornices were thrown down yesterday.

"The main facts of the earthquake as felt in this city, are that four persons were killed by the falling of cornices and chimneys, that a dozen brick buildings on made ground are shattered so that they are untenantable; that the cornices of two buildings have been thrown down, and many walls cracked, much plastering loosened and many window panes broken.

"On the other hand, no person was seriously injured in a house, and the great majority of the buildings on the natural upland show no signs of having been damaged in the least.

"The spires of the churches, towers of the Masonic Temple, Merchants Exchange and Synagogue Emanuel, the four and five story buildings on Montgomery and Kearny Streets, are uninjured.

"The foundations of buildings should, on the made ground, be as solid as possible; and high chimneys should be secured by iron bars, fastened on with bands and running down below to top of wall. Brick buildings should be tied together by strong iron rods, their walls should be thick, the best mortar should be used and the height should not exceed three stories."

—*Daily Alta California*, October 22, 1868.

1865 Earthquake depicted by contemporary cartoonist.

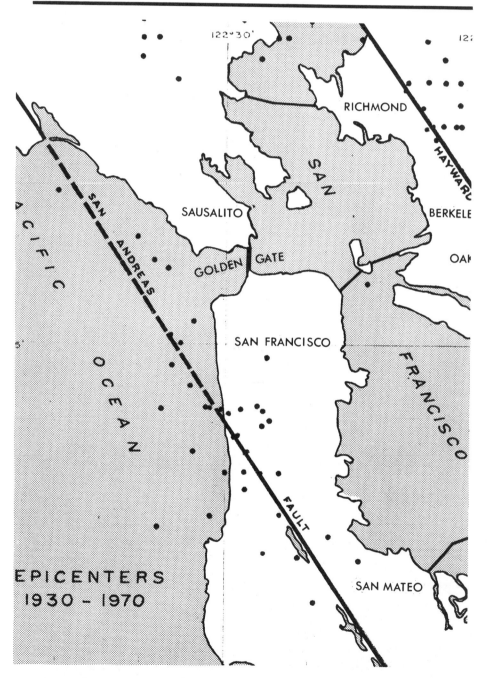

San Andreas Fault. (Dots mark epicenters of activity between 1930 and 1970.)

Tent city on Nob Hill after 1906 Earthquake.

1906

April 18, 1906

Time - 5.12:06 a.m. - 5.13:11 a.m.

Magnitude - 8.25 Richter scale

Duration - 48 seconds

Fire temperature - 2700°F (52 original fires were officially reported, over 300 breaks in water mains, and more than 23,000 service pipes broken.)

Buildings destroyed by fire - 28,000

Area of destruction - 4.11 square miles

Gas and electric arc street lamps destroyed - 2,465 gas; 180 electric arc

Cost of destruction - $350,000,000

Amount of rubble - 10 to 11 million cubic yards of rubble had to be removed before reconstruction could commence.

Air temperature - 8:00 a.m. 51.5°; 8:00 p.m. 61.8°

Deaths - Killed outright 315; Shot for crime 6; Shot by mistake 1; Missing 352; Total: 674

They all predicted it. Eastern insurance men always said "San Francisco is bound to burn down or up. It is a wooden city and some day a fire will get beyond control of your fire department, excellent as it is." (Coast Review, May 1906)

1957

March 22. The strongest shock since the 1906 earthquake was experienced by San Francisco and the Bay Area at 11:45.20 on the morning of Friday, March 22, 1957. It registered 5.3 on the Richter scale and for a whole new generation of the local population it was the greatest earthquake they had ever experienced. Earlier in the day two other quakes had been felt, the first at 8:38 a.m. was 3 on the Richter scale and the second at 10:48 a.m., was 3.75 on the Richter scale.

No lives were lost, there were no serious injuries, and structural damage to homes was slight, although a large number of homes in the Westlake-Palisades-Daly City area suffered more or less superficial damage, being generally confined to exterior plaster. Damage to buildings in San Francisco was noted throughout the city, but was probably most extensive in the western portions.

Family portrait following 1868 Earthquake.

Richter Scale

Richter Scale Magnitude	Equivalent Energy			
1.0	.6 ounces TNT	5.5	.1,000 tons	TNT
1.5	.2 pounds TNT	6.0	.6,270 tons	TNT
2.0	.13 pounds TNT	6.5	.31,550 tons	TNT
2.5	.63 pounds TNT	7.0	.199,000 tons	TNT
3.0	.397 pounds TNT	7.5	.1,000,000 tons	TNT
3.5	.1,990 pounds TNT	8.0	.6,270,000 tons	TNT
4.0	.6 tons TNT	8.5	.31,550,000 tons	TNT
4.5	.32 tons TNT	9.0	.199,000,000 tons	TNT
5.0	.199 tons TNT			

(Based on California Division of Mines and Geology data)

Mercalli Earthquake Intensity Scale

The following scale can be used in populated areas to judge the strength of earthquakes before the official Richter reading is given.

1. Not felt except by a very few under especially favorable conditions.

2. Felt only by those at rest on upper floors. Delicately suspended objects may swing.

3. Noticeably felt indoors on upper floors. Automobiles may rock slightly. Vibration like passing of truck.

4. Felt indoors by many, few outdoors. Dishes, windows, doors disturbed; walls make creaking sound. Standing motor-cars rocked noticeably.

5. Felt by nearly everyone. Some windows, dishes broken; a few instances of cracked plaster. Pendulum clocks may stop.

6. Felt by all. Heavy furniture may move, a few instances of fallen plaster or damaged chimneys. Damage slight.

7. Everybody runs outdoors. Damage negligible in buildings of good design and construction; slight to moderate in well-built ordinary structures; considerable in poorly built or badly designed structures; some chimneys broken. Felt by those in automobiles.

8. Damage slight in specially designed structures; considerable in ordinary buildings, with partial collapse; great in poorly built structures. Panel walls thrown out of frame structures. Fall of chimneys, factory stacks, columns, monuments, walls. Heavy furniture overturned. Sand and mud ejected in small amounts. Changes in well water. Persons driving automobiles disturbed.

9. Damage considerable in specially designed structures; well-designed frame structures thrown out of plumb; great in substantial buildings, with partial collapse. Buildings shifted off foundations. Ground cracked conspicuously. Underground pipes broken.

10. Some well-built wooden structures destroyed; most masonry and frame structures destroyed with foundations; ground badly cracked. Rails bent. Landslides considerable from river banks and steep slopes. Shifted sand and mud. Water splashed over banks.

11. Few, if any, masonry, structures remain standing. Bridges destroyed. Broad fissures in ground. Under-ground pipelines completely out of service. Earth slumps and land slips in soft ground. Rails bent greatly.

12. Damage total. Waves seen on ground surfaces. Lines of sight and level distorted. Objects thrown upward into air.

Institutions

Cemeteries

On March 26, 1900, the Board of Supervisors passed Bill No. 54, Ordinance No. 25, "Prohibiting the Burial of the Dead Within the City and County of San Francisco from and after the First day of August, 1901." It was approved by Mayor James D. Phelan, on March 30, 1900.

In 1914 the Board of Health sent out notices to all persons owning or claiming lots in Calvary, Masonic, Odd Fellow and Laurel Hill cemeteries to remove within 14 months from January 17, 1914, all bodies as they had been declared to be "a public nuisance and a menace and detriment to the public health and welfare."

Today, there remain within the city limits two cemeteries. They are:

Mission Dolores Cemetery. Located alongside Mission Dolores Church, Dolores Street, between 16th and 17th Streets. First burial in Mission Dolores cemetery took place on December 21, 1776.

National Cemetery, Presidio of San Francisco. 25 acres, the first interment was on July 23, 1852. It was made a National Cemetery in 1884.

Early Burial Grounds

North Beach - 50 vara lot on corner of Powell & Lombard. (Vara = 137½ feet square)

Telegraph Hill - Southerly slope.

Russian Hill - Summit of.

Calvary Cemetery *(Catholic).* 48 acres bounded by Geary, Turk, St. Josephs, and Masonic Ave. Cemetery dedicated November 8, 1860. Bodies moved to Holy Cross Cemetery, San Mateo County.

Chinese Cemetery. Located at the rear of Laurel Hill Cemetery from Parker Avenue west. Later moved to Golden Gate Cemetery.

Gibbath Olom Cemetery *(Hills of Eternity - Jewish).* Located at Dolores and Church, and 19th and 20th Streets. Opened February 26, 1861, closed December 31, 1888.

Golden Gate Cemetery *(Clement Street Cemetery & City Cemetery).* Roughly 200 acres of land purchased by the

Masonic Cemetary. (St. Ignatius Church in background.)

city in 1868 for cemetery purposes. Located at Clement Street and 33rd Ave. In 1909 the supervisors secured consent of the various cemetery organizations for the use of the land as a park. Today many bodies remain buried beneath the turf of Lincoln Golf Park.

Greek Cemetery. Located on ground purchased from Archbishop Alemany, south of Odd Fellows Cemetery on a sand hill, (Stanyan & Golden Gate Avenue). Access was through Odd Fellows Cemetery. Cemetery later moved to Golden Gate Cemetery.

Hebrew Cemetery. Two 50 vara lots located at Broadway & Vallejo, Franklin & Gough. Cemetery used for the period 1850-1860.

Laurel Hill Cemetery. See Lone Mountain.

Lone Mountain Cemetery. Bounded by California, Geary, Parker and Presidio Aves. Cemetery dedicated May 30, 1854. Renamed Laurel Hill Cemetery in 1867. Bodies moved to Cypress Lawn Cemetery, San Mateo County. Tombstones used on seawall.

Masonic Cemetery. Masonic Cemetery Association organized January 26, 1864, on 30 acres bounded by Turk and Fulton, Parker and Masonic Ave.

Nevai Shalome Cemetery *(Home of Peace - Jewish).* Located at Dolores & Church and 18th and 19th Streets. Opened July 25, 1860, closed December 31, 1888.

Odd Fellows Cemetery. Cemetery dedicated November 19, 1865. Located at Geary & Turk, Parker & Arguello. Bodies moved to Greenlawn Cemetery in Colma. Stonework from cemetery used on seawall at Aquatic Park.

Yerba Buena Cemetery. 10 acres bounded by Market, Larkin and McAllister Streets. Burials made 1850-1861. Bodies exhumed and moved to Golden Gate Cemetery in 1870.

Birth and Death Records Available for San Francisco

Births. All local records prior to April 18, 1906 were destroyed, with the exception of July 1st, 1905, to March 31, 1906. These are on file with the State Registrar of Vital Statistics, Sacramento, California.

Deaths. Only the following death records are available, most were destroyed in the 1906 earthquake and fire.

Book 1 - Nov. 8, 1865 to Sept. 30, 1869.

Book 2 - Oct. 1, 1869 to Apr. 30, 1873.

Book 3 - April 1, 1882 to June 30, 1889 (Coroner's cases only).

Book M - August 1, 1894 to June 30, 1896.

Book O - July 1, 1898 to March 16, 1900.

Book P - Mar. 17, 1900 to Oct. 22, 1901.

Book Q - Oct. 23, 1901 to June 30, 1903.

Book R - July 1, 1903 to June 30, 1904.

Churches

(Limited to those of historical or architectural interest.)

Chapel of Our Lady
Presidio of San Francisco

The original adobe chapel put up in 1776 collapsed in the 1812 earthquake. The second chapel built on the same spot burned in 1846 and was replaced in 1873 by a New England styled chapel, which served as a house of worship for both Catholic and Protestant military men until 1931. The present remodeled chapel is now used for Catholic services only.

First Baptist Church of San Francisco
Market and Octavia Streets

The first church building was erected on Washington, near Stockton, in 1849. It was followed by a new church located on Eddy, between Jones and Leavenworth, which was dedicated July 29, 1877. After the destruction of their church in the 1906 earthquake and fire, the congregation sought out a new location and purchased property at Octavia and Market Streets. Ground was broken on August 30, 1909 and today's church, of classic design was dedicated on September 14, 1910.

First Unitarian Church
1187 Franklin Street

First located at Stockton near Sacramento in a building dedicated July 17, 1853, later moving to Geary Street near Stockton in 1864.

Today's stone church located at 1187 Franklin Street was dedicated February 9, 1889. Damage to the amount of $16,300.00 was suffered in 1906 when a portion of the bell tower crashed through the roof, but the church reopened September 16, 1906. Thomas Starr King, the church's most famous clergyman, is buried beneath a small marble sarcophagus in front of the church.

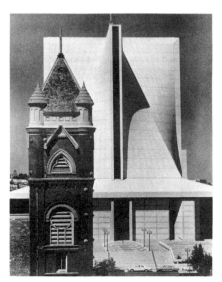

Cathedral Hill. (St. Mark's Lutheran in foreground, silhouetted against St. Mary's Cathedral.)

Holy Trinity Russian (Eastern) Orthodox Cathedral
1520 Green Street

Built in 1868 at 1715 Powell Street, the Holy Trinity Russian Orthodox Cathedral was the first Russian cathedral built in the United States.

The Cathedral was completely destroyed in the earthquake and fire of 1906, but its seven bells were saved and installed in the new $10,000 church relocated at 1520 Green Street in 1909.

Mission San Francisco de Assisi
Mission Dolores
Dolores and Sixteenth Streets

Fray Francisco Palou established the first Mission Dolores, a brush shelter, at about 18th and Church Streets in June 1776. This site served until the present adobe mission was completed in 1791.

Grace Cathedral
California and Taylor Streets

The second Episcopal church to be known as Grace was constructed in 1860 at California and Stockton Streets. From the time Bishop William I. Kip placed his Bishop's Chair in the new church in 1861 it was known as Grace Cathedral, until destroyed by the earthquake and fire of 1906.

The new Grace Cathedral, built on land donated by the Crocker family (California, Sacramento, Jones, Leavenworth), had its cornerstone laid by Bishop William Ford Nichols on Jan. 24, 1910. Lewis P. Hobart, the architect, described the Gothic-spired church as "a truly American Cathedral." The third largest Episcopal Cathedral in the United States was consecrated on Friday, November 20, 1964 and Sunday, November 22, 1964.

The adobe Mission Dolores.

The Church, built completely by Indians, is 114 feet long, 22 feet wide, with adobe walls four feet thick.

On April 4, 1952, Mission Dolores was designated a Minor Basilica by Pope Pius XII. It was the fourth such designation in the United States and the first west of the Mississippi.

Notre Dame des Victoires
566 Bush Street

The exterior of today's church, built in 1913, is copied from Notre Dame de Fourvieres, in Lyons, France. The first church building located on the same site was consecrated by Archbishop Alemany on May 4, 1856 and destroyed in 1906.

Old First Presbyterian
Van Ness Avenue and Sacramento

The first church building was shipped around the Horn and erected at Stockton, between Broadway and Pacific. Dedication services were held January 19, 1851. It was destroyed by fire in less than six months and a new church was dedicated October 12, 1851.

Another dedication took place May 13, 1858 when an ornate brick building began service as the new church.

The final move in 1882 brought the church to the corner of Van Ness Avenue and Sacramento Street where it was destroyed by fire in 1906. It was rebuilt in 1911 and is said to be "the finest piece of Byzantine architecture on the West Coast."

Old St. Patrick's
820-22 Eddy Street
(next to Holy Cross Church)

The oldest frame church building in San Francisco began as St. Patrick's Church on the site where the Palace Hotel now stands. Built in 1851, the parish limits were bounded by Pine, Ninth, Mission Creek, and the Bay. It

was moved in 1873 to Eddy, between Octavia and Laguna, and called St. John the Baptist Church. In 1891 it moved again to its present location where it served as Holy Cross Church until the new church was completed in 1899. It now serves as Holy Cross Parish Hall.

Russian Holy Virgin Cathedral of the Church in Exile
6210 Geary Boulevard

The cornerstone of the new Russian Orthodox Cathedral at Geary, between 26th and 27th Avenues, was laid June 25, 1961. Oleg N. Ivanitsky, the architect, noted "the cathedral will be built to the highest standards of Russian ecclesiastical architecture," and "will be the largest and most beautiful on the Pacific Coast." Previously the Holy Virgin Cathedral was located at Fulton near Fillmore, where the church building was originally built as an Episcopal Church called St. Stephen's in 1880.

St. Boniface Church
133 Golden Gate Avenue

The first St. Boniface church, at Sutter, between Montgomery and Kearny Streets, was dedicated April 15, 1860.

Relocating on Golden Gate Avenue, three churches have been dedicated on this site. The first on June 5, 1870; the second on October 23, 1887; and the present church, in Rhineland Romanesque style of pressed stone, on November 1, 1908.

St. Dominic's Church
Bush & Steiner Streets

The Dominican Fathers opened a small wooden church at Bush and Steiner Streets in 1873. In 1886 a large brick church was dedicated and used until destroyed in 1906 by the earthquake. The present 8-spired Gothic church has been in use since 1928.

St. Francis of Assisi
610 Vallejo Street

The first parish church built within the limits of Yerba Buena was dedicated June 17, 1849. In 1972, after 123 years of continuous service, a bronze plaque was unveiled proclaiming the church as Registered Landmark No. 5. The white, twin-towered Gothic church, whose walls withstood the 1906 earthquake and fire, is the only church in the United States where a mass is said in Chinese.

St. Ignatius Church
Fulton Street and Parker Avenue

A parish church on Market Street until made a college church in October, 1863. The new relocated St. Ignatius was constructed at Van Ness and Hayes and dedicated on February 1, 1880. Destroyed in 1906, the grey brick church was rebuilt at Fulton and Parker Avenue at a cost of $300,000 and dedicated in 1914.

St. John's Presbyterian
1-25 Lake Street

Since 1905, the site of this Gothic shingle church has been the southwest corner of Arguello and Lake. First located at Post and Mason Streets in 1870, it was relocated at California and Octavia, in 1889. Damaged in 1906 by the earthquake it was formally dedicated April 28, 1907.

St. Luke's Episcopal Church
Van Ness at Clay

Founded in 1868 on Pacific between Polk and Van Ness, it moved to its present site in 1884. The new church, which opened in 1900, was destroyed in 1906 but four years later the present stone church was dedicated.

St. Mark's Evangelical Lutheran
1111-1135 O'Farrell Street

In 1866 three Lutheran congregations united, taking the name St. Mark's Evangelical Lutheran Church. The present site was purchased in 1893 and the Van Ness Avenue and O'Farrell Street Gothic designed church was dedicated in 1895.

St. Mary's Cathedral
Geary and Gough

The Catholic cathedral has been located in four different locations since 1849. The first Cathedral of San Francisco was the little frame shanty built as St. Francis' Church by Father Langlois in 1849.

From 1853 to 1891 the present Old St. Mary's Church, at California and Grant Avenue, served as the cathedral. On January 11, 1891 the new cathedral at Van Ness Avenue and O'Farrell Street was dedicated. It was used for 71 years until destroyed by fire September 7, 1962.

The present cathedral, located atop Cathedral Hill, at Geary and Gough Streets, was dedicated May 5, 1971. The architects were Angus McSweeney, Paul Ryan, and Jack Lee. The $7-million building unites the Nave, Sanctuary, Trancept, Baptistry, and Narthex in one space, crowned by a colorful skylight shaped in the form of a cross. The windows represent the four elements: the blue north window, water; the light colored south window, the sun; the red west window, fire; the green east window, earth. The cathedral seats 2,400 people.

St. Patrick's
756 Mission Street

The present church properties were purchased in 1862 and the church dedicated by Archbishop Alemany on March

17, 1872. Destroyed in 1906 the church was rebuilt using many of the original bricks. Fire scars are still apparent on the original walls of this Victorian Gothic structure.

St. Paulus Evangelical Lutheran Church
999 Eddy Street

This Gothic church, dedicated in 1894, was saved from the 1906 fire but was nearly destroyed by fire in 1940. St. Paulus is a wooden reproduction of the Cathedral at Chartres.

Sts. Peter & Paul Church
666 Filbert Street

Designed by Charles Fantoni after the earthquake and fire, this church is sometimes called "The Italian Cathedral." The Romanesque designed church was dedicated March 30, 1924. Previously, when founded in 1884, it had been located at Grant Avenue and Filbert Street.

Swedenborgian Church
2107 Lyon Street

A. Page Brown was the architect of this rustic little church which seats only 80 people. It was built in 1894 with emphasis on natural objects, many with religious symbolism. William Keith paintings grace the north wall. The church was first established in 1849 and by 1865 was housed in a small, wooden building on O'Farrell, between Taylor and Mason

Streets. Thirty years later funds were raised for the new building.

Temple Emanu-El
Arguello and Lake

Built in 1925 at a cost of $3,000,000 to replace the earlier Temple at Sutter and Powell Streets destroyed in 1906. The architects for this Byzantine stucco building were Schnaittacher, Bakewell and Brown. The building was completed in 1927.

Temple Sherith Israel (Loyal Remnant of Israel)
California and Webster Streets

Albert Pissis served as the architect of this brownstone domed Temple whose cornerstone was laid February 22, 1904. The synagogue was consecrated on September 24, 1905 on which occasion the principal address was delivered by Jacob Voorsanger.

Suffering only $1,000 damage to the roof during the 1906 earthquake, this building received public attention when it served as the courthouse for the Ruef-Schmidt trials.

Trinity Episcopal Church
1668 Bush Street

In 1849 located at the southwest corner of Powell and Jackson, later moved to Pine near Montgomery. By 1867 this building was felt to be too small, so a new church rose at Post and Powell. Since 1892 the sandstone Norman styled church has stood at Bush and Gough Streets.

Hospitals

California Podiatry Hospital
19 Farren Street

Specialized hospital for the surgical treatment of diseases and disorders of the feet, established in 1914.

The Children's Hospital
3700 California Street

Dating back to 1875 when, on March 23, the first organizational step was taken. Opened as the Pacific Dispensary at 509 Taylor Street, then moved to 201½ Stockton Street, and later to 228 Post Street. In 1885 the present site of the hospital was secured and a new building was dedicated in October, 1911. New wings and buildings have been added since.

The Chinese Hospital
835 Jackson Street

Opened on April 18, 1925 to provide medical and hospital care for the Chinese population in San Francisco and neighboring communities. It is an outgrowth of the dispensary for the care and treatment of the poor which was first opened in 1900 by the Chinese Six Companies.

Franklin Hospital
Castro and Duboce Avenue

Until World War I known as the German Hospital. Cornerstone laid at Brannan Street on August 29, 1857; the second German Hospital was constructed in 1877 at 14th & Noe Streets followed by a third which was dedicated on June 27, 1908. The new Franklin Hospital, now called Ralph K. Davies Medical Center, opened February, 1969.

French Hospital
Geary Blvd. between 5th and 6th Avenues

Founded in 1851 by Etienne Dervec on Rincon Hill, as San Francisco's first private hospital. The hospital was relocated in 1856 at Bryant and Fifth Streets, and moved to its present location in 1895. The new French Hospital was dedicated May 4, 1963.

Garden Hospital - Jerd Sullivan Rehabilitation Center
2750 Geary Boulevard

In 1890, a circle of King's Daughters (international nonsectarian order) voted to devote themselves to the care of in-curable men and women and geriatric patients. The first home was situated on the corner of Francisco and Stockton Streets, relocating later at Golden Gate Avenue near Broderick Street, and still later at 1024 Franklin Street. Known as the Garden Hospital since the early 1940's, the 132-bed hospital is now called the Garden Hospital - Jerd Sullivan Rehabilitation Center.

Golden Gate Community Hospital
1065 Sutter Street

Organized as the Sutter Hospital on November 14, 1927 by the Doctors Jacobs. It was also called the Doctors Hospital until the name was changed to Golden Gate Community Hospital in 1960.

Harkness Community Hospital & Medical Center
1400 Fell Street

Built in 1910 as the central hospital for medical service of the Southern Pacific Railway, the Pacific System. The Harkness Annex was built in 1931, a gift of Edward S. Harkness. In 1967 the name of the hospital was changed to Harkness Community Hospital. The hospital closed Aug. 26, 1974.

Kaiser Permanente Medical Center
2425 Geary Boulevard

The Kaiser Industrial Organization consists of about 100 active companies and subsidiaries. The major companies are Kaiser Aluminum, Kaiser Steel, Kaiser Cement and Gypsum and Kaiser Engineers. Kaiser's unusual interest in community health is most prominently evident in the Kaiser Foundation Medical Care Program, also known as the Kaiser-Permanente Medical Care Program. The six-story $2,300,000 hospital built in the Anza Vista District opened in 1954.

Letterman General Hospital
Presidio of San Francisco

General Order No. 182 issued by the War Department on December 1, 1898 created Letterman General Hospital, named after Major Jonathan Letterman. It was the first hospital to be named after a military dignitary. The new 10-story hospital, located near the Lombard Street Gate, was completed in 1969 at a cost of $13,000,000. Construction of an additional wing began in 1972.

Marshal Hale Memorial Hospital
3733 Sacramento Street

Organized on January 12, 1881 as the Homoeopathic Medical College and incorporated under the laws of the State of California on January 20, 1881. New articles of incorporation were drawn up in November 1887, and the name changed to the Hahnemann Hospital College of San Francisco. Located on Haight Street above Octavia (115 Haight) until 1901 when the college moved to Sacramento and Maple Streets. The Children's Hospital Auxiliary purchased the college building in 1922. A new building was constructed on California Street and still later, in the 1970's the hospital was relocated in new quarters on Sacramento Street. Hospital renamed Marshall Hale Memorial Hospital in March 1975.

Mount Zion Hospital & Medical Center
1600 Divisadero

On November 3, 1887, forty three San Franciscans met to talk of founding a Jewish Hospital, and did so in the home of Dr. Julius Rosenstein at Sutter and Hyde Streets. In 1898 new quarters were located on Sutter, between Scott and Divisadero Streets. In 1913 a $300,000 brick building at Post and Scott Streets was completed which today stands surrounded by new wings and buildings.

Pacific Medical Center
Clay and Webster Streets

The Stanford University Hospital was organized as Lane Hospital in 1893 as a teaching hospital in connection with Cooper Medical College. Stanford Hospital was built and opened in December, 1917 for the care of private patients under the leadership of Dr. Levi Cooper Lane. On May 1, 1960 the Stanford Lane Hospital became the Presbyterian Medical Center. Ground for the new hospital was broken February 27, 1970 and it opened in April, 1973.

St. Elizabeth Infant Hospital
100 Masonic Avenue

Established in 1921 at 2530 Van Ness Avenue is a home for unmarried pregnant girls by the Daughters of St. Vincent de Paul. The new building at 100 Masonic Avenue was constructed in 1928 and has since been remodeled.

St. Francis Hospital
Hyde & Pine Streets

Founded in 1905 by a group of physicians and operated as a private hospital until 1938. In that year it was reorganized as a non-profit, non-sectarian general hospital. The new $11,000,000 hospital was dedicated in April, 1969.

St. Joseph's Hospital
355 Buena Vista Avenue

Located on Buena Vista Heights the hospital is a non-profit, charitable corporation organized under the laws of the State of California, July 26, 1906, and is operated by the Franciscan Sisters of the Sacred Heart.

St. Luke's Hospital
3555 Army Street

Established in 1871 as a benevolent non-profit institution, under the auspices of the Episcopal Church. It was originally located in two houses on Bernal Heights.

In 1875 the hospital was moved to its present location and a new building completed in 1913. Dedication of the present hospital took place August 28, 1970.

St. Mary's Hospital
Hayes & Stanyan Streets
Opened in quarters of old City & County Hospital in 1857. A new hospital was constructed in 1860 at First and Bryant Streets, and destroyed in the 1906 fire. A building on Sutter Street housed the hospital until the present structure was completed in 1918. The hospital is run by the Sisters of Mercy.

San Francisco General Hospital
22nd Street and Potrero
The first San Francisco Hospital building was erected in 1872. The cornerstone of the present building was laid November 20, 1909. The hospital is owned and operated by the City and County of San Francisco. A new hospital is now under construction.

Shriners' Hospital
1701 - 19th Avenue
Organized in 1923 by the Ancient Arabic Order, Nobles of the Mystic Shrine, the hospital was specifically designed to treat orthopedic conditions of children under 14 years of age. The new hospital for burned children opened in December, 1970.

Southern Pacific Hospital
See Harkness Hospital.

Stanford Hospital
See Presbyterian Medical Center.

The U.S. Marine Hospital
Lake and 14th Avenue
Created under the Dept. of the Treasury to combat cholera, yellow fever, and general unsanitary conditions existing among seamen. The corner stone for the first U.S. Marine Hospital was laid April 7, 1853 and the building completed Dec. 12, 1853. The hospital was located on Rincon Hill until moved in 1875 to the Presidio.

U.S. Veterans Administration Hospital
42nd and Clement
Completed in 1934 at a cost of $898,800 and dedicated September 17th of that year. This is one of the first government projects to be designed with studied consideration of earthquake hazard and prevention of earthquake damage. The hospital has since been expanded and renovated.

University of California Medical Center
Parnassus and 3rd Avenue
Dr. Hugh Toland founded the Toland Medical College on Stockton Street in 1864. This college was deeded to U.C. as a medical department in 1873. Mayor Adolph Sutro donated 26 acres of land to the university, where the medical center now stands. The University Hospital was built in 1917 followed by the Langley Porter Neuropsychiatric Institute, Moffitt Hospital, Medical Sciences Bldg., etc. The hospital is financed by the Regents of the University of California through earnings and University funds.

Libraries

City College of San Francisco Library

50 Phelan Avenue

Agriculture, art, business, education, music, paramedical, science and technology, social and behavioral sciences. 46,000 volumes. M-Th, 7:30 a.m. - 9:00 p.m.; Friday, 7:30 a.m. - 4:30 p.m.; Sunday, 1:00 - 5:00 p.m.

Golden Gate College Library

536 Mission Street

Business, economics, accounting history. 60,550 volumes. M-F, 8:00 a.m. - 10:00 p.m.; Saturday & Sunday, 10:00 a.m. - 5:00 p.m.

Lone Mountain College, Monsignor Joseph M. Gleason Library

2800 Turk Street

Many special collections—early Americana, Californiana, French Revolution and Prince of Muscowa Collection of Napoleonia and French Revolution, Société de l'histoire de France, Joan of Arc, early Mexican history, Delphian Classics, Greek and Latin literature and philology, Patrologia Latina and Acta Sanctorum (complete) Amplissima Collectio Conciliorum Mansi. 146,000 volumes. M-Th, 8:00 a.m. - 10:00 p.m.; Friday, 8:00 a.m. - 5:00 p.m.; Sat., 9:30 a.m. - 5:00 p.m.; Sun., 8:00 a.m. - 10 p.m.

San Francisco Art Institute, Ann Bremer Memorial Library

800 Chestnut Street

Art, humanities. 17,500 volumes. M-Th, 9:00 a.m. - 9:00 p.m.; Friday, 9:00 a.m. - 5:00 p.m.; Sat., 10:00 a.m. - 2:00 p.m.

San Francisco Conservatory of Music Library

1201 Ortega Street

6,900 volumes, 1,850 tape reels and phonograph records. M-Th, 9:00 a.m. - 5:00 p.m., 7:00 - 9:00 p.m.; Friday, 9:00 a.m. - 5:00 p.m.; Sat., 9:00 a.m. - 1:00 p.m.

San Francisco State College Library

1630 Holloway Avenue

Art, business, economics, education, humanities, science and technology, social and behaviorial sciences. 382,040 volumes.

Simpson Bible College. Start-Kilgour Memorial Library

801 Silver Avenue

Education, humanities, religion. 27,000 volumes. M-F, 7:45 a.m. - 9:45 p.m.; Sat., 8:30 a.m. - 4:30 p.m.

University of San Francisco, Richard A. Gleason Library

Golden Gate and Parker Avenues

Special Collections: St. Thomas More and Robert Graves. 301,581 volumes. M-Th, 7:30 a.m. - 10:30 p.m.; Friday, 7:30 a.m. - 6:30 p.m.; Sat., 9:30 a.m. - 5:00 p.m.; Sun., 1:00 - 10:30 p.m.

California State Division of Mines and Geology Library

Ferry Building

28,000 volumes relating to the earth sciences, history of California mining, and the early surveys of the West. M-F, 8:00 a.m. - 5:00 p.m.; 10:00 a.m. - 12:00 first Saturday of the month.

United States Army Corps of Engineers District Library

100 McAllister Street

Military history, Federal law, technical & scientific books. 11,000 volumes. M-F, 8:00 a.m. - 4:30 p.m.

United States Federal Water Pollution Control Administration, Pacific Southwest Region Library

760 Market Street

Water resources for California, Nevada, Hawaii, Arizona, Utah and parts of Colorado and New Mexico. 3,000 volumes. M-F, 8:00 a.m. - 4:30 p.m.

Society of California Pioneers, Joseph A. Moore Memorial Library

456 McAllister Street

California history with emphasis on San Francisco. 12,500 volumes. M-F, 10:00 a.m. - 4:00 p.m.

Alliance Française Bibliothèque (French Library)

414 Mason Street

Books in French. 20,000 volumes. M-F, 10:00 a.m. - 4:00 p.m.; Saturday 1:00 p.m. - 3:00 p.m.

American Russian Institute, Reference Library

90 McAllister Street

Russian history. 7,000 volumes. M-F, 10:00 a.m. - 4:00 p.m.; Saturday, 1:00 p.m. - 3:00 p.m.

British Consulate-General, Information Section

120 Montgomery Street

British history. 2,000 volumes. M-F, 9:00 a.m. - 5:00 p.m.

Center of Asian Art & Culture Library, Brundage Collection

Golden Gate Park

Oriental Art and Culture. 7,000 volumes. M-F, 1:00 - 4:45 p.m.

African-American Historical and Cultural Society Library

680 McAllister Street

Black history. 4,000 volumes. M-F, 9:00 a.m. - 6:00 p.m.

Mechanics Institute Library

57 Post Street (Open to the public with membership)

General information library. 164,000 volumes. M-S, 9:00 a.m. - 10:00 p.m.; Sunday 1:00 p.m. - 5:00 p.m.

San Francisco Lighthouse Center for the Blind, Braille Library

745 Buchanan Street

Braille, talking and large-print books. 1,400 volumes. M-F, 9:00 a.m. - 12:00; 1:00 - 4:00 p.m.

World Trade Libraries

Embarcadero Center

World trade, economics, ports and harbors, transportation, foreign directories and telephone books. 15,690 volumes. M-F, 9:00 a.m. - 5:30 p.m.

San Francisco Public Library

Twenty-seven branches and two mobile units: bookmobile (12,231 volumes) and "The Whole World" vehicle. 1,355,966 volumes system-wide; 7,840 periodical titles.

Main Library
Civic Center

General Reference and Catalog Information: 558-3191. M-F, 9:00 a.m. - 9:00 p.m.; Saturday, 9:00 a.m. - 6:00 p.m.

Special departments; art & music: (558-3687); children's room: (558-3510) (hours on Friday, 1:00 - 6:00 p.m.); history and social sciences: (558-4927); literature, philosophy & religion: (558-3511); newspapers and periodicals: (558-3774); San Francisco History Room and special collections: (558-3949) (hours: Tues. - Sat., 9:00 a.m. - 6:00 p.m.; closed Mon.); science & government documents: (558-3321); registration and book return: (558-3477).

Special collections: genealogy and heraldry (12,000 books), Schmulowitz collection of wit and humor (13,000 books), Grabhorn printing collection (1600 items), calligraphy and lettering, Californiana (25,000 items), foreign language collection (25,000 books), California and Western state map collection, large-print books, college catalogs, civil service books, records, back-issue newspapers and documents on microfilm, scores and sheet music, framed art prints for borrowing. Services: telephone reference service (558-3191), copying machines, rental typewriters, meeting rooms. 753,344 volumes.

Anza Branch
550-37th Avenue, 558-3330

Books, magazines, records. 21,528 volumes. Mon., Thurs., Fri., 1:00 p.m. - 6:00 p.m.; Tues., 1:00 p.m. - 9:00 p.m.; Wed., Sat., 10:00 a.m. - 6:00 p.m.

Bernal Branch
500 Cortland Avenue, 558-4992

Books, records, periodicals in Spanish and Filipino, basement meeting rooms, adjacent playground. 15,077 volumes. Mon., Tues., 1:00 p.m. - 6:00 p.m.; Wed., 1:00 - 8:00 p.m.; Thurs., Fri., 1:00 - 6:00 p.m.; Sat., 10:00 a.m. - 6:00 p.m.

Business Branch
530 Kearny Street, 558-3946

Specializes in books about business, includes vertical files of clippings, pamphlets, documents. 11,112 volumes, 1600 current annual reports. M-F, 9:00 a.m. - 6:00 p.m.

Chinatown Branch
1135 Powell Street, 558-4938

Books, records, newspapers and periodicals in Chinese, basement study room, librarian speaks several dialects of Chinese. 22,659 volumes. Mon., 1:00 - 9:00 p.m.; Tues., Wed., 10:00 a.m. - 9:00 p.m.; Thurs., Fri., 1:00 - 6:00 p.m.; Sat., 10:00 a.m. - 5:00 p.m.

Eureka Valley Branch
3555-16th Street, 558-4992

Books, records, collections in Spanish and Filipino, young adult reading. 27,282 volumes. Mon., Thurs., Fri., 1:00 p.m. - 6:00 p.m.; Tues., 1:00 p.m. - 9:00 p.m.; Wed., 10:00 a.m. - 6:00 p.m.; Sat., 10:00 a.m. - 6:00 p.m.

Excelsior Branch
4400 Mission Street, 558-4798.

Books, magazines, records. 30,957 volumes. Mon., 1:00 - 9:00 p.m.; Tues., Wed., 10:00 am - 9:00 p.m.; Thurs., 10:00 a.m. - 6:00 p.m. Fri., 1:00 - 6:00 p.m.; Sat., 10:00 a.m. - 6:00 p.m.

Glen Park Branch

2909 Diamond Street, 558-4716

Books, records, magazines. 10,776 volumes. Mon., 2:00 - 6:00 p.m.; Tues., 2:00 - 8:00 p.m.; Wed., 2:00 - 6:00 p.m.; Thurs., 2:00 - 8:00 p.m.; Fri., 2:00 - 6:00 p.m.; Sat., closed.

Golden Gate Valley Branch

1801 Green Street, 558-4663

Books, magazines, records. 22,870 volumes. Mon., 1:00 - 6:00 p.m.; Tues., 1:00 - 9:00 p.m.; Wed., 10:00 a.m. - 6:00 p.m.; Thurs., Fri., 1:00 - 6:00 p.m.; Sat., 10:00 a.m. - 6:00 p.m.

Ingleside Branch

387 Ashton Avenue, 558-4629

Books, magazines, records. 13,938 volumes. Mon., Tues., 1:00 - 6:00 p.m.; Wed., 10:00 a.m. - 12:00, 1:00 p.m. - 6:00 p.m.; Thurs., Fri., 1:00 - 6:00 p.m.; Sat., closed.

Marina Branch

Chestnut near Webster, 558-4595

Books, magazines, records. 26,157 volumes. Mon., 1:00 - 9:00 p.m.; Tues., Wed., 10:00 am. - 9:00 p.m.; Thurs., 10:00 a.m. - 6:00 p.m.; Fri., 1:00 - 6:00 p.m.; Sat., 10:00 a.m. - 6:00 p.m.

Merced Branch

155 Winston Drive, 558-4576

Books, magazines, records. 27,942 volumes. Mon., 1:00 - 9:00 p.m.; Tues., Wed., 10:00 a.m. - 9:00 p.m.; Thurs., 10:00 am. - 6:00 p.m.; Fri., 1:00 - 6:00 p.m.; Sat., 10:00 a.m. - 6:00 p.m.

Mission Branch

3359-24th Street, 558-4183

General collection, plus books and newspapers in Spanish; magazines, records. 30,962 volumes. Mon., 1:00 - 9:00 p.m.; Tues., Wed., 10:00 a.m. - 9:00 p.m.; Thurs., 10:00 a.m. - 6:00 p.m.; Fri., 1:00 - 6:00 p.m.; Sat., 10:00 a.m. - 6:00 p.m. Children's Room: Mon., Thurs., Fri., 2:00 - 6:00 p.m.; Tues., 10:00 a.m. - 6:00 p.m. Wed., 2:00 - 8:00 p.m.; Sat., 10:00 a.m. - 6:00 p.m.

Noe Valley Branch

451 Jersey Street, 558-4143

Books, magazines, records. 18,048 volumes. Mon., Tues., Thurs., Fri., 1:00 p.m. - 6:00 p.m.; Wed., 10:00 a.m. - 12:00, 1:00 - 6:00 p.m.; Sat., closed.

North Beach Branch

200 Mason Street, 558-4062

Books, magazines, records, newspapers in Italian. 21,889 volumes. Mon., 1:00 - 9:00 p.m.; Tues., Wed., 10:00 a.m. - 6:00 p.m.; Thurs., 10:00 a.m. - 6:00 p.m.; Fri., 1:00 - 6:00 p.m.; Sat., 10:00 a.m. - 6:00 p.m.

Ocean View Branch

111 Broad Street, 558-3840

Books magazines, records. 9,643 volumes. Mon., - Fri., 2:00 p.m. - 6:00 p.m.; Sat., closed.

Ortega Branch

3223 Ortega Street, 558-3869

Books, magazines, records. 23,043 volumes. Mon., 1:00 - 6:00 p.m.; Tues., Wed., 10:00 a.m. - 9:00 p.m.; Thurs., 10:00 - 6:00 p.m.; Fri., 1:00 p.m. - 6:00 p.m.; Sat., 10:00 a.m. - 6:00 p.m.

Park Branch

1833 Page Street, 558-3620

Books, magazines, records. 21,298 volumes. Mon., closed; Tues., 1:00 - 9:00 p.m.; Wed., 10:00 a.m. - 6:00 p.m.; Thurs., Fri., 1:00 - 6:00 p.m.; Sat., 1:00 p.m. - 6:00 p.m.

Parkside Branch

1200 Taraval Street, 558-3696

Books magazines, records. 21,298 volumes. Mon., 1:00 - 9:00 p.m.; Tues., Wed., 10:00 a.m. - 9:00 p.m.; Thurs., 10:00 a.m. - 6:00 p.m.; Fri., 1:00 - 6:00 p.m.; Sat., 10:00 a.m. - 6:00 p.m.

Portola Branch

2434 San Bruno Avenue, 558-3525

Books, magazines, records, 15,231 volumes. Mon., closed; Tues., Thurs., Fri., Sat., 1:00 p.m. - 6:00 p.m.

Potrero Branch

1616-20th Street, 558-3363

Books, magazines, records. 14,629 volumes. Mon., closed; Tues., 1:00 p.m. - 9:00 p.m.; Wed., 10:00 a.m. - 12:00, 1:00 p.m. - 6:00 p.m.; Thurs., Fri., Sat., 1:00 p.m. - 6:00 p.m.

Presidio Branch

3150 Sacramento Street, 558-3359

Books, magazines, records. 23,541 volumes. Mon., Tues., 1:00 p.m. - 9:00 p.m.; Wed., 10:00 a.m. - 6:00 p.m.; Thurs., Fri., 1:00 - 6:00 p.m.; Sat., 10:00 a.m. - 6:00 p.m.

Richmond Branch

351 Ninth Avenue, 558-3393

Books, records, magazines. 26,829 volumes. Mon., 1:00 - 9:00 p.m.; Tues., Wed., 10:00 a.m. - 9:00 p.m.; Thurs., 10:00 a.m. - 6:00 p.m.; Fri., 1:00 - 6:00 p.m.; Sat., 10:00 a.m. - 6:00 p.m. Children's Room: Mon., Thurs., Fri., 2:00 - 6:00 p.m.; Tues., 10:00 a.m. - 6:00 p.m.; Wed., 2:00 - 8:00 p.m.; Sat., 10:00 a.m. - 6:00 p.m.

Sunset Branch

1305-18th Avenue, 558-3250

Books, magazines, records. 22,906 volumes. Mon., 1:00 - 9:00 p.m.; Tues.,

Wed., 10:00 a.m. - 9:00 p.m.; Thurs., 10:00 a.m. - 6:00 p.m.; Fri., 1:00 - 6:00 p.m.; Sat., 10:00 a.m. - 6:00 p.m. Children's Room: Mon., Thurs., Fri., 2:00 - 6:00 p.m.; Tues., 10:00 a.m. - 6:00 p.m.; Wed., 2:00 - 8:00 p.m.; Sat., 10:00 a.m. - 6:00 p.m.

Visitacion Valley Branch

45 Leland Avenue, 558-3218

Books, magazines, records. 13,392 volumes. Mon., Tues., Thurs., Fri., 1:00 p.m. - 6:00 p.m.; Wed., 10:00 a.m. - 12:00, 1:00 p.m. - 6:00 p.m.; Sat., closed.

Waden Branch

5075 Third Street, 558-5085

Books, magazines, records. Heavy on black history and literature. Architecture (AIA) prize-winning building. 18,329 volumes. Mon., Thurs., Fri., 1:00 - 6:00 p.m.; Tues., 1:00 p.m. - 9:00 p.m.; Wed., 10:00 a.m. - 6:00 p.m.; Sat., 10:00 a.m. - 6:00 p.m.

West Portal Branch

190 Lenox Way, 558-3120

Books, magazines, records. 25,801 volumes. Mon., 1:00 - 9:00 p.m.; Tues., Wed., 10:00 a.m. - 9:00 p.m.; Thurs., 10:00 a.m. - 6:00 p.m.; Fri., 1:00 - 6:00 p.m.; Sat., 10:00 a.m. - 6:00 p.m.

Western Addition Branch

1550 Scott Street, 558-5685

Books, Magazines, records. Heavy on Black and Japanese history and literature. 23,079 volumes. Mon., 1:00 - 9:00 p.m.; Tues., Wed., 10:00 a.m. - 9:00 p.m.; Thurs., 10:00 a.m. - 6:00 p.m.; Fri., 1:00 - 6:00 p.m.; Sat., 10:00 a.m. - 6:00 p.m.

San Francisco Law Library (County)

City Hall, Room 436

228,271 volumes. M-F, 8:30 a.m. - 5:15 p.m.

San Francisco Maritime Museum Library

Foot of Polk Street

Books, photographs, maps. M-F, 10:00 a.m. - 5:00 p.m.

Sutro Library (State)

Golden Gate Avenue at Temescal

Local history and genealogy, English and Mexican history. 100,000 volumes. M-F, 9:00 a.m. - 6:00 p.m.

Colleges and Universities

Antioch College - West

149 - 9th Street

Sometimes called "The University Without Walls" for it has abandoned many of the traditions of institutionalized teaching. It provides education for students wherever they may be: at work, in their houses, through internships, independent study and field experience, with areas of special social problems, at one or more colleges, and in travel and service abroad and in the United States. Antioch College - West is comprised of Antioch West/San Francisco, Antioch West/Los Angeles, Antioch West/Headstart Training Program, and Antioch West/Camarillo.

California Institute of Asian Studies

3494 - 21st Street

The California Institute of Asian Studies is an outgrowth of the Cultural Integration Fellowship which was founded in San Francisco in 1951. The Institute was formed in San Francisco in April, 1968. It specializes in Asian culture and civilization and in East-West comparative studies in philosophy, religion, psychology, sociology, aesthetics, and other humanistic disciplines.

California Podiatry College and Hospital

1770 Eddy Street

Established as California College of Chiropody in 1914 with name changing to California Podiatry College and Hospital in 1960. Private, coeducational college offers a 4-year program.

California State University, San Francisco

1600 Holloway Avenue

Instruction began in 1899 when the school was chartered as San Francisco State Normal School. In 1921 the name was changed to San Francisco State Teachers College, in 1935 it was called San Francisco State College, and on June 1, 1972 it received a new title, California State University, San Francisco. It is a coeducational state liberal arts college.

Cogswell Polytechnical College

3000 Folsom Street

Founded and endowed in 1887 by Dr. H. D. Cogswell, a San Francisco dentist. It was the first technical school of higher education west of St. Louis. The school's first building at Folsom & 26th Streets was demolished in 1941.

Golden Gate University

536 Mission Street

Established in 1881 as an evening high school by the YMCA, changing to college level in 1901. By 1908 it was called YMCA School and College, incorporating as Golden Gate College in 1923.

Hastings College of the Law

198 McAllister Street

The oldest law school west of the Rockies was established March 26, 1878 as the University of California's law department. It is now a coeducational professional college in quarters that were dedicated March 26, 1953 at McAllister & Hyde Streets.

Heald Colleges

1215 Van Ness Avenue

Edward Payson Heald came to California from Oregon in 1863 and opened a coeducational business college, the first of its kind in the West. Today's college offers diploma courses in accounting, business administration, secretarial science, courtroom reporting, office machines, computer programming, computer operation.

Lincoln University

281 Masonic Avenue

Lincoln University is a private, nonprofit, nondenominational institution of higher learning which is operated under a Board of Trustees. It is divided into several divisions, including the College of Liberal Arts, the Graduate Program, and the Law School. Established by Dr. Benjamin F. Lickey in 1919, it was first located in the downtown area, then at 2518 Jackson Street until moving to Masonic Avenue in 1972.

Lone Mountain College

Lone Mountain

The 24½-acre campus atop Lone Mountain was established by the Religious of the Sacred Heart in 1930. It began as a private liberal arts college for women but has since changed to a coeducational institution. The name was changed from San Francisco College for Women, in September, 1970, to Lone Mountain College.

Music and Arts Institute

2622 Jackson Street

Founded in 1939 at Golden Gate College, it was incorporated separately in 1939. Located in the Pacific Heights area since 1949, the college offers the complete program leading to the Bachelor of Music Degree with majors in piano, instrument, voice, composition, music theory, piano pedagogy, accompanying and coaching.

San Francisco Art Institute

800 Chestnut Street

Established in 1871 by a group of artists and writers as the San Francisco Art Association. Given the Mark Hopkins home at California and Mason Streets in 1893, the Art Association occupied that site until the 1906 earthquake and fire destroyed the building. Renamed the California School of Fine Arts it moved into its present building on Russian Hill in 1926. In 1960 the Art Association and the College combined under one name, The San Francisco Art Institute. In 1969 a new addition to the building was opened.

San Francisco City College

Ocean and Phelan Avenues

In 1935 the San Francisco Board of Education established the San Francisco Junior College. It is a two-year school with tuition-free instruction in the fields of liberal arts, hotel and restaurant operation, technical engineering, home economics, photography, commercial and graphic arts, dental assistant training, and criminology.

San Francisco College of Mortuary Science

1450 Post Street

Coeducational college founded in 1930 by Dr. L. W. Hosford. College was constructed exclusively for the education, advancement and development of the mortuary profession in all its phases.

San Francisco Conservatory of Music
1201 Ortega Street

A coeducational professional school offering training in conducting, composition, all instruments, theory, and voice. Established in 1917 by Ada Clement, it was first located at 3435 Sacramento Street, moving to 1201 Ortega in October, 1956.

San Francisco Law School
20 Haight Street

Organized in 1906, it became the first night law school to be chartered (in 1909) under the laws of the State of California. This school prepares men and women for the practice of law, and trains students in the legal nature of public affairs.

Simpson Bible College
801 Silver Avenue

Four-year liberal arts and Bible College for men and women affiliated with the Christian and Missionary Alliance.

University of California, San Francisco Medical Center
Third and Parnassus Avenues

Dr. H. H. Toland founded his medical school on Nov. 5, 1864 serving as faculty president and professor of surgery. In 1872 he transferred his Toland Medical School on Stockton Street to the State of California. The college moved to its present site in 1898, and, since 1902, has been fully supported by the University of California. Through a program of expansion the Center now provides clinical services at San Francisco General Hospital, research programs at 14 Bay Area hospitals, and expert doctor consultation is provided upon request.

University of San Francisco
Fulton Street and Parker Avenue

The City's oldest institution of higher learning was founded in May, 1855 by Rev. Anthony Maraschi, S.J. Located in the 1850's at 4th & Market Streets, the school later moved to Hayes and Van Ness, where it was destroyed by fire in 1906. Relocating on 21 acres atop the hill at Fulton and Parker, it became a university in 1930 and adopted the City's name. Coeducational since 1964, the University includes Colleges of Liberal Arts, Science, and Business Administration, and Schools of Law and Nursing.

Arts & Entertainment

Expositions

CALIFORNIA MIDWINTER INTERNATIONAL EXPOSITION
1894

Admission: 50¢ Adults, 25¢ children (ages 6-12).

While in Chicago as National Commissioner at large to the Columbian Exposition of 1893, Michael H. de Young conceived the idea of a similar exposition for San Francisco. It was San Francisco's first World Fair.

During the month of June meetings of citizens, presided over by the Mayor were held: the State Board of Trade took favorable action, committees were appointed and a plan of organization adopted. M. H. DeYoung was created President and Director General; Irwin C. Stump, Vice President, and R. Cornely, Associate Director-General in charge of Foreign Affairs. On July 10, Concert Valley, in the heart of Golden Gate Park, was selected as the site of the California Midwinter International Exposition. Ground was broken on August 24, 1893 at the spot where the bronze statue "Roman Gladiator" now stands in front of the De Young Museum. After the task of grading and leveling had been completed, the erection of the five large buildings was commenced. They were situated on the four sides of a quandrangle, called the Grand Court, in the center of which was the Electric Tower, which rose 266 feet into the air. Within the quadrangle the grounds were laid out in terraces, and planted with palms and other semi-tropical plants. Outside the exhibition buildings were located the various concessions and county buildings.

The following foreign nations participated in the exposition which opened January 27, 1894: Brazil, France, Ottoman Empire, Oriental Countries, Serbia, Montenegro and Roumania, Canada, Austro-Hungary, Great Britain, Italy, Russia, Portugal, Siam, Spain, Switzerland, Belgium, Hawaii, and Japan.

Besides the California counties which displayed, there were four states which added colorful exhibits to this first fair. They were: Nevada, Utah, Montana, and Arizona.

Contemporary drawing of the Midwinter International Exposition of 1894.

PANAMA PACIFIC INTERNATIONAL EXPOSITION - 1915

Admission: 50¢ Adults, 25¢ Children (ages 5-12).

On December 29, 1909 President William Howard Taft said, "San Francisco has shown such a spirit that if the exposition is held there it will be a great success." Within five years, lacking three days, San Francisco the stricken city of 1906, had, Phoenix-like, risen from her ashes and been officially chosen as the place in which to hold an Exposition to commemorate the completion of the Panama Canal.

The location was the "Harbor View" site, now the Marina District. It was a natural amphitheater with a floor about three miles long and from a third to a half-mile wide, backed by the hills of the Pacific Heights, and flanked at each end by government reservations. The grounds comprised 635 acres, divided into three sections. In the center were grouped the 11 great exhibit palaces and Festival Hall. To the west, spreading fan-shaped along the Bay, were located the pavilions of foreign nations and the buildings of the States, while still beyond these were the live stock exhibit buildings and race track, covering 65 acres, the aviation field, and the drill field. To the east of the exhibit palaces were the amusement concessions known as "The Zone". The Exposition established a record in the history of world expositions by being structurally complete three months beforehand, and completely ready on the opening day, February 20, 1915.

The following foreign nations participated in the Exposition: Argentina, Austria, Australia, Bolivia, Brazil, Bulgaria, Canada, China, Cuba, Denmark, Germany, Great Britain, Holland, India, Italy, Japan, New Zealand Norway, Panama, Persia, Portugal, Siam, Spain and Sweden.

There were forty-three states and territories counted as participants and these were: Alabama, Arizona, Arkansas, California, Colorado, Delaware, Florida, Georgia, Hawaii, Idaho, Illinois, Indiana, Iowa, Kansas, Kentucky, Louisiana, Maryland, Massachusetts, Michigan, Nebraska, Nevada, New Jersey, New York, South Carolina, North Dakota, Ohio, Oklahoma, Oregon, Pennsylvania, Philippines, Rhode Island, North Carolina, Tennessee, Texas, Utah, Virginia, West Virginia, Wisconsin, Wyoming, Washington, Minnesota, Mississippi, Missouri, and Montana.

The Exposition had attracted 18,876,438 persons when it closed December 4, 1915 with a reading of a toast from President Woodrow Wilson:

"The Panama-Pacific International Exposition:

"Which in its conception and successful accomplishment gave striking evidence of the practical genius and artistic taste of America;

"Which in its unusual and interesting exhibits afforded impressive illustration of the development of the arts of peace; and

"Which in its motive and object was eloquent of the new spirit which is to unite East and West and make all the world partners in the common enterprises of progress and humanity."

WHAT WAS SAID ABOUT 1915 EXPOSITION

"They who builded this Panama-Pacific Exposition were so wise in adopting all the good features and avoiding those which marred the preceding ones that to me it seems as near perfection as the mind and hand of man have ever wrought. This is the university of the world. It has a chair fully endowed to meet the wants and needs of each. The eye, the ear, the mind, the heart, the soul, each may have its horizon here enlarged."—Vice-President Thomas R. Marshall.

"I am really sorry that the English language is so mean in superlatives that I cannot tell you thoroughly what I think of your Exposition. You have an

*Tower of Jewels and Fountain of Energy at the Panama
Pacific International Exposition, 1915.*

Exposition which, more than any other Exposition we have had in all these
years, is conceived in a spirit of the finest art, and executed with the highest
degree of intelligence."—Secretary of the Treasury William G. McAdoo.

"It is the greatest revelation of beauty that has ever been seen on
earth."—Edwin Markham.

"It is indescribably beautiful. It is so beautiful that it gives you a choky
feeling in your throat as you look at it."—New York *World*.

GOLDEN GATE INTERNATIONAL EXPOSITION - 1939-1940

Admission: 50¢ Adults, 25¢ children under 12.

President Franklin D. Roosevelt said in his 1938 visit to Treasure Island, "I think you people out here on the Pacific Coast, when you start to do something, do it better than anyone else in the United States." He was speaking of the nearly completed Golden Gate International Exposition which was to commemorate the completion of the two San Francisco Bay Bridges and to be held on a man-made island dredged out of San Francisco Bay.

Mayor Angelo J. Rossi in his opening day greeting to Exposition visitors on February 18, 1939 said, in part:

"To us is given the honor and responsibility of staging the Golden Gate International Exposition and acting as host city in welcoming the world to participate in a celebration dedicated to the future of the Pacific empire.

"In the spirit of western hospitality we invite the world to share the beauty and grandeur of Treasure Island in 1939.

"As chief executive of the host city, it affords me genuine pleasure to assure visitors that a heartfelt welcome awaits their coming to the Exposition. Speaking for the citizenry of San Francisco, we look forward to upholding western tradition of cordiality and friendship. We know that the journey will be worth while, that the visit will be replete with interest and entertainment, and that memories will be stored with treasures of the Golden

Scale model for the Golden Gate International Exposition.

Gate International Exposition and the attractions of California and the west's vacationlands."

The Exposition closed October 29, 1939 and re-opened May 25, 1940 as a new "streamlined" exposition. The 1940 Fair was a new venture in the old buildings on the old site. A new plan of operations had to be created, new attractions had to be secured, old structures had to be given new beauty and color. The 1940 management had four months to conceive and build an entirely new and different show. When the Exposition closed on September 29, 1940, more than 17 million visitors had been attracted to the Treasure Island fairs.

1939 State & Territorial Participation

Arizona	Missouri	Utah
California	Montana	Washington
Colorado	Nevada	Wyoming
Idaho	New Mexico	Territory of Hawaii
Illinois	Oregon	

1939 Foreign Participation

Argentina	El Salvador	Netherlands East Indies
Australia	France	New Zealand
Brazil	French Indo-China	Norway
Chile	Guatemala	Panama
British Columbia	Italy	Peru
Republic of Columbia	Japan	Philippines
Czechoslovakia	Johore	Portugal
Denmark	Mexico	Sweden
Ecuador	Netherlands	

1940 State & Territorial Participation

Arizona	Nevada	Washington
California	Oregon	Territory of Hawaii
Illinois	Utah	Alaska
Missouri		

1940 Foreign Participation

Belgium	British West Indies	Denmark
Brazil	Colombia	Ecuador
British India	Czechoslovakia	France

French Indo-China	Malaysia	Philippines
Great Britain	Mexico	Portugal
Holland	Netherlands East Indies	Russia
Hungary	Norway	Turkey
Italy	Persia	Switzerland
Japan	Peru	

"The Golden Gate International Exposition was the dream of many states and cities and counties, and boys and girls and men and women. Lights are made by men in beauty and last for just a little while. Memories come from God and live forever. So will our memories of this beauty live until Time's End!"— Leland W. Cutler, President 1939 Exposition

"Yesterday's bright version of Treasure Island today becomes an enduring memory. To have added another chapter to San Francisco's prismatic history is something in which we can all take pride. 'A thing of beauty is a joy forever: Its loveliness increases; it will never Pass into nothingness": . . . 'The feast is over and the lamps expire!"—Marshall Dill, President 1940 Exposition

Films Made In (or about) San Francisco

Adventure (1945) Clark Gable, Greer Garson
Barbary Coast (1935) Miriam Hopkins, Edward G. Robinson, Joel McCrea
The Birds (1963) Rod Taylor, Jessica Tandy, Suzanne Pleshette
Bullitt (1968) Steve McQueen, Robert Vaughn, Jacqueline Bisset
Butterflies Are Free (1972) Goldie Hawn, Eddie Albert
Charlie Chan at Treasure Island (1939) Sidney Toler, Cesar Romero
Chinatown at Midnight (1950) Hurd Hatfield, Jean Willes, Tom Powers
The Conversation (1972) Gene Hackman
Daddy's Gone A-Hunting (1969) Scott Hylands, Carol White, Paul Burke
Dark Intruder (1965) Leslie Nielsen, Judi Meredith
Dark Victory (1947) Lauren Bacall, Humphrey Bogart
Days of Wine and Roses (1962) Jack Lemmon, Lee Remick, Jack Klugman
Dealing (1972) Barbara Hershey, Robert F. Lyons
Dirty Harry (1971) Clint Eastwood, Harry Guardino, Andy Robinson
Experiment in Terror (1962) Glenn Ford, Lee Remick, Stephanie Powers
Face of Fear (1971) Elizabeth Ashley, Ricardo Montalban, Jack Warden

Flower Drum Song (1961) Nancy Kwan, Jack Soo, Benson Fong, Miyoshi Umeki
Fools (1970) Jason Robards, Katherine Ross, Scott Hylands
Freebie and the Bean (1973) Monty Stickles, James Caan, Alan Arkin
'Frisco Kid (1935) James Cagney, Margaret Lindsay
Gentlemen Jim (1942) Errol Flynn, Jack Carson, Alexis Smith
Good Neighbor Sam (1964) Jack Lemmon, Romy Schneider, Dorothy Provine
Greed (1923) Gibson Gowland, Jean Hersholt, Zasu Pitts
Ground Zero (1973) Ron Casteel, Yvonne D'Angers
Guess Who's Coming to Dinner? (1967) Spencer Tracy, Katherine Hepburn,
    Sidney Poitier
Harold and Maud (1971) Ruth Gordon, Bud Cort, George Segal
Hello 'Frisco (1924) "Slim" Summerville, Bobby Dunn
Hello, 'Frisco, Hello (1943) Alice Faye, John Payne, Jack Oakie
House Across the Bay (1940) George Raft, Joan Bennett
House on Telegraph Hill (1951) Richard Basehart
I Remember Mama (1948) Irene Dunne, Barbara Bel Geddes, Oscar Homolka
In Old San Francisco (1927) Sojin, Anna May Wong
Incident in San Francisco (1971) Christopher Connelly, Richard Kiley
It Came From Beneath the Sea (1955) Kenneth Tobey, Faith Domergue, Donald Curtis
Kiss Them For Me (1957) Gary Grant, Suzy Parker, Jayne Mansfield
The Laughing Policeman (1972) Walter Matthau
The Mack (1973) Max Julian, Richard Pryor, Carol Speed
Magnum Force (1973) Clint Eastwood, Hal Holbrook
Maltese Falcon (1941) Humphrey Bogart, Mary Astor, Peter Lorre
Man From 'Frisco (1944) Michael O'Shea, Anne Shirley, Gene Lockhart
Man's Favorite Sport (1964) Rock Hudson, Paula Prentiss, John McGiver
Nightmare in Blood (1973) Morgan Upton, Jerry Walter
The Norliss Tapes (1973) Roy Thinnes
Old San Francisco (1927) Dolores Costello, Warner Oland
One Is A Lonely Number (1972) Trish Van Devere, Paul Jenkins
The Organization (1971) Sidney Poitier, Barbara McNàir
Owl and the Pussycat (1970) Barbara Streisand, George Segal
Pal Joey (1957) Frank Sinatra, Rita Hayworth, Kim Novak
Pete and Tillie (1972) Carol Burnett, Walter Matthau
Petulia (1968) Julie Christie, Richard Chamberlain, George C. Scott
Play It Again Sam (1972) Woody Allen, Diane Keaton, Tony Roberts
Pleasure of His Company (1961) Fred Astaire, Debbie Reynolds, Lilli Palmer
Point Blank (1968) Lee Marvin, Angie Dickinson, Carroll O'Connor
The Poor Devil (1972) Sammy Davis, Jr.
Psych-Out (1968) Susan Strasberg, Dean Stockwell
San Francisco (1936) Clark Gable, Jeannette McDonald, Spencer Tracy
The Second Coming of Suzanne (1972) Gene Barry

The Sisters (1938) Bette Davis, Jane Bryan, Anita Louise, Errol Flynn
Skidoo (1969) Jackie Gleason, Carol Channing, Peter Lawford
Take the Money and Run (1969) Woody Allen, Janet Margolin
That Certain Summer (1973) Hal Holbrook, Martin Sheen, Scott Jacoby, Hope Lange
They Call Me Mr. Tibbs (1970) Sidney Poitier, Barbara McNair, Martin Landau
THX-1138 (1971) Robert Duvall, Donald Pleasance, Maggie McOmie
Vertigo (1958) Jimmy Stewart, Kim Novak, Barbara Bel Geddes
Waterfront (1944) John Carradine, J. Carrol Naish
What's Up Doc? (1972) Barbara Streisand, Ryan O'Neal
The World In His Arms (1952) Gregory Peck, Ann Blyth, Anthony Quinn

San Francisco International Film Festival

The Film Festival is a civic, non-profit corporation, sponsored by the San Francisco Art Commission. It is the only film festival in North America that is sanctioned by the International Federation of Film Producers Associations, and has been held yearly since 1957. In the past films have been shown at the Metro Theater, Coronet Theater, and Masonic Auditorium, but since 1971 the permanent home for this festival is the Palace of Fine Arts.

Museums

African-American Historical Society

680 McAllister Street

Exhibits pertaining to African and Afro-American history. Open Monday-Friday 1-5, free admission.

American Indian Historical Society

1451 Masonic Avenue

National headquarters of the society, collecting records and items relating to American Indian history. Changing displays of Indian art as well as baskets, blankets and beads. Open Thursday-Sunday, 2-5, free admission.

Balclutha

Pier 43

The San Francisco Maritime Museum's floating display of maritime mementoes exhibited in the three-masted square rigger *Balclutha* tied up at Pier 43. Open daily, 9:30 a.m. - 11:30 p.m. Admission: Adults 75¢, children 6-12, 25¢.

Bank of California Gold and Coin Museum

400 California

Collection of gold coin, currency, ingots and nuggets. Also exhibited are examples of currencies and coinage from Alaska, British Columbia, Oregon Territory, California, Colorado, and the State of Deseret. Open Monday-Friday, 10-3, free admission.

Cable Car Barn
Washington & Mason Streets

A working museum where the visitor may watch the machinery that winds the cables for San Francisco's moving Historical Landmark. In addition there is photographic display outlining the history of San Francisco's transit systems. Open daily, 8 a.m. to midnight, free admission.

California Academy of Sciences
Golden Gate Park

Many connected buildings, each featuring fine scientific collections. They are Steinhart Aquarium, Morrison Planetarium, North American Hall, African Hall, and the newest, Cowell Hall. Open every day of the year, 10-5. Admission: Adults 50¢, children 25¢, free admission first Saturday each month.

California Geology Museum
Ferry Building

The mineral resources of California are on display along with exhibits of products manufactured from these minerals. Museum maintained by the California Division of Mines and Geology. Open Monday-Friday, 8-5, first Saturday of each month 10-12, free admission.

California Historical Society (Whittier Mansion)
2090 Jackson Street

Examples of the work of California artists of the past in changing exhibits, shown in the first California town house to be built entirely of stone on a steel framework. Imported wood paneling and German silver fittings add to the beauty of the interior. Open Tuesday-Saturday, 10-4, free admission.

California Palace of the Legion of Honor
Lincoln Park

Fine art collection and the largest collection of graphic arts in the Western United States. Open every day of the year, 10-5. Free admission.

California State Automobile Association History Room
150 Van Ness Avenue

Photos and other mementoes of early motoring.

Chinese Historical Society of America
17 Adler Place

Located in an alley between Grant and Columbus Avenues this unique museum is full of artifacts and photographs which relate to the history of the Chinese in Western America. Open Tuesday-Sunday, 1-5, free admission.

M. H. de Young Memorial Museum
Golden Gate Park

Collections of European and American art, the Avery Brundage Collection of Asian Art, and a wing devoted primarily to temporary exhibitions. Open every day of the year, 10-5, free admission.

Fort Point
Presidio, beneath the Golden Gate Bridge

The fort is now in the process of being restored to the condition of Civil War days. Exhibits of military history pertaining to the fort and the military are on display. Open Monday-Friday, 11:30 a.m. - 12:30 p.m., Saturday and Sunday, 1-5, free admission.

Palace of the Legion of Honor, modeled after the classic 18th century Palais de la Legion d'Honneur in Paris.

Josephine D. Randall Jr. Museum
Museum Way (off Roosevelt Way)

Small displays of Paleontology, Geology and Indian artifacts. In addition there are small animals which can be touched or held. Open Tuesday-Saturday, 10-5, Sunday 12-4:30, free admission.

Maritime Museum
Foot of Polk Street

Housed in a building built to resemble a ship at anchor, this museum offers fine collections of ship models, scrimshaw, navigational aids, ship photos and maps. Open every day, 10-5, free admission.

Mission Dolores
Dolores and 16th Streets

The cornerstone of the present church was laid by Father Palou, April 25, 1782, making this the oldest building in San Francisco. The altar, decorations and books are from Spain and Mexico. A small cemetery connects with the church. Open May-Oct., 9-5, Nov.-Apr. 10-4. Admission: 25¢.

Museum of Russian Culture
2450 Sutter Street

History and culture of Russia, especially 20th Century book and manuscript repository. Open Tuesday, 5-9, free admission

Fort Point, nestled below the Golden Gate Bridge.

Octagon House
2645 Gough

The Colonial Dames of America, California Branch, have restored this eight-sided house, built in 1861, as their headquarters. On display are items made before 1800, including Hepplewhite, Queen Anne and Chippendale furniture, as well as silver and pewter. Open, first Sunday and second and fourth Thursday of each month, 1-4, free admission.

Palace of Arts and Science (Exploratorium)
Baker and Beach

The Exploratorium is under the direc-tion of the Palace of Arts and Science Foundation. The exhibits are designed so that the public can manipulate and interact with them. This is a new type of science museum combining the arts and the sciences by linking both with the way people see, hear, feel and move. Open, Wed. - Sun., 1 - 5, free admission.

San Francisco Fire Department Pioneer Memorial Museum
655 Presidio Avenue

Fire-fighting apparatus and displays of historic photographs and ephemeral matter all relating to the history of San Francisco's fire department since 1850. Open daily, 1-4, free admission.

San Francisco Maritime State Historic Park
Hyde Street Pier

The *Eureka*, *C. A. Thayer*, *Wapama*, and the *Alma* are four ships rich in maritime history that are now open to the public for viewing. Each ship serves as a floating museum with exhibits pertaining to that ship's history. Open: Summer, 10-10; Winter, Monday-Thursday 10-6, Friday-Saturday, 10-midnight, Sunday 10-8. Admission: Adults 50¢, children 25¢.

San Francisco Museum of Art
Veterans Building

Modern art and contemporary trends in painting and sculpture. Open Tuesday-Friday 10-10, Saturday 10-5, Sunday 1-5, free admission.

Society of California Pioneers
456 McAllister Street

Membership in this society is limited to male descendants of those resident in California prior to January 1, 1850. Their exhibit area features changing displays of memorabilia and photographs of San Francisco and California history. Open Monday-Friday, 10-4, free admission.

Wells Fargo History Room
420 Montgomery Street

An impressive display of Wells Fargo history through memorabilia of bandits, lawmen, treasure boxes, etc. Also included are the working tools of the early Gold Rush miners. Open banking days, 10-3, free admission.

A World of Oil
555 Market Street

The history of the petroleum industry in drawings, photographs, and three life-sized dioramas. Also featured are electronic displays and a film. Open Monday-Friday, 10-4, free admission.

Municipal Band

Municipal music was first suggested to the Board of Supervisors in 1910 by the Musicians' Union of San Francisco, and was also a plank in the platform of the Labor Party in its campaign of 1909. Nothing was done, however, until the Rolph Board of Supervisors came into office, and $10,000 of its budget for the fiscal year 1912-13 was set apart for this purpose.

The Board of Supervisors referred the matter of arrangements and organization of the municipal band to the Public Welfare Committee. That committee later recommended John A. Keogh as the director of the Municipal Band and the appointment was finally confirmed by the Board of Supervisors on Monday, July 8, 1912.

The first concert of the San Francisco Municipal Band took place on Sunday, July 21, 1912, at Washington Square. Dr. S. A. Musante of the North Beach Promotion Association delivered a brief address of welcome, inviting the assembled people to remain and enjoy the concert.

For 58 years the Municipal Band

performed for visiting kings, queens, presidents, and other dignitaries, but in June, 1970, it was voted out of existence by the San Francisco Art Commission, which had supervision of the band since 1932.

Opera & Ballet

In San Francisco operatic performances were given as early as 1850. However, the first grand opera was Bellini's "La Sonnambula" presented at the Adelphi on February 12, 1851. During the 1850's and 1860's a troupe would sometimes give as many as thirteen seasons of opera in one year, making this city the center of opera in the West. The most important opera houses before 1906 were the Metropolitan I & II, Maguire's Opera House, Academy of Music, The Tivoli, and the Grand Opera House.

The first season of municipal opera opened on September 26, 1923 at the Civic Auditorium. Gaetano Merola directed the performance of Puccini's "La Boheme." Opera continued to be performed at the Civic Auditorium until the Opera House was built in 1932, with the exception of the years 1928 and 1929 when the company was in Dreamland Auditorium (now Winterland). The first opera presented in the new Opera House was "La Tosca." The cast was headed by Muzio, Dino Borgioli and Alfredo Gandolfi, and directed by Gaetano Merola.

Index of Conductors 1923-1972

Adler, Kurt Herbert: 1943-53, 1958, 1960-61.
Barbini, Ernesto: 1954-55.
Bartoletti, Bruno: 1970.
Basile, Arturo: 1959.
Beckman, Irving: 1970.
Beecham, Sir Thomas: 1943.
Bellugi, Piero: 1965.
Bernardi, Mario: 1967-68.
Blechschmidt, Hans: 1931-32.
Bodanzky, Artur: 1935.
Bonynge, Richard: 1963-64, 1966, 1971, 1972.
Breisach, Paul: 1946-52.
Cillario, Carlo Felice: 1970-71.
Cimara, Pietro: 1942-48, 1951-52.

Cimini, Pietro: 1925-29, 1931-32, 1934, 1937.
Cleva, Fausto: 1942-43, 1949-55.
Coppola, Anton: 1969.
Curiel, Glauco: 1952-58.
De Fabritiis, Oliviero: 1956, 1962.
Dell'Orefice, Antonio: 1929-31, 1933.
DiRosa, Ottavio: 1960.
Dohnanyi, Christoph von: 1971.
Ehrling, Sixten: 1969.
Faldi, Aldo: 1968.
Ferencsik, Janos: 1962-63.
Fournet, Jean: 1958.
Giovaninetti, Reynald: 1972.
Gregor, Bohumil: 1969-70.
Grossman, Herbert: 1967.

Herbert, Walter: 1942.
Horenstein, Jascha: 1966.
Kritz, Karl: 1945-46, 1949-54, 1956-58.
Lawner, George: 1961.
Leinsdorf, Erich: 1938-41, 1948, 1951,
    1955, 1957.
Leitner, Ferdinand: 1964.
Lert, Richard: 1935-36.
Levine, James: 1970-71.
Lopez-Cobos, Jesus: 1972.
Ludwig, Leopold: 1958-65, 1967-68.
Mackerras, Charles: 1969, 1971.
Martin, Wolfgang: 1959.
Martinon, Jean: 1965.
Marzollo, Dick: 1947-48.
McArthur, Edwin: 1939.
Merola, Gaetano: 1923-49, 1952.
Molinari-Pradelli, Francesco: 1957,
    1959-66.
Montemezzi, Italo: 1941-42, 1947.
Monteux, Pierre: 1954.
Morel, Jean: 1955.
Mueller, Leo: 1954.
Murray, Earl: 1959.
Papi, Gennaro: 1936-41.

Patane, Giuseppe: 1967-69.
Pelletier, Wilfred: 1928-31, 1933, 1947.
Peress, Maurice: 1972.
Perisson, Jean: 1966-71, 1972.
Perlea, Jonel: 1950.
Prêtre, Georges: 1963-64.
Pritchard, John: 1970.
Reiner, Fritz: 1936-38.
Rescigno, Nicola: 1950-51.
Riedel, Karl: 1929-30, 1936, 1944.
Sanzogno, Nino: 1971, 1972.
Schaefer, Hans George: 1960.
Schuller, Gunther: 1967-70.
Schwieger, Hans: 1956.
Sebastian, Georges: 1944-46, 1958.
Serafin, Tullio: 1953.
Solti, Georg: 1953.
Stein, Horst: 1965-68.
Steinberg, William: 1944-49, 1956-57.
Suitner, Otmar: 1969-71, 1972.
Szenkar, Eugen: 1954.
Van Den Burg, Willem: 1939.
Varviso, Silvio: 1959-61, 1971.
Wallenstein, Alfred: 1951.
Wilson, Charles: 1971.

San Francisco Ballet

The San Francisco Ballet Company, founded in 1933 by Adolph Bolm, is the oldest resident classical ballet company in America. It was originally established as an auxiliary to the Opera, but now acts as an independent organization.

Symphony

The first popular concert by the San Francisco Symphony Orchestra, founded by the Musical Association of San Francisco, was presented December 29, 1911 at the Cort Theater. Mme. Martha Richardson, the prima donna soprano of the Paris Opera Company appeared as soloist.

In 1921 Supervisor J. Emmet Hayden originated the idea of San Francisco supporting and conducting a series of Symphony Orchestra concerts. These concerts were begun on November 8, 1922 in the Exposition Auditorium (Civic Auditorium). Since the opening of the Opera House in 1932 all performances of the symphony orchestra are held there.

Conductors

Henry Hadley, "Father of Municipal Music" 1911-1915.

Alfred Hertz, 1915-1930.
Basil Cameron, 1930-1931.
Issay Dobrowen, 1931-1936.
Pierre Monteux, 1936-1951.
Enrique Jorda, 1951-1962.

Josef Krips, 1962-1970.
Seiji Ozawa, 1970-1975
"San Francisco is really the best city in America. There is a very free feeling in this city. People who live here have very free minds, which is very important for me to make music. I love San Francisco."

San Francisco Art Festival

The first municipally sponsored Art Show, a project of the Art Commission, was held in the Civic Center Plaza, October 17-20, 1946. Since that date this municipal event has been held yearly and has stimulated and promoted interest in the Fine Arts among the citizens of San Francisco.

Sports

Football

Early San Francisco football teams regularly played against the University of California football varsity team at locations throughout this city. The first Stanford-California game was held in San Francisco at the Haight Street Grounds on March 19, 1892. These highly publicized games were played in San Francisco until 1904 when the California Field opened in Berkeley.

Football Fields

Recreation Park 8th & Harrison Streets.
Haight Street Grounds Stanyan Street across from Golden Gate Park.
Central Park 8th & Market Streets.
16th & Folsom Street Grounds.

Richmond Field 6th Avenue and Lake.
Golden Gate Park.
Ewing Field, Masonic Avenue.
Kezar Stadium.
Candlestick Park.

Candlestick Park

Baseball

San Francisco's first organized baseball game was played at 16th &

Harrison Streets in the Mission.

This game was followed by others played at sand lots throughout the city until proper diamonds were established in the following parks:

25th & Folsom Streets Opened Nov. 26, 1868.

Central Park 8th & Market Streets. Opened 1885.

Haight Street Grounds Stanyan Street across from Golden Gate Park. Opened April 3, 1887.

Recreation Park, 8th & Harrison Streets Opened Oct. 3, 1897.

Recreation Park, 15th & Valencia Streets. 1907.

Ewing Field Masonic Ave. Opened May 16, 1914.

Seals Stadium 16th & Bryant Streets. Opened April 7, 1931.

Candlestick Park Opened April 12, 1960.

Golf Courses

Public Courses

Golden Gate Park (9 holes) Opened April 4, 1951.

Harding Park (18 holes) Opened July 18, 1925.

(Named for President Warren G. Harding who died in San Francisco.)

Lincoln Park (18 holes) Opened as a 6-hole course in 1909 and enlarged to 18 holes in 1913.

McLaren Park (9 holes) Opened Sept. 1961.

Sharp Park (18 holes) (San Mateo County) Opened in 1932.

Private Courses

Olympic Club Course Two 18-hole courses were constructed in 1923, the "Lake Course" and the "Ocean Course."

Presidio Golf Club Established June 28, 1905.

San Francisco Golf Club Established in 1895 as a 9-hole course laid out in the Presidio of San Francisco. Moved in 1905 to Junipero Serra Blvd., south of Ocean Ave.

Race Tracks

Race tracks were functioning early in the 1850's and continued to do so until the last track closed in 1905. The first racing ovals appeared in the Mission District, followed by those in the Outside Lands, and still later by the Ingleside Track.

Bay District - First & Fifth Avenues, Anza & Fulton Streets. Opened November 12, 1873. Closed May 27, 1896.

Bayview - 24th & 28th Streets and Ingalls & Railroad Avenues. Opened Sept. 3, 1864.

Half Mile - 24th & 28th Avenues & Point Lobos & Clement.

Ingleside - Ocean Ave. & Junipero Serra Blvd. Opened Nov. 28, 1895. Closed Dec. 31, 1905.

Ocean View - Ocean Ave., Sloat Blvd., 26th & 34th Avenues. Opened May 23, 1865.

Pioneer - Mission, Bryant, 24th & Army.

The Willows, or Union Track - 19th & 23rd Streets, Mission & Harrison Streets.

Swimming Pools

Opened

Balboa (indoor) June 15, 1958	**Garfield** (indoor) Dec. 2, 1957
San Jose Ave. & Havelock Street	26th & Harrison
Coffman (indoor) Nov. 15, 1958	**Hamilton** (indoor) Oct. 16, 1955
Visitacion Ave. & Hahn Street	Geary Blvd. & Steiner

Sutro Baths in their heyday.

The Baths as seen by cartoonist E. Jessup.

King (outdoor)   Aug. 3, 1968
   3rd & Carroll Streets
Larsen (indoor)   Nov. 15, 1958
   19th Ave. & Wawona
Mission (outdoor)   June 18, 1916
   Mission Playground
   (19th & Angelica Streets)
North Beach (indoor)   Dec. 5, 1956
   Mason & Lombard Streets
   (remodeled)

Rossi (indoor)   Sept. 22, 1957
   Arguello Blvd. & Anza
Fleishhacker Pool (closed since 1972) The
   city's largest outdoor pool containing
   6,500,000 gallons of warmed salt
   water. Pool measures 1,000 feet long
   by 150 feet wide. It opened April 23,
   1925.

Baths Almost Forgotten

Crystal Baths Powell & Bay. Opened
   1886/Closed 1906
Crystal Palace Salt Water Baths 775 Lombard. Opened 1924/Closed Jan. 8,
   1956.
Harbor View Hot Salt Water Baths NW
   corner Baker & Jefferson Streets.
   Opened 1890/Closed 1912
Lick Baths 10th Street near Howard.

Opened Nov. 1890/Closed Nov. 30,
   1919
Lurline Baths NW corner Larkin & Bush.
   Opened 1893/Closed 1936
Palace Baths Filbert near Powell.
   Opened 1887/Closed 1906
Sutro Baths Point Lobos Avenue.
   Opened Mar. 14, 1896/Closed Sept.
   1, 1952

Yachting

Since the 1850's, the American period, the 450 square miles of water in San Francisco Bay have lured week-end sailors to race in sport a variety of sailing craft.

The participants very early organized themselves into informal sailing clubs, followed by these more permanent organizations.

Yacht Clubs

Pioneer Yacht Club Organized Sept. 9, 1852.
San Francisco Yacht Club Organized July 16, 1869.

Pacific Yacht Club Organized June, 1878
Corinthian Yacht Club March 16, 1886
St. Francis Yacht Club May 13, 1927

Sailing

Lake Merced Sport Center adjacent to Harding Park Golf Course on Skyline Blvd.

Transportation

Airports

San Francisco International Airport

Early sites proposed for San Francisco's Airport were located at Millbrae, South San Francisco, Beresford, Lomita Park, San Mateo Point, San Bruno, Bay Farm Island, the Marina, and Redwood City. The site approved by the Board of Supervisors through Ordinance No. 7428 was the 150 acres owned by the Mills Estate, located in San Mateo County above the Bay tidelands. The adjoining 1,000 acres of submerged land that could be later reclaimed were an important factor in deciding the airports location.

The new San Francisco Municipal Airport (called Mills Field) was dedicated May 7, 1927 and operation began June 7 of that year.

The March 15, 1929 Supplement to the Third Edition of Airplane Landing Fields of the Pacific West describes the San Francisco Airport as: "Three Runways - (1) 5700' x 200 ', (2) 1800' x 200' (3) Emergency runway across highway 1200' x 250'. Surface on all runways excellent. Completely equipped administration building and hospital. Restaurant. Mechanical service. Weather Bureau representative located here for survey of meteorlogical and aerological conditions on San Francisco peninsula. Gasoline and oil supplied by Standard Oil Company at airport."

In 1930 the city began a 10-year purchase program of the then existing 1,112 acres of airport land. By June 9, 1937 the name of the airport had been officially changed from Mills Field to San Francisco Airport.

Today's airport comprises approximately 2,400 acres with control of 2,800 acres of Bay tidelands. Since 1970 the airport has been controlled by a five-member Airports Commission. Previously the Public Utilities Commission had been responsible for its development, given this duty by the 1932 charter.

A new Master Plan initiated after voter approval of a $98-million airport development bond issue in November, 1967 has allowed for terminal, runway, and garage expansion.

Bart

(Bay Area Rapid Transit)

BART's function is to move people rapidly from place to place. This is done by a 75-mile rail complex which follows the region's natural transportation corridors along existing highway and railroad rights-of-way and through an underwater tube. There are 34 stations on the line, 17 in Alameda County, 8 in San Francisco, 8 in Contra Costa County, and 1 in Daly City, San Mateo County. Three transfer points are available, all in Oakland.

BART was financed by a $792-million bond issue approved by the voters on November 6, 1962 and $180-million in Bay Bridge tolls to pay for the Trans-Bay Tube. Additional money has been granted by the U.S. Department of Housing and Urban Development.

BART was first governed by a 12-man board of directors appointed by the County Board of Supervisors and City Mayors. Today 9 directors are elected by the voters.

BART train passes under a freeway it is designed to supercede.

Bart - Tracks

Track: welded rail 1517 ft. in length
Track gauge: wide gauge 5 ft. 6 in.
Ties: prestressed concrete weighing 525 pounds each.
Power: Electric third rail carrying 1,000 volts D.C.

Cost: approximately $32 million
Designers: Parsons Brinckerhoff-Tudor-Bechtel.
First track laid: February 19, 1965 (Contra Costa County)

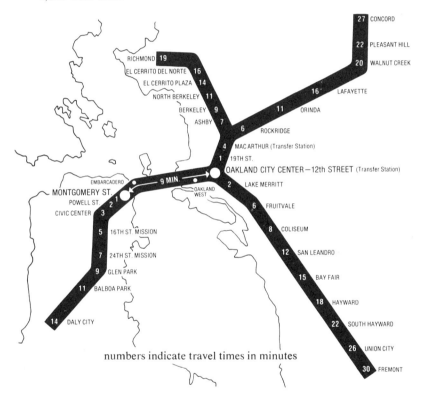

numbers indicate travel times in minutes

Bart - Transbay Tube

Length: Largest underwater rapid transit tube in the world: 3.6 miles in tube (19,113 feet), 6 miles overall including approaches.

Construction: 57 binocular-shaped sections of tubular steel and reinforced concrete, about 350 feet long by 48 feet wide by 24 feet high each. Constructed by Bethelem Steel Company.

Depth: Deepest point is 130 feet below the Bay surface.

Starting date: First scoopful of mud raised from Bay for tube construction April 15, 1966.

Completion date: Last tube connected April 3, 1969.

Contractors: Transbay Contractors (4 contracting firms)

Cost: $89.9 million

Openings: Public walk in tube Nov. 9, 1969 with some 20,000 participating. First train through tube June 9, 1972 taking 1 hour, 15 minutes. First three-car train with more than 50 BART officials, newsmen and technicians aboard traveled between the Seventh Street Station in Oakland and the Montgomery Street Station in San Francisco in six minutes, 55 seconds. Opening day through tube Monday, Sept. 16, 1974.

Bart - Cars

Length: 72 feet
Width: 10½ feet
Height: 10½ feet
Ceiling Height: 6 feet 9 inches
Weight: 56,000 pounds

Seating capacity: 72 people
Average Speed: 80 mph
Cost of 250 cars: $66.7 million
Manufacturer: Rohr Corporation, Chula Vista, California

Bridges

Golden Gate Bridge

In 1918 the San Francisco Board of Supervisors voted for studies to determine if a span could be built across the Golden Gate.

Later in 1923, Bridging the Golden Gate Association was formed when Frank P. Doyle, president of the Chamber of Commerce of Santa Rosa, called and presided at a meeting of representatives from San Francisco and North Bay counties in the Chamber's Assembly Room.

A construction permit was issued by Patrick Hurley, U.S. Secretary of War, on August 11, 1930, and in November of the same year a bond issue in the amount of $35-million (bonds paid off July 1, 1971) was approved by a vote of 107,930 for and 35,305 against.

The engineer, Joseph B. Strauss (Clifford Paine, assistant) commenced work on the bridge January 5, 1933 when steam shovels began digging the Marin anchorage.

Statistics

Style: Suspension
Length: 7 miles including approaches; 6450 ft. bridge itself
Width: 90 ft., center to center of cables
Longest single span: 4200 ft.
Height of towers: 746 ft. above water
Deepest pier: 100 ft. below water
Largest pier: 90 x 185 ft.; height from base: 144 ft.

Number of piers: 2
Steel used: over 100,000 tons
Cable wire: length 80,000 miles; weight 22,000 tons
Size cables: 36½ inches diameter; 7660 ft. long
Number of wires: 27,572 strands, 2/10 inch diameter
Concrete: 693,000 cubic yards

Paint color: international orange
Man hours: 25,000,000
Men killed during building: 11
Sway: 27.7 ft.

Work begun: January 5, 1933
Last rivet (gold) placed: May 27, 1937
Pedestrian day: May 27, 1937

Annual Vehicular Traffic

1938 .3.5 million	1972 .34.5 million
1969 . . . . .32.0 million	

Commuter Head Counts
Southbound, 6 to 10 a.m., auto-bus-ferry

March 1972, workday average . .33,153

March 1973, workday average . .34,560

Increase 1,407

Estimated increase using transit .1,300

Number of additional autos
  from 1972 90

Notes: Estimated number of passengers per auto is 1.28. Thus, 1280 transit passengers remove 1000 autos from bridge.

Vehicular Congestion

1. Highway officials consider 150 vehicles per lane per hour to be maximum for efficiency, and 1800 to be overload situation. With overload, traffic slows. This leads to more congestion, slower-moving traffic.

2. Normal peak traffic southbound on four lanes of bridge is from 7:45 a.m. to 8:15 a.m., currently estimated at about 1700 vehicles per lane per hour.

3. Bus and ferry commuters now estimated at 7650 daily, thus removing nearly 6000 vehicles (at 1.28 passengers per car) from commute-hour peaks between 6:30 and 8:30 a.m.

4. Conclusion by bridge officials: Additional bus and ferry transit essential to keep bridge traffic moving.

View from South Tower of the Golden Gate Bridge.

Two bridges in the building, in 1935.

Subsidies for Transit

1. For 1972-73, bridge officials estimate 31 cents per ferryboat passenger, 54 cents per bus passenger.

2. 1976-77, they expect ferryboat passenger subsidies to be about the same as bus passenger subsidies, 50 to 55 cents per ticket.

3. Subsidies come from bridge revenues, mostly the 75-cent one-way-only toll, with a minor amount for the bus transit system from state gasoline tax rebates to Marin County.

Value of the Bridge

1937 - $35 million (the construction cost), to be paid through tolls.

1973 - $200 million (replacement cost), paid off in 1971.

Plaque: Bronze with cement made of ingredients from every county in the State, fastened to the toll plaza of the Golden Gate Bridge at a ceremony conducted by the grand officers of the Native Sons on May 27, 1937. It reads:

"Dedication by the Native Sons of the Golden West; as tribute to the engineering genius which gave to the State of California the Golden Gate Bridge—longest bridge span in the world—we, the Native Sons of the Golden West make this dedication in recognition of the beauty and utility of this great structure and the scientific achievement for which it stands. May 27, 1937"

Bridge dedicated: May 28, 1937 after President Roosevelt pressed a button in Washington at 12 Noon.

San Francisco-Oakland Bay Bridge

Senate Bill 1762 was introduced into the Senate December 15, 1927 after various plans for better and faster communication across San Francisco Bay, other than ferries, were suggested.

This bill granted to the City and County of San Francisco the right to construct a bridge across San Francisco Bay, and approaches from Rincon Hill in the City and County of San Francisco to a point near the South Mole of San Antonio Estuary, in the county of Alameda.

Construction was begun on the bridge July 9, 1933. It was completed in

San Francisco-Oakland Bay Bridge nearing completion.

three years, four months, and three days, opening November 12, 1936. Cardinal Eugenio Pacelli (later Pope Pius XII) blessed the bridge at the West Tower No. 1, October 28, 1936.

Statistics

Style: 2 Suspension; 1 Cantilever; 5 Truss Spans; 14 Deck Spans
Length of Main Structure: 22,720 feet
Length over water: 4½ miles
Total length: 43,500 feet or 8½ miles

West Bay Crossing
Height of towers above water: 474 and 519 feet
Depth of piers below water: 100 to 235 feet

Height of center anchorage above water: 281 feet
Length of center spans: 2,310 feet
Length of side spans: 1,160 feet
Sway: 27.7 feet

East Bay Crossing
Length of main span: 1,400 feet
Clearance above high water: 185 feet
Depth of piers: 50 to 235 feet

San Francisco-Oakland Bay Bridge today.

Third Street Bridge

(At China Basin)

The first Third Street Bridge was a Page double-leaf bascule bridge erected in 1904 by the Atchison, Topeka & Santa Fe Railway Company, and presented free to the City by agreement for maintenance and operation.

The contract for the new Third Street Bridge was awarded on November 25, 1931 to Barrett & Hilp. The bridge opened May 12, 1933.

Third Street Bridge

(At Islais Creek)

This bridge was redesigned and opened as a six-lane (instead of four) roller-bearing span, on March 3, 1950. Duncanson-Harrelson were awarded the $1,250,000 job of converting the bridge which splits in the center.

Cable Cars

Andrew Smith Hallidie developed his system of cable roads now in use in this city in 1873. The first trial run of his dummy was down the Clay Street hill between Jones and Kearny, a distance of 2,880 feet on August 2, 1873, at 4 A.M. Later the same day, the dummy with a car attached made another round trip, this time with a large crowd in attendance. There were many changes and alterations made to the system before complete success crowned Mr. Hallidie's endeavors and public recognition was forthcoming.

In 1881 at the San Francisco Industrial Exhibition the Honorable W. W. Morrow stated, ". . . what a revolution it [the cable car] has made in the mode of transporting passengers in this city! The hills have fallen down before it, and they are now even more accessible, and certainly more desirable for residence than the level portions of the city."

The cable cars were made a National Historic Landmark on October 1, 1964.

Cable Car Specifications

	Single-End Cars	Double-End Cars
Weight:	12,180 pounds	11,500 pounds
Seating capacity:	30	34
Length over bumpers:	27 feet	30 feet 5 inches

*Cable car crossroads of the world: California and Powell streets,
where three lines intersect.*

Length over closed section:	12 feet	10 feet 7 inches
Length over open section:	15 feet	9 feet
Width over steps:	7 feet 10 inches	8 feet
Truck centers:	11 feet 8 inches	19 feet
Height:	10 feet 3 inches	10 feet 3 inches
Size & type of wheel:	22 inches, cast steel	
Track gauge:	3 feet 6 inches	
Cable speed:	840 feet per minute or 9 mph	

Steepest grades:

59 Powell-Mason Line:
Powell bet. Bush & Pine   17.5%
60 Powell-Hyde Line
Hyde bet. Bay & Francisco   21.3%
61 California
California bet. Grant & Stockton 18.2%

Cable Turntables
(Single-end cars require a turn table at each end)
1. Powell-Market   3. Beach-Hyde
2. Bay-Taylor   4. Washington-Mason carhouse

Street Railroads

In 1860 the Market Street Railroad Company was formed and consisted of five cable lines: Valencia, Castro, Haight, Hayes, McAllister; and one horse line: 5th Street, Market to Townsend.

In the consolidation of 1893 the following companies were taken over: Omnibus Railroad Company, North Beach and Mission Company, Central Railroad Company, and the Ferries and Cliff House Company.

The first electric line in San Francisco was the San Francisco and San Mateo Railroad Company, built by Behrend Joost in 1891. It ran from Steuart and Market streets to the county line, via Steuart, Harrison, Fourteenth, Guerrero and San Jose Avenue. It was purchased by the "Baltimore Syndicate" in 1896 and later formed the nucleus for the United Railroads, which on March 18, 1902, began operating all lines in the city, with the exceptions of the Presidio & Ferries line, California Street cable line, and the Geary Street line.

The City Charter adopted in 1900 declared for ultimate municipal ownership for all public utilities, but it was not until December, 1909, that a $2,000,000 bond issue was passed.

The Municipal Street Railway was inaugurated December 28, 1912. Mayor Rolph spoke to the crowd saying: "It is in reality 'the people's road', built by the people and with the people's money. The first cable road in the country was built in San Francisco, and now, the first municipal railway of the country is built in San Francisco. Our operation of this road will be closely watched by the whole country. It must prove a success. We must run it by proper methods. When we have it built from the Ferry to the Ocean, it will be the best single route in the city, and we must extend it wherever possible, until it becomes a great municipal system."

The merger of the Market Street Railway Company with the Municipal Railway occurred on September 29, 1944.

Tunnels

Broadway Tunnel

Construction started: May 1950
Opened: Dec. 21, 1952 to vehicular and pedestrian traffic
Cost: $5,253,552
Engineer: Ralph G. Wadsworth
Width: 28½ ft. each bore

Length: twin bores 1,616 ft. with approaches 3,300 ft. through Russian Hill from Powell Street on the East to Polk Street on the West.

Duboce (or Sunset) Tunnel

Construction started: June 5, 1926
Opened: Oct. 21, 1928 to street cars
only
Length: 4,232 feet from Duboce & Noe
Street to Carl & Cole Streets.
Width: 25 feet

Height: 23 ft. above invert, net
clearance above rail 18 ft.
9 in.
Cost: Approximately $1,651,983.00
Engineer: M. M. O'Shaughnessy

Fort Mason Tunnel
(Belt Line Railroad)

Completed: Nov. 1, 1914
Length: 1,537 feet Van Ness Ave. to
Laguna

Width: 17 feet
Cost: $273,149.30

Mile Rock Sewerage Tunnel

Contract awarded: Feb. 11, 1914

Engineer: M. M. O'Shaughnessy

Height: 9 feet

Width: 11 feet

Length: 4,550 feet (North of the
Fulton Street Pumping Station
the storm water outfall extends
from Cabrillo street under the
Sutro Heights to the outfall
of the sea front)

San Francisco Subway
(Embarcadero Tunnel)

Construction started: Dec. 6, 1923
Opened: May 2, 1925 (to auto traffic
only)
Length: 1,004 ft.
Width: 23 ft.
Height: 13 ft.
Grade in approaches: 3¾%
Floor thickness: 5 ft.

Side wall thickness: 2½ ft.
High tide level below top of Subway:
6 ft.
Cost: $375,000
Filling-in operation started:
April 9, 1957
Engineer: Frank G. White

Stockton Tunnel

Contract awarded: April 11, 1913
Length: 911 ft. Stockton Street
between Bush & Sacramento
Streets.
Width: 50 ft.
Cost: In excess of $600,000

Completed: Dec. 28, 1914 (First
tunnel in San Francisco
to accommodate vehicular
and pedestrian traffic)
Engineer: M. M. O'Shaughnessy

Twin Peaks Tunnel

Ground broken: Nov. 30, 1914
Completed: July 14, 1917
Celebration: July 15, 1917
First street car through:
    Feb. 3, 1918
Engineer: M. M. O'Shaughnessy

Length: (2¼ miles)
    Market & Castro to Lenox
    Way & Ulloa
Height: 15 ft.
Width: 25 ft.
Cost: $3,372,000

Rail Tunnels

SOUTHERN PACIFIC

Mariposa Street & Iowa Street to 22nd Street & Iowa Street
  Length: 1817.30 ft.
  Width: 30 ft.
23rd Street & Pennsylvania Ave. to 25th Street & Pennsylvania Ave.
  Length: 1086.40 ft.
  Width: 30 ft.
Phelps Street and Palou Ave. to Williams Ave. and Reddy Street
  Length: 2364 ft.

Gould Street and Jamestown Ave. to Bayshore Ave. and Tunnel Ave.
  Length: 3540 ft.
  Width: 30 ft.

WESTERN PACIFIC

18th Street and Arkansas Street to Sierra Street and Texas Street
  Length: 1625 ft.
  Width: 17 ft.

A San Francisco Bibliography

Architecture

AIDALA, THOMAS. *Great Houses of San Francisco*. New York: Knopf, 1974.

BAIRD, JOSEPH ARMSTRONG, JR. *Time's Wondrous Changes: San Francisco Architecture 1776-1915*. San Francisco: Calif. Historical Society, 1962.

BRUGMANN, BRUCE AND GREGGAR SLETTELAND. *The Ultimate Highrise, San Francisco's Mad Rush Toward the Sky*. San Francisco: Bay Guardian, 1971.

ELLERY, NATHANIEL. *Permanency in Building Construction*. San Francisco, 1913.

GEBHARD, DAVID. *A Guide to Architecture in San Francisco and Northern California*. Santa Barbara and Salt Lake City: Peregrine Smith, Inc., 1973.

KIRKER, HAROLD. *California's Architectural Frontier: Style and Tradition in the Nineteenth Century*. San Marino, Cal.: The Huntington Library, 1960.

MCCUE, BOONE & TOMSICK. *Tall Buildings in San Francisco*. San Francisco: Chamber of Commerce, 1971.

OLMSTED, ROGER. *Here Today; San Francisco's Architectural Heritage*. San Francisco: Chronicle Books, 1968.

VAIL, WESLEY D. *Victorians; An Account of Domestic Architecture in Victorian San Francisco, 1870-1890*. San Francisco: W. D. Vail, 1964.

WATKINS, MRS. ELEANOR PRESTON. *The Builders of San Francisco and Some of Their Early Homes*. San Francisco, Calif.: 1935.

WOODBRIDGE, JOHN M. *Buildings of the Bay Area; A Guide to the Architecture of the San Francisco Bay Region*. New York: Grover Press, 1960.

Arts

ARMSBY, LEONORA WOOD. *We Shall Have Music*. San Francisco: Pisani Printing and Pub. Co., 1960.

BLOOMFIELD, ARTHUR J. *Fifty Years of the San Francisco Opera*. San Francisco: San Francisco Book Co., 1972.

BLOOMFIELD, ARTHUR J. *The San Francisco Opera, 1923-1961.* New York: Appleton-Century-Crofts, 1961.

GAGEY, EDMOND M. *The San Francisco Stage.* New York: Columbia Univ. Press, 1950.

GLEASON, RALPH J. *The Jefferson Airplane and the San Francisco Sound.* New York: Ballantine Books, 1969.

LEWIS, OSCAR. *Bay Window Bohemia; An Account of the Brilliant Artistic World of Gaslit San Francisco.* Garden City, New York: Doubleday, 1956.

MACMINN, GEORGE R. *Theater of the Golden Era in California.* Caldwell, Ida.: Caxton, 1941.

SCOTT, MELLIER, GOODIN. *Partnership in the Arts; Public and Private Support of Cultural Activities in the San Francisco Bay Area.* Berkeley: Institute of Governmental Studies, Univ. of Calif., 1963.

U.S. WORK PROJECTS ADMINISTRATION, CALIFORNIA. *History of Music in San Francisco.* San Francisco: Work Projects Administration of Northern California, 1939-1942.

Barbary Coast

ASBURY, HERBERT. *The Barbary Coast; An Informal History of the San Francisco Under-World.* New York: Knopf, 1933.

DILLON, RICHARD. *Embarcadero.* New York: Coward-McCann, 1959.

EVANS, ALBERT S. *A La California. Sketches of Life in the Golden State.* San Francisco: A. L. Bancroft & Co., 1874.

GENTRY, CURT. *The Madams of San Francisco; An Irreverent History of the City by the Golden Gate.* Garden City, New York: Doubleday, 1964.

LLOYD, B. E. *Lights and Shades of San Francisco.* San Francisco: A. L. Bancroft & Co., 1876.

VILAS, MARTIN S. *The Barbary Coast of San Francisco.* 1915.

WILSON, JACKSON STITT. *The Barbary Coast in a Barbarous Land.* Los Angeles: Socialist Party of California, 1913?.

Bridges

BROWN, ALLEN. *Golden Gate, A Biography of a Bridge.* Garden City, New York: Doubleday, 1965.

GOLDEN GATE BRIDGE. *Report of the Chief Engineer to the Board of Directors of the Golden Gate Bridge and Highway District, California, Sept. 1937.* San Francisco: 1938.

MENSCH, E. CROMWELL. *The Golden Gate Bridge. A Technical Description in Ordinary Language*. San Francisco: 1937.

MENSCH, E. CROMWELL. *The San Francisco-Oakland Bay Bridge. A Technical Description in Ordinary Language*. San Francisco: 1936.

WADE, LAWRENCE L. *Bridges of San Francisco Bay*. San Francisco: Falcon, 1966.

Cable and Street Cars

ARNOLD, BION J. *Report on the Improvement and Development of the Transportation Facilities of San Francisco*. San Francisco: 1913.

BEEBE, LUCIUS MORRIS. *Cable Car Carnival*. Oakland, Calif.: Grahame Hardy, 1951.

CABLE RAILWAY COMPANY, SAN FRANCISCO. *System of Traction Railways for Cities and Towns*. San Francisco: 1881?.

FRANKLIN, SID. *Market Street Railroad Company: A History*. San Francisco: 1941.

HANSCOM, W. W. *Archaeology of the Cable Car*. Pasadena, Calif.: Socio-Technical Books, 1970.

INTERURBANS. *Market Street Railway Revisited*, edited by Ira L. Swett. South Gate, Calif.: 1972.

KAHN, EDGAR M. *Cable Car Days in San Francisco*. Stanford, Calif.: Stanford Univ. Press, 1940.

NEVILL, WALLACE E. *When the Jackson Street Cable Stopped, Or, The Car Conductor's Dream*. San Francisco: Printed for the author by the Coming Light Publishing House, n.d.

PARKER, FRANK. *Anatomy of the San Francisco Cable Car*. Stanford: Delkin, 1946.

PERINI, JIMO. *San Francisco Grip*. San Francisco: San Francisco Grip Publishers, 1969.

SMALLWOOD, CHARLES. *The White Front Cars of San Francisco*. South Gate, Calif.: Interurbans, 1971.

SMITH, J. BUCKNALL. *A Treatise Upon Cable or Rope Traction as Applied to the Working of Street and Other Railways*. London, 1887.

SWAN, CHRISTOPHER. *Cable Car*. San Francisco: Ten Speed Press, 1973.

VILAS, MARTIN S. *Municipal Railway of San Francisco*. Martin Samuel Vilas, 1915.

Chinatown

BODE, WILLIAM WALTER. *Lights and Shades of Chinatown*. San Francisco: Crocker, 1896.

COOLIDGE, MARY ROBERTS. *Chinese Immigration.* New York: Holt, 1909.

DILLON, RICHARD H. *The Hatchet Men; The Story of the Tong Wars in San Francisco Chinatown.* New York: Coward-McCann, 1962.

DOBIE, CHARLES CALDWELL. *San Francisco's Chinatown.* New York: D. Appleton-Century, 1939.

FANG, JOHN T., EDITOR. *Chinatown Handy Guide, San Francisco.* San Francisco: Chinese Pub. House, 1959.

GENTHE, ARNOLD. *Pictures of Old Chinatown.* New York: Moffatt Yard, 1909.

GIBSON, REV. OTIS. *Chinese in America.* Cincinnati: Hitchcock and Walden, 1877.

HOY, WILLIAM. *The Chinese Six Companies. A Short General Historical Resume of the Origin, Function and Importance in the Life of the California Chinese.* San Francisco: Chinese Consolidated Benevolence Association, 1942.

IRWIN, WILL. *Old Chinatown. A Book of Pictures by Arnold Genthe.* New York: Moffat, Yard and Co., 1908.

JUE, GEORGE K. *Chinatown; Its History, Its People, Its Importance.* San Francisco: San Francisco Chamber of Commerce, 1951.

LEE, ROSE HUM. *The Chinese in the United States of America.* Hong Kong: Hong Kong Univ. Press, Oxford Univ. Press, 1960.

LLOYD, BENJAMIN E. *Lights and Shades in San Francisco.* San Francisco: A. L. Bancroft & Co., 1876.

NEE, VICTOR G. AND BRETT DE BARY. *Longtime Californ'; A Documentary Study of an American Chinatown.* New York: Pantheon Books, 1972, 1973.

PALMER, PHIL. *Chinatown, San Francisco.* Berkeley, Calif.: Howell-North, 1960.

SANDMEYER, ELMER CLARENCE. *The Anti-Chinese Movement in California.* Urbana: Univ. of Illinois, 1939.

STODDARD, CHARLES WARREN. *A Bit of Old China.* San Francisco: A. M. Robertson, 1912.

Churches or Parishes

ANTHONY, CHARLES V. *Fifty Years of Methodism. A History of the Methodist Episcopal Church Within the Bounds of the California Annual Conference from 1847-1897.* San Francisco: Methodist Book Concern, 1901.

BORDEN, STANLEY T. *Trinity Presbyterian Church; 90 Years in San Francisco's Mission District.* San Francisco: 1958?.

BUFFORD, CHARLES M. *A Hundred Years of Congregationalism in San*

Francisco, 1849-1949. Prepared for Centennial meeting of First Congregational Church, San Francisco, held at Portsmouth Plaza, July 31, 1949.

CARRERS, JOHN F. *The Story of Old St. Mary's*. San Francisco: Paulist Fathers, n.d.

CARROLL, LUKE M. *Holy Cross Parish, Lone Mt. District of San Francisco*. Published in honor of the Golden Jubilee, October 1937, n.d.

CURRY, JAMES. *History of the San Francisco Theological Seminary of the Presbyterian Church in the U.S.A. and its Alumni Association*. Vacaville, Calif.: Reporter Publishing Company, 1907.

DORN, J. GEORGE. *One Hundred Years in San Francisco, California; A History of St. Mark's Evangelical Lutheran Church, 1849-1949*. San Francisco: 1949.

HISTORICAL RECORDS SURVEY. *A Directory of Churches and Religious Organizations in San Francisco, California, 1941. San Francisco, Calif.: The Northern California Historical Records Survey, 1941.*

IRWIN, REV. D. HANSON, EDITOR. *The Pacific Coast Pulpit*. New York: Chicago: Fleming H. Revell Co., 1893.

MCCARTHY, FRANCIS FLORENCE. *Hunter's Point*. San Francisco: Flores Paramount Press, 1942.

MCGLOIN, JOHN BERNARD. *Jesuits by the Golden Gate; The Society of Jesus in San Francisco, 1849-1969*. San Francisco: Univ. of San Francisco, 1972.

MCSWEENEY, THOMAS DENIS. *Cathedral on California Street. The Story of St. Mary's Cathedral, San Francisco, 1854-1891, and of Old St. Mary's A Paulist Church, 1894-1951*. Fresno, Calif.: Academy of California Church History, 1952.

A Memorial of the Golden Jubilee, St. Paulus Church Dedication, The Eleventh of February 1894-1944; And, Church Handbook for 1944. San Francisco: 1944.

MONTESANO, PHIL. *The Black Churches in Urban San Francisco, 1860-1865; Their Educational, Civic, and Civil Rights Activities*. Typescript, n.d.

MONTROSE, DONALD. *The Story of a Parish; Its Priests and Its People. . .* Pub. at St. Boniface Parish, J. Quatannens, 1961.

RIORDAN, JOSEPH W. *The First Half Century of St. Ignatius Church and College*. San Francisco: H.S. Crocker Co., 1905.

SAN FRANCISCO. FIRST UNITARIAN SOCIETY. *One Hundred Years of the First Unitarian Church of San Francisco, 1850-1950*. San Francisco: Printed at the Grabhorn Press, 1950.

SAN FRANCISCO. HOWARD STREET METHODIST EPISCOPAL CHURCH. *"The Retrospect" A Glance at Thirty Years of the History of Howard Street Methodist Episcopal Church of San Francisco*. San Francisco: A. Buswell & Co., printers and binders, 1883.

SAN FRANCISCO. ST. BONIFACE CHURCH. *Golden Anniversary, 1908-1958*. San Francisco: The Franciscan Fathers, 1958.

WILLIAMS, ALBERT. *A Pioneer Pastorate and Times, Embodying Contemporary Local Transactions and Events.* San Francisco: Wallace & Hassett, 1879.

VOORSANGER, JACOB. *The Chronicles of Emanu-El; Being an Account of the Rise and Progress of the Congregation Emanu-El, Which was Founded in July, 1850, and Will Celebrate its Fiftieth Anniversary December 23, 1900. San Francisco: Press of C. Spaulding & Co., 1900.*

ZARCHIN, MICHAEL MOSES. *Glimpses of Jewish Life in San Francisco.* 2nd rev. ed. Oakland, Calif., Judah L. Magnes Memorial Museum, 1964.

Climate

FELTON, ERNEST L. *California's Many Climates.* Palo Alto, Calif.: Pacific Books, Pub., 1965.

MCADIE, ALEXANDER G. *The Climate of San Francisco.* Washington: Gov. Printing Office, 1899.

MCADIE, ALEXANDER G. *The Clouds and Fogs of San Francisco.* San Francisco: A. M. Robertson, 1912.

Earthquakes

AITKEN, FRANK W. AND EDWARD HILTON. *History of the Earthquake and Fire in San Francisco. An Account of the Disaster of April 18, 1906 and its Immediate Results.* San Francisco: Hilton, 1906.

BANKS, CHARLES E. AND OPIE READ. *The History of the San Francisco Disaster and Mount Vesuvius Horror. . .* Chicago: 1906.

BOREL, ANTOINE. *"San Francisco is No More", The Letters of Antoine Borel, Jr., 1905-1906.* Menlo Park, Calif., 1963.

BRONSON, WILLIAM. *The Earth Shook, The Sky Burned.* Garden City: Doubleday, 1959.

BROWN, HELEN H. *The Great San Francisco Fire; An Account of the San Francisco Earthquake and Fire of April 1906. . .* San Francisco: Leo Holub, 1956.

BURGESS, DON L. *Ashes of San Francisco.* Prairie City: Decker Press, 1948.

BYERLY, PERRY. *History of Earthquakes in the San Francisco Bay Area.* 1952.

CALIFORNIA STATE EARTHQUAKE INVESTIGATION COMMISSION. *Report of the California Earthquake of April 18, 1906.* Washington, D.C., Carnegie Institution, 1908-10.

GILBERT, GROVE KARL. *The San Francisco Earthquake and Fire of April 18,*

1906, and Their Effects on Structures and Structural Materials. . . Washington: Government Printing Office, 1907.

Glimpses of San Francisco Disaster, Graphically Depicting the Great California Earthquake and Fire, Original Photographs of the World's Greatest Conflagration. . . Chicago: Laird & Lee, 1906.

GREELY, ADOLPHUS W. *Earthquake in California April 18, 1906.* Washington: Government Printing Office, 1906.

HIMMELSWRIGHT, ABRAHAM LINCOLN ARTMAN. *San Francisco Earthquake and Fire. A Brief History of the Disaster.* New York: Roebling Construction Co., 1906.

IACOPI, ROBERT. *Earthquake Country.* Menlo Park, Calif.: Lane Books, 1964.

JORDAN, DAVID STARR. *California Earthquake of 1906.* San Francisco: A. M. Robertson, 1907.

KEELER, CHARLES AUGUSTUS. *San Francisco Through Earthquake and Fire.* San Francisco: Elder, 1906.

KENNEDY, JOHN CASTILLO. *The Great Earthquake and Fire, San Francisco, 1906.* New York: Morrow, 1963.

LIVINGSTON, RICHARD. *A Personal History of the San Francisco Earthquake and Fire in 1906.* San Francisco: Windsor Press, 1941.

LYMAN, W.W. *Recollections of the San Francisco Earthquake and Fire of 1906.* James E. Brard, 1972.

MORRIS, CHARLES. *The San Francisco Calamity by Earthquake and Fire.* . . 1906.

MORROW, WILLIAM W. *The Earthquake of April 18, 1906, and the Great Fire in San Francisco on That and Succeeding Days.* . . San Francisco: 1906.

NEIL, HENRY. *Complete Story of the San Francisco Earthquake.* . . *April 18, 1906.* . . *With a Full Account of the Generous Aid Supplied to the Sufferers by the People of the United States.* . . Chicago: Bible House, 1906.

RODRIGUEZ, MARIE LOUISE BINE. *The Earthquake of 1906.* San Francisco: James H. Barry Co., 1951.

RYDER, DAVID WARREN. *They Wouldn't Take Ashes for an Answer.* San Francisco: Fireman's Fund Insurance Co., 1948.

San Francisco and Vicinity Before and After Its Destruction. Portland, Me., L. H. Nelson, 1906.

STEINBRUGGE, KARL V. *Earthquake Hazard in the San Francisco Bay Area: A Continuing Problem in Public Policy.* Berkeley: Univ. of Calif.: 1968.

STETSON, JAMES BURGESS. *Narrative of my Experiences in the Earthquake and Fire at San Francisco.* Palo Alto, Calif.: Lewis Osborne, 1969.

SUTHERLAND, MONICA. *The Damndest Finest Ruins.* New York: Coward-McCann, 1959.

THOMAS, GORDON. *The San Francisco Earthquake.* New York: Stein and Day, 1971.

TYLER, SYDNEY. *San Francisco's Great Disaster. . . With an Interesting Chapter on the Causes of This and Other Earthquakes. . .* Phila.: Ziegler, 1906.

WILSON, JAMES RUSSEL. *San Francisco's Horror of Earthquake and Fire. . .* Phila.: National Publishing Co., 1906.

ZEIGLER, WILBUR GLEASON. *Story of the Earthquake and Fire. . .* San Francisco: Murdock, 1906.

Expositions

The Blue Book; A Comprehensive Official Souvenir View Book of the Panama-Pacific International Exposition at San Francisco, 1915. . . San Francisco: R. A. Reid, 1915.

JAMES, JACK AND E. V. WELLER. *Treasure Island the Magic City 1939-40. The Story of the Golden Gate International Exposition.* San Francisco: Pisani, 1941.

JAMES, JULIET HELENA. *The Meaning of the Courts of the Golden Gate International Exposition, 1939.* Berkeley, Calif.: [Professional Press], 1939.

LEVY, LOUIS. *Chronological History of the Panama-Pacific International Exposition.* San Francisco: Panama-Pacific International Exposition, 1911.

MARKWART, A. H. *Building an Exposition.* San Francisco: Panama-Pacific International Exposition, 1915.

NEUHAUS, EUGEN. *The Art of Treasure Island.* Berkeley: Univ. of Calif., 1939.

Official History of the Midwinter International Exposition January to July 1894. Compiled from Official Records of the Exposition and Published by the Authority of the Executive Committee. San Francisco: Crocker, 1894.

REINHARDT, RICHARD. *Treasure Island: San Francisco's Exposition Years.* San Francisco: Scrimshaw Press, 1973.

TODD, FRANK MORTON. *Story of the Exposition being the Official History of the International Celebration Held at San Francisco in 1915 to Commemorate the Discovery of the Pacific Ocean and the Construction of the Panama Canal.* New York: Putnam, 1921.

Flora and Fauna

CLYDE, DALE PETERS AND HOPE B. PURMONT. *Birding in the Bay Area.* Healdsburg, Calif.: Naturegraph Co., 1964.

CONRADSON, DIANE R. *Exploring Our Baylands.* Palo Alto: Palo Alto Chamber of Commerce, 1966.

GILLIAM, HAROLD. *The Natural World of San Francisco.* Garden City, New York: Doubleday, 1967.

MAILLIARD, JOSEPH. *Handbook of the Birds of Golden Gate Park.* San Francisco: Published by the Academy, 1930.

METCALF, WOODBRIDGE. *Native Trees of the San Francisco Bay Region.* Berkeley and Los Angeles: Univ. of Calif. Press, 1959.

Golden Gate Park

BLAIR, HOSEA. *Monuments and Memories of San Francisco: Golden Gate Park.* San Francisco: 1955.

DOSS, MARGOT PATTERSON. *Golden Gate Park At Your Feet.* San Francisco: Chronicle Books, 1970.

GIFFIN, GUY AND HELEN. *Story of Golden Gate Park.* San Francisco: Phillipps & Van Orden, 1949.

JOHNSON, ROBERT BARBOUR. *The Magic Park.* San Francisco: Century Press, 1940.

LIPPMANN, C. R. *A Trip Through Golden Gate Park: An Outstanding Achievement in Landscape Architecture.* San Francisco: Print Corp., 1937.

PRUETT, HERBERT E. *The Golden Gate Park.* [Berkeley]: Pruett-MacGregor, 1968.

STELLMANN, EDITH KINNEY. *Katie of Birdland: An Idyl of the Aviary in Golden Gate Park.* San Francisco: H. S. Crocker Co., [1917].

WILSON, KATHERINE. *Golden Gate the Park of a Thousand Vistas.* Caldwell, Ida.: Caxton, 1947.

Graft

BEAN, WALTON. *Boss Ruef's San Francisco; The Story of the Union Labor Party, Big Business, and the Graft Prosecution.* Berkeley: Univ. of Calif. Press, 1952.

BONNETT, THEODORE. *The Regenerators a Study of the Graft Prosecution in San Francisco.* San Francisco: Pacific Printing Co., 1911.

The Fate of the San Francisco Grafters, Benedict Arnold of his Native City . . . San Francisco: Cubery & Co., 1908.

HICHBORN, FRANKLIN. *"The System" as Uncovered by the San Francisco Graft Prosecution.* San Francisco: J. H. Barry, 1915.

Report on the causes of Municipal corruption in San Francisco, as disclosed by the investigations of the Oliver Grand Jury, and the prosecution of certain persons for bribery and other offenses against the state. 1910.

THOMAS, LATELY. *A Debonair Scoundrel.* New York: Holt, Rinehart and Winston, 1962.

Guides

ADAMS, BEN. *San Francisco; An Informal Guide*. New York: Hill and Wang, 1968.

AUSTIN, LEONARD. *Around the World in San Francisco*. Stanford, Calif.: James Ladd Delkin, 1940.

BENET, JAMES. *A Guide to San Francisco and the Bay Region*. New York: Random House, 1963.

DELKIN, JAMES LADD. *Flavor of San Francisco, A Guide to "The City"*. Palo Alto: Stanford Univ. Press, 1943.

GENTRY, CURT. *The Dolphin Guide to San Francisco and the Bay Area: Present and Past*. Garden City, New York: Dolphin Books, 1969.

HANSELL, FRANZ. *Opinionated Guide to San Francisco*. Sausalito, Calif.: Comstock Editions, 1973.

HANSELL, FRANZ T. *The Great Family Fun Guide to San Francisco*. Sausalito, Calif.: Comstock Editions, 1974.

HITTELL, JOHN S. *A Guide Book to San Francisco*. San Francisco: The Bancroft Co., 1883.

HOLDEN, BARBARA AND MARY-JANE WOEBCKE. *A Child's Guide to San Francisco*. Berkeley: Diablo Press, 1968.

JUNIOR LEAGUE OF SAN FRANCISCO, INC. *A Family Guide to the San Francisco Bay Area*. San Carlos, Calif.: Nourse Pub. Co., 1962.

PURDY, HELEN THROOP. *San Francisco As It Was, As It Is, and How To See It*. San Francisco: Elder, 1912.

Rand McNally Guide to San Francisco, Oakland, Berkeley, and Environs of the Bay Cities. . . New York: 1925.

SUNSET BOOKS. *San Francisco*. Edited by Jack McDowell. Menlo Park, Calif.: Lane, 1969.

WATKINS, TOM H. *San Francisco in Color*. New York: Hastings House, 1968.

WRITERS' PROGRAM OF THE W.P.A. IN NORTHERN CALIFORNIA. *San Francisco The Bay and Its Cities*. Rev. 3rd ed. New York: Hastings House, 1973.

Harbor

CAMP, WILLIAM MARTIN. *San Francisco Port of Gold*. New York: Doubleday, 1947.

DILLON, RICHARD H. *Embarcadero*. New York: Coward-McCann, 1959.

DYKSTRA, JOHN B. *Which Way The Bay?* Berkeley, Calif.: Urbanac Press, 1964.

FEDERATED HARBOR IMPROVEMENT ASSOCIATIONS, SAN FRANCISCO. *San Francisco Harbor; Its Commerce and Docks with a Complete Plan for Development*. San Francisco: 1908.

GILLIAM HAROLD. *Between the Devil and the Deep Blue Bay; The Struggle to Save San Francisco Bay*. San Francisco: Chronicle Books, 1969.

GILLIAM, HAROLD. *San Francisco Bay*. Garden City, New York: Doubleday, 1957.

GRADY, HENRY FRANCIS & R. M. CARR. *Port of San Francisco. A Study of the Traffic Competition, 1921-33*. Berkeley: Univ. of Calif., 1934.

HAMILTON, JAMES WILLIAM AND W. J. BOLCE. *Gateway to Victory. The Wartime Story of the San Francisco Port of Embarkation*. Stanford, 1946.

HARLAN, GEORGE H. AND CLEMENT FISHER, JR. *Of Walking Beams and Paddle Wheels. A Chronicle of San Francisco Bay Ferryboats*. San Francisco: Bay Books Limited, 1951.

KEMBLE, JOHN HASKELL. *San Francisco Bay. A Pictorial Maritime History*. Cambridge, Maryland: Cornell Maritime Press, 1957.

ODELL, RICE. *The Saving of San Francisco Bay; A Report on Citizen Action and Regional Planning*. Washington: Conservation Foundation, 1972.

RIESENBERG, FELIX. *Golden Gate The Story of San Francisco Harbor*. New York: Knopf, 1940.

SCOTT, MELLIER GOODIN. *The Future of San Francisco Bay*. Berkeley: Univ. of Calif., Institute of Governmental Studies, 1963.

WRIGHT, BENJAMIN COOPER. *San Francisco's Ocean Trade, Past and Future 1848-1911*. San Francisco: Carlisle, 1911.

Hills

CARROLL, LUKE M. *Holy Cross Parish and Lone Mountain District of San Francisco*. San Francisco: 1937.

DEERING, MARGARET P. *The Hills of San Francisco*. San Francisco: 1936.

HART, ANN CLARK. *Lone Mountain, The Most Revered of San Francisco's Hills*. San Francisco: The Pioneer Press, 1937.

MYRICK, DAVID F. *San Francisco's Telegraph Hill*. Berkeley, Calif.: Howell-North Books, 1972.

RYDER, DAVID WARREN. *The Story of Telegraph Hill, A Bit of Old San Francisco*. San Francisco: L'Esperance, Silvertson & Beran, 1948.

SAN FRANCISCO CHRONICLE. *Hills of San Francisco*. San Francisco: Chronicle Publishing Co., 1959.

SAROYAN, WILLIAM. *Hilltop Russians in San Francisco*. Palo Alto, Calif.: Stanford Univ. Press, 1941.

SHUMATE, ALBERT. *A Visit to Rincon Hill and South Park*. San Francisco: Tamalpais Press, 1963.

Hippies

BEGGS, REV. LARRY. *Huckleberry's for Runaways.* New York: Ballantine Books, 1969.

BRONSTEEN, RUTH. *The Hippy's Handbooks: How to Live on Love.* New York: Canyon Book Co., 1967.

CAVAN, SHERRI. *Hippies of the Haight.* St. Louis: New Critics Press, 1972.

GUSTAITIS, RASA. *Turning On.* Toronto, Ontario: The Macmillan Company, 1969.

PERRY, HELEN W. *The Human Be-In.* New York: Basic Books, 1970.

SMITH, DAVID E. AND JOHN LUCE. *Love Needs Care; A History of San Francisco's Haight-Ashbury Free Medical Clinic and Its Pioneer Role in Treating Drug-Abuse Problems.* Boston-Toronto: Little Brown and Company, 1971.

VON HOFFMAN, NICHOLAS. *We Are The People Our Parents Warned Us Against.* Chicago: Quadrangle Books, 1968.

WOLF, LEONARD. *Voices from the Love Generation.* Boston: Little Brown, 1968.

WOLFE, BURTON H. *The Hippies.* New York: American Library, 1968.

YABLONSKY, LEWIS. *The Hippie Trip.* New York: Pegasus, 1968.

Hotels and Restaurants

CROSS, RALPH H. *The Early Inns of California, 1844-1869.* San Francisco: Lawton Kennedy, 1954.

EDWARDS, CLARENCE EDGAR. *Bohemian San Francisco Its Restaurants and Their Most Famous Recipes.* San Francisco: Elder, 1914.

GOODRICH, MARY. *The Palace Hotel.* San Francisco: The Crandall Press, 1930.

GOURMET INTERNATIONAL. *Gourmet International's Recommended Restaurants of San Francisco.* Gourmet International, A Division of Research Unlimited, 1963.

LEWIS, OSCAR. *Bonanza Inn.* New York: A. A. Knopf, 1939.

MUSCATINE, DORIS. *A Cook's Tour of San Francisco; The Best Restaurants and Their Recipes.* New York: Scribner, 1969.

O'CONNELL, DANIEL. *The Inner Man. Good Things to Eat and Drink and Where to Get Them.* San Francisco: The Bancroft Co., 1891.

THOMPSON, RUTH. *Eating Around San Francisco.* Los Angeles: Lymanhouse, 1937.

UNNA, WARREN. *The Coppa Murals: A Pageant of Bohemian Life in San Francisco at the Turn of the Century.* San Francisco: Book Club of California, 1952.

Islands

BLUECLOUD, PETER. *Alcatraz Is Not An Island.* Wingbow Press, 1972.

BRUCE, JOHN CAMPBELL. *Escape from Alcatraz; A Farewell to the Rock.* New York: McGraw-Hill, 1963.

DODGE, ROBERT. *From Manhattan to Alcatraz.* New York: Holt, Rinehart & Winston, 1973.

ELLIS, STEVE. *Alcatraz: Number 1172.* Los Angeles: Holloway House Pub. Co., 1969.

GODWIN, JOHN. *Alcatraz: 1868-1963.* Garden City, New York: Doubleday, 1963.

HOOVER, MILDRED B. *The Farallon Islands, Calif.* Stanford, Calif.: Stanford Univ. Press, 1932.

JOHNSTON, JAMES A. *Alcatraz Island Prison, and the Men Who Live There.* New York: Scribner's, 1949.

KILLINGER, EMILY TIBBEY. *The Islands of San Francisco Bay.* San Francisco: 1934.

MCDEVITT, E. *The Naval History of Treasure Island.* Treasure Island, Calif., U.S. Naval Training and Distribution Center, San Francisco, 1946.

RAY, MILTON S. *The Farallones: The Painted World and Other Poems of California.* San Francisco: Printed by John Henry Nash, 1934.

U.S. Naval Training Station established 1899. Yerba Buena Island, San Francisco, California. Rear-Admiral Henry Glass, commandant. San Francisco: Willeford & Winchell, 1902.

Journalism

BRANCH, EDGAR M. *Clemens of the Call; Mark Twain in San Francisco.* Berkeley, Calif.: Univ. of Calif. Press, 1969.

BRUCE, JOHN R. *Gaudy Century, The Story of San Francisco's Hundred Years of Robust Journalism.* New York: Random House, 1948.

BURGESS, GELETT. *Gelett Burgess Behind the Scenes; Glimpses of Fin-de-Siecle San Francisco.* San Francisco: Printed by Grabhorn-Hoyem for the Book Club of California, 1968.

CLEMENS, SAMUEL LANGHORNE [Mark Twain]. *The Washoe Giant in San Francisco.* San Francisco: G. Fields, 1938.

CUMMINS, ELLA STERLING. *The Story of the Files. . . A Review of Californian Writers and Literature. . .* Issued under the Auspices of the World's Fair Commission of California, Columbian Exposition, 1893.

DUFFUS, ROBERT L. *The Tower of Jewels.* New York: W. W. Norton & Co., 1960.

HART, JEROME ALFRED. *In Our Second Century*. San Francisco: The Pioneer Press, 1931.

JOHNSON, KENNETH M. *The Sting of the Wasp; Political and Satirical Cartoons from the Truculent Early San Francisco Weekly*. San Francisco: Book Club of California, 1967.

OLDER, FREMONT. *Growing Up*. San Francisco: San Francisco Call-Bulletin, 1931.

WALKER, FRANKLIN. *San Francisco's Literary Frontier*. New York: A. A. Knopf, 1939.

YOUNG, JOHN P. *Journalism in California*. San Francisco: Chronicle Pub. Co., 1915.

Labor

CRONIN, BERNARD C. *Father Yorke and the Labor Movement in San Francisco 1900-1910*. Washington, D.C.: Catholic Univ., 1943.

CROSS, IRA B. *A History of the Labor Movement in California*. Berkeley: Univ. of Calif., 1935.

EAVES, LUCILE. *A History of California Labor Legislation, With an Introductory Sketch of the San Francisco Labor Movement*. Berkeley: The Univ. Press, 1910.

ELIEL, PAUL. *The Waterfront and General Strikes, San Francisco, 1934*. San Francisco: Hooper Printing Co., 1934.

RYAN, FREDERICK LYNNE. *Industrial Relations in the San Francisco Building Trades*. Norman: Univ. of Oklahoma Press, 1935.

RYAN, PAUL WILLIAM. *The Big Strike*. Olema, Calif.: Olema Pub. Co., 1949.

SCHNEIDER, BETTY. *Industrial Relations in the West Coast Maritime Industry*. Berkeley: Institute of Industrial Relations, Univ. of Calif., 1958.

Mission Dolores

BOLTON, HERBERT EUGENE. *Font's Complete Diary. A Chronicle of the Building of San Francisco*. Berkeley, Calif.: Univ. of California Press, 1931.

ENGELHARDT, ZEPHYRIN. *San Francisco or Mission Dolores*. Chicago: Franciscan Herald Press, 1924.

MERRILL, GEORGE A. *The Story of Lake Dolores and Mission San Francisco de Asis*. Redwood City, Calif.: Hedge Printing Co., n.d.

PALOU, FRANCISCO. *Life of Fray Junipero Serra*. Translated by Maynard J. Geiger. Washington: Academy of American Franciscan History, 1955.

SERRA, JUNIPERO. *Writings of Junipero Serra*. Ed. by A. Tibesar. Wash.: Academy of American Franciscan History, 1955.

THOMAS, P. J. *Our Centennial Memoir. Founding of the Missions. San Fran-cisco de Assis in its Hundredth Year. The Celebration of its Foundation. Historical Reminiscences of the Missions of California.* San Francisco: P. J. Thomas, 1877.

Palace of Fine Arts

BURDEN, ERNEST E. *San Francisco's Wildflower; The Palace of Fine Arts.* San Francisco: Phoenix Pub. Co., 1967.

MAYBECK, BERNARD R. *Palace of Fine Arts and Lagoon: Panama-Pacific International Exposition, 1915.* San Francisco: Paul Elder, 1915 .

NEWHALL, RUTH WALDO. *San Francisco's Enchanted Palace.* Berkeley, Calif.: Howell-North Books, 1967.

Presidio and Fort Point

BLAIR, HOSEA. *Monuments and Memories of San Francisco: The Presidio.* San Francisco: 1956.

BROWNE, MARTHA FAY R. *The Golden Gate and its Old Fort.* San Francisco: 1933.

DAVIS, JOHN FRANCIS. *The Founding of San Francisco Presidio and Mission Sesquicentennial Address by John F. Davis.* San Francisco: Pernau-Walsh Printing Co., 1926.

GARDNER, FRED. *The Unlawful Concert; An Account of the Presidio Mutiny Case.* New York: Viking Press, 1970.

U.S. WORKS PROJECT ADMINISTRATION. WRITER'S PROGRAM, CALIFORNIA. *The Army at the Golden Gate; A Guide to Army Posts in the San Francisco Bay Area.* Compiled by workers of the Writers' Program of the Work Projects Administration in Northern California. San Francisco: 1940.

Schools & Universities

BARLOW, WILLIAM. *An End to Silence; The San Francisco State College Movement in the '60s.* New York: Pegasus, 1971.

BOYLE, KAY. *The Long Walk at San Francisco State, and Other Essays.* New York: Grove Press, 1970.

DOHRMANN, F. *Three Years on a Board; Being the Experiences of the San Francisco Board of Education, 1922-24.* San Francisco: Dohrmann, 1924.

KARAGUEUZIAN, DIKRAN. *Blow It Up! The Black Student Revolt at San Francisco State College and the Emergence of Dr. Hayakawa.* Boston: Gambit, 1971.

RIORDAN, JOSEPH W. *The First Half Century of St. Ignatius Church and College*. San Francisco: H. Crocker, 1905.

SUMMERSKILL, JOHN. *President Seven*. New York: World Pub. Co., 1971.

SWETT, JOHN. *History of the Public School System of California*. San Francisco: A. L. Bancroft, 1876.

Streets

BLOCK, EUGENE B. *The Immortal San Franciscans for Whom the Streets were Named*. San Francisco: Chronicle Books, 1971.

CARLISLE, HENRY C. *San Francisco Street Names*. San Francisco: American Trust Co., 1954.

DICKSON, SAMUEL. *The Streets of San Francisco*. Stanford, Calif.: Stanford Univ. Press, 1955.

Vigilantes

ACADEMY PACIFIC COAST HISTORY PUBLICATIONS. *Papers of the San Francisco Committee of Vigilance of 1851*. Berkeley: Univ. of Calif., 1919.

COBLENTZ, STANTON ARTHUR. *Villains and Vigilantes; The Story of James King of William and Pioneer Justice in California*. New York: Wilson Erickson, 1936.

McGOWAN, EDWARD. *Narrative of Edward McGowan, Including a Full Account of the Author's Adventures and Perils While Persecuted by the San Francisco Vigilance Committee of 1856*. San Francisco: Published by the Author, 1857.

MYERS, JOHN. *San Francisco's Reign of Terror*. Garden City, New York: Doubleday, 1966.

NUNIS, DOYCE BLACKMAN. *The San Francisco Vigilance Committee of 1856; Three Views by William T. Coleman, William T. Sherman, and James O'Meara*. Los Angeles: Los Angeles Westerners, 1971.

O'MEARA, JAMES. *Vigilance Committee of 1856 by a Pioneer California Journalist*. San Francisco: Barry, 1887.

SCHERER, JAMES AUGUSTIN BROWN. *"The Lion of the Vigilantes"; William T. Coleman and the Life of Old San Francisco*. Indianapolis and New York: The Bobbs-Merrill Co., 1939.

SMITH, FRANK MERIWEATHER. *San Francisco Vigilance Committee of '56, With Some Interesting Sketches of Events succeeding 1846*. San Francisco: Barry Baird, 1883.

STEWART, GEORGE RIPPEY. *Committee of Vigilance; Revolution in San Francisco 1851*. Boston: Houghton Mifflin, 1964.

TERRY, DAVID S. *Trial of David S. Terry by the Committee of Vigilance, San Francisco.* San Francisco: 1856.

VALENTINE, ALAN CHESTER. *Vigilante Justice.* New York: Reynal, 1956.

WEBB, STEPHEN P. *A Sketch of the Causes, Operations and Results of the San Francisco Vigilance Committee in 1856.* Written in 1874. Reprinted from the Essex Institute Historical Collections. 1948.

WILLIAMS, MARY FLOYD. *History of the San Francisco Committee of Vigilance of 1851.* Berkeley: Univ. of Calif., 1921.

Walks

DOSS, MARGOT PATTERSON. *The Bay Area at Your Feet.* San Francisco: Chronicle Books, 1970.

DOSS, MARGOT PATTERSON. *Golden Gate Park at Your Feet.* San Francisco: Chronicle Books, 1970.

DOSS, MARGOT PATTERSON. *Paths of Gold.* San Francisco: Chronicle Books, 1974.

DOSS, MARGOT PATTERSON. *San Francisco at Your Feet; Great Walks in a Walker's Town.* New York: Grove Press, 1964.

DOSS, MARGOT PATTERSON. *Walks for Children in San Francisco.* New York: Grove Press, 1970.

Water

MCALPINE, WILLIAM JARVIS. *A Memoir on the Water Supply of the City of San Francisco.* San Francisco : C. A. Murdock, 1879.

O'SHAUGNESSEY, MICHAEL MAURICE. *Hetch Hetchy Its Origin and History.* San Francisco: 1937.

SCHUSSLER, HERMAN. *The Water Supply of San Francisco, Calif. Before, During and After the Earthquake of April 18, 1906 and the Subsequent Conflagration.* New York: M. Brown , 1906.

TAYLOR, RAY W. *Hetch Hetchy.* San Francisco: Ricardo J. Orozco, 1926.

General Histories

ALTROCCHI, JULIA COOLEY. *Spectacular San Franciscans.* New York: Dutton, 1949.

ATHERTON, GERTRUDE. *Golden Gate Country.* New York: Duel Sloan, 1945.

ATHERTON, GERTRUDE. *My San Francisco.* Indianapolis: Bobbs-Merrill, 1946.

BANCROFT, HUBERT HOWE. *History of California, Volume 6.* San Francisco: The History Co., 1888.

BANCROFT, HUBERT HOWE. *California Inter Pocula.* San Francisco: Bancroft, 1888.

The Bay of San Francisco, The Metropolis of the Pacific Coast, And Its Suburban Cities. Chicago: Lewis Pub. Co., 1892.

BEEBE, LUCIUS MORRIS. *San Francisco's Golden Era: A Picture of San Francisco Before the Fire.* Berkeley, Calif.: Howell-North, 1960.

BOLLENS, JOHN C. *The Problem of Government in the San Francisco Bay Region.* Berkeley: Univ. of Calif., 1948.

BOLTON, HERBERT E. *Outpost of Empire; The Story of the Founding of San Francisco.* New York: A. A. Knopf, 1931.

BYINGTON, LEWIS FRANCIS. *The History of San Francisco.* Chicago: S. J. Clark Co., 1931.

CAEN, HERBERT E. *Baghdad by the Bay.* New York: Doubleday, Doran, 1949.

CAEN, HERBERT E. *Don't Call It Frisco.* Garden City, New York: Doubleday, 1953.

CAEN, HERBERT E. AND DONG KINGMAN. *San Francisco, City on Golden Hills.* Garden City, New York: Doubleday, 1967.

CAREY, JOSEPH. *By the Golden Gate; or, San Francisco, The Queen City of the Pacific Coast. . .* Albany, New York: 1902.

CHIANG, I. *The Silent Traveler in San Francisco.* New York: W. W. Norton, 1964.

COY, OWEN C. *California County Boundaries. A Study of the Division of the State into Counties and of the Subsequent Changes in their Boundaries.* Berkeley, Calif. Hist. Survey Commission, 1923.

CROW, MARTHA NELL. *Howard Hillman's San Francisco At-a-Glance.* New York: D. McKay Co. 1971.

DICKSON, SAMUEL. *San Francisco is Your Home.* Stanford, Calif.: Stanford University Press, 1947.

DICKSON, SAMUEL. *San Francisco Kaleidoscope.* Stanford, Calif.: Stanford University Press, 1949.

DOBIE, CHARLES CALDWELL. *San Francisco A Pageant.* New York: Appleton-Century, 1939.

DWINELLE, JOHN WHIPPLE. *The Colonial History of San Francisco, Being a Synthetic Argument in the District Court of the United States for the Northern District of California for Four Square Leagues of Land Claimed by that City.* San Francisco: Towne & Bacon, 1863.

ELDREDGE, ZOETH SKINNER. *The Beginnings of San Francisco from the Expedition of Anza 1774 to the City Charter of April 15, 1850.* San Francisco: Eldredge, 1912.

HART, ANN CLARK. *Clark's Point; A Narrative of the Conquest of California and of the Beginning of San Francisco.* San Francisco: Pioneer Press, 1937.

HITTELL, JOHN S. *The Commerce and Industries of the Pacific Coast of North America; Comprising the Rise, Progress, Products, Present Conditions, and Prospects of the Useful Arts on the Western Side of our Continent. . .* San Francisco: A. L. Bancroft & Co., 1882.

HITTELL, JOHN S. *A History of the City of San Francisco and Incidentally of the State of California.* San Francisco: A. L. Bancroft, 1878.

IRWIN, WILL. *The City That Was. A Requiem of Old San Francisco.* New York: Huebsch, 1906.

JACOBSON, PAULINE. *City of the Golden Fifties.* Berkeley: Univ. of Calif., 1941.

JONES, IDWA. *Ark of Empire, San Francisco's Montgomery Block.* New York: Doubleday & Co., 1951.

JUDNICH, MARTIN WILLIAM. *The San Francisco Government; A Summary of the San Francisco City and County Charter, The Laws and Ordinances, And the Work of the Various Departments.* San Francisco: Ken-Books, 1967.

KINNAIRD, LAWRENCE. *History of the Greater San Francisco Bay Region.* New York: Lewis Historical Pub. Co., 1966.

LEWIS, OSCAR. *San Francisco: Mission to Metropolis.* Berkeley, Calif.: Howell-North Books, 1966.

LEWIS, OSCAR. *This Was San Francisco; Being First-Hand Accounts of the Evolution of One of America's Favorite Cities.* New York: David McKay, 1962.

LONGSTREET, STEPHEN. *The Wilder Shore: A Gala Social History of San Francisco's Sinners and Spenders, 1849-1906.* Garden City, New York: Doubleday, 1968.

MILLARD, BAILEY. *History of the San Francisco Bay Region.* San Francisco: The American Historical Society, Inc., 1924.

NORRIS, KATHLEEN. *My San Francisco.* New York: Doubleday, 1932.

O'BRIEN, ROBERT. *This is San Francisco.* New York: Whittlesey House, 1948.

OLDER, CORA MIRANDA. *San Francisco: Magic City.* New York: Longmans, Green, 1961.

PARTON, MARGARET. *Laughter on the Hill, A San Francisco Interlude. . .* New York: Whittlesey House, 1945.

PETERSON, JOYCE. *The San Francisco I Love.* New York: Tudor Pub. Co., 1970.

PHILLIPS, CATHERINE COFFIN. *Portsmouth Plaza, The Cradle of San Francisco.* San Francisco: John Henry Nash, 1932.

PHILLIPS, CATHERINE COFFIN. *Through the Golden Gate. San Francisco 1769-1937.* San Francisco: Suttonhouse, 1938.

POTTER, ELIZABETH. *The San Francisco Skyline*. New York: Dodd, 1939.

ROYCE, JOSIAH. *California from the Conquest in 1846, to the Second Vigilance Committee in San Francisco*. Boston: Houghton, Mifflin, 1886.

SCOTT, MELLIER GOODIN. *The San Francisco Bay Area: A Metropolis in Perspective*. Berkeley: Univ. of Calif. Press, 1959.

SCOTT, STANLEY, ED. *The San Francisco Bay Area: Its Problems and Future*. Berkeley: Univ. of Calif. Press, 1972.

SOULE, FRANK. *The Annals of San Francisco*. New York, San Francisco: D. Appleton & Co., 1855.

STELLMAN, LOUIS JOHN. *Port O'Gold; A History Romance of the San Francisco Argonauts*. Boston: Badger, 1922.

WELLS, EVELYN. *Champagne Days of San Francisco*. New York: Appleton-Century, 1943.

WILSON, NEIL C. *Here is the Golden Gate; Its History, Its Romance and Its Derring-Do*. New York: Morrow, 1962.

WOON, BASIL. *San Francisco and the Golden Empire*. New York: Harrison Smith, 1935.

YOUNG, JOHN PHILIP. *San Francisco, A History of the Pacific Coast Metropolis*. San Francisco: Clarke Pub. Co., 1912.

Biographies (General)

BANCROFT, HUBERT HOWE. *Chronicles of the Builders of the Commonwealth*. San Francisco: History Co., 1891-92.

BLAKE, EVARTS I. ED. *San Francisco, A Brief Biographical Sketch of Some of the Most Prominent Men*. San Francisco: Pacific Publishing Co., 1902.

BYINGTON, LEWIS FRANCIS. *The History of San Francisco*. Chicago, San Francisco: L. J. Clarke Pub. Co., 1931.

COWAN, ROBERT ERNEST. *Forgotten Characters of Old San Francisco*. Los Angeles: Ward Ritchie Press, 1938.

DE FORD, MIRIAM. *They Were San Franciscans*. Caldwell, Idaho: The Caxton Printers Ltd., 1941.

DICKSON, SAMUEL. *San Francisco is Your Home*. Stanford, Calif.: Stanford Univ. Press, 1947.

DICKSON, SAMUEL. *San Francisco Kaleidoscope*. Stanford, Calif.: Stanford Univ. Press, 1949.

DICKSON, SAMUEL. *Tales of San Francisco*. Stanford, Calif.: Stanford Univ. Press, 1957.

DILLON, RICHARD H. *Humbugs and Heroes: A Gallery of California Pioneers*. Garden City, New York: Doubleday, 1970.

HUNT, ROCKWELL, ED. *California and Californians*. Chicago, New York: Lewis Pub. Co., 1926.

LEWIS, OSCAR. *The Big Four*. New York: A. A. Knopf, 1941.

LEWIS, OSCAR. *Silver Kings*. New York: A. A. Knopf, 1947.

Men Who Made San Francisco. San Francisco: Brown and Power, 1911-12.

MURRAY, W. H. *The Builders of a Great City. San Francisco's Representative Men, The City, Its History and Commerce*. San Francisco: Journal of Commerce Pub. Co., 1891.

QUIGLEY, DR. *The Irish Race in California, and on the Pacific Coast*. San Francisco: A. Roman & Co., Pub., 1878.

San Francisco: Its Builders Past and Present, Pictorial and Biographical. Chicago, San Francisco: S. J. Clarke Co., 1913.

SHUCK, OSCAR TULLY. *Historical Abstract of San Francisco*. San Francisco: 1897.

SHUCK, OSCAR TULLY. *Sketches of the Leading and Representative Men of San Francisco. . .* San Francisco: 1875.

STARR, LANDO. *Blue Book of San Franciscans in Public Life*. San Francisco: McLaughlin Pub. Co., 1941.

SWASEY, W. F. *Early Days and Men of California*. Oakland: Pacific Press, 1891.

Personal Narratives

BARRY, T. A. AND B. A. PATTEN. *Men and Memories of San Francisco in the Spring of '50*. San Francisco: A. L. Bancroft, 1873.

BENARD DE RUSSAILH, ALBERT. *Last Adventure. San Francisco in 1851*. Translated from the original journal of Albert Benard de Russailh, by Clarkson Crane. San Francisco: The Westgate Press, 1931.

BOLTON, HERBERT E. *Font's Complete Diary, A Chronicle of the Founding of San Francisco*. Berkeley, Univ. of Calif. Press, 1931.

BOSQUI, EDWARD. *Memoirs*. San Francisco: 1904.

BROWN, JOHN HENRY. *Reminiscences and Incidents of "The Early Days" of San Francisco. . . Actual Experience of an Eye-Witness from 1845 to 1850*. San Francisco: Mission Journal Pub. Co., 1886.

BRYANT, EDWEIN. *What I Saw in California. . . in the Years 1846-47*. New York: D. Appleton, 1948.

CHAMISSO, ADELBERT VON. *A Sojourn at San Francisco Bay, 1816*. San Francisco: The Book Club of Calif., 1936.

DAVIS, WILLIAM HEATH. *Sixty Years in California, A History of Events and Life in California*. San Francisco: A. J. Leary, 1889.

DOWNEY, JOSEPH T. *Filings from an Old Saw: Reminiscences of San Francisco and California's Conquest*. San Francisco: J. Howell, 1956.

GREELEY, HORACE. *An Overland Journey from New York to San Francisco in the Summer of 1859*. Edited, and with notes and an introduction by Charles T. Duncan. New York: Alfred A. Knopf, 1964.

HARLAN, JACOB W. *California '46 - '88.* San Francisco: Bancroft, 1888.

HART, JEROME A. *In Our Second Century. From an Editor's Note Book.* San Francisco: Pioneer Press, 1931.

LEALE, JOHN. *Recollections of a Tule Sailor.* San Francisco: Fields, 1939.

LEVY, HARRIET LANE. *920 O'Farrell Street.* New York: Doubleday, 1947.

LLOYD, BENJAMIN E. *Lights and Shades in San Francisco.* San Francisco: Bancroft, 1876.

MAHR, AUGUST CARL. *The Visit of the "Rurik" to San Francisco in 1816.* Stanford, Calif.: Stanford Univ. Press, 1932.

MARRYAT, SAMUEL FRANCIS. *Mountains and Molehills or Recollections of a Burnt Journal. . .* London: Longman, 1855.

MASSEY, ERNEST DE. *A Frenchman in the Gold Rush.* Translated by Marguerite Eyer Wilbur. San Francisco: Calif. Historical Society, 1927.

MEGQUIER, MARY JANE. *Apron Full of Gold: The Letters of Mary Jane Megquier from San Francisco, 1849-1856.* San Marino: Huntington Library, 1949.

MURDOCK, CHARLES A. *A Backward Glance at Eighty.* San Francisco: Elder, 1921.

NEVILLE, AMELIA. *The Fantastic City.* New York: Houghton Mifflin, 1932.

PRIETO, GUILLERMO. *San Francisco in the Seventies. The City as Viewed by a Mexican Political Exile.* Edited by Edwin S. Morby. San Francisco: Nash, 1938.

ROOT, HENRY. *Personal History and Reminiscences with Personal Opinions on Contemporary Events 1845-1921.* San Francisco: 1921.

TAYLOR, BAYARD. *Eldorado, or Adventures in the Path of Empire.* New York: Putman, 1850.

TAYLOR, BENJAMIN FRANKLIN. *Between the Gates. . .* Chicago: Griggs, 1878.

TAYLOR, WILLIAM. *Seven Years' Street Preaching in San Francisco, California.* Edited by W. P. Strickland. New York: Carlton & Porter, 1856.

WILLIAMS, SAMUEL. *The City of the Golden Gate. A Description of San Francisco in 1875.* San Francisco: Book Club of San Francisco, 1921.

WILSON, LUZENA STANLEY. *Luzena Stanley Wilson, '49er; Memories Recalled Years Later for her Daughter Correnah Wilson Wright.* Mills College, Calif.: The Eucalyptus Press, 1937.

WISTAR, ISAAC. *Autobiography 1827-1905.* Phila.: 1914.

Index

Photographic Credits

Cover photograph provided by the San Francisco Convention and Visitors Bureau.

San Francisco Chronicle   14, 15, 29, 31, 65, 73, 90, 91, 97, 98, 105, 106, 115, 125, 127, 167, 177, 180, 202, 218, 219, 225, 227.

San Francisco Convention and Visitors Bureau   18, 21, 24, 95, 122, 123, 124, 132, 138, 186 (top), 211, 212, 217, 228, 230.

San Francisco Public Library   35, 39, 40, 44, 48, 51, 52, 54, 59, 61, 62, 67, 72, 74, 92, 102, 103, 131, 180, 184, 186 (bottom), 204, 205, 222, 226.